Feiffer is in favor of

H-BOMB TESTING ☑

JUVENILE DELINQUENCY ☑

and

FLASH FLOODS ☑

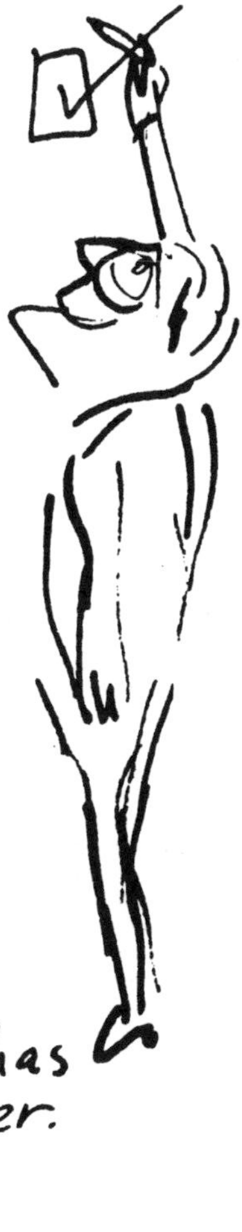

publish

FEIFFER

NOW!

Show that irresponsibility has a place in your newspaper.

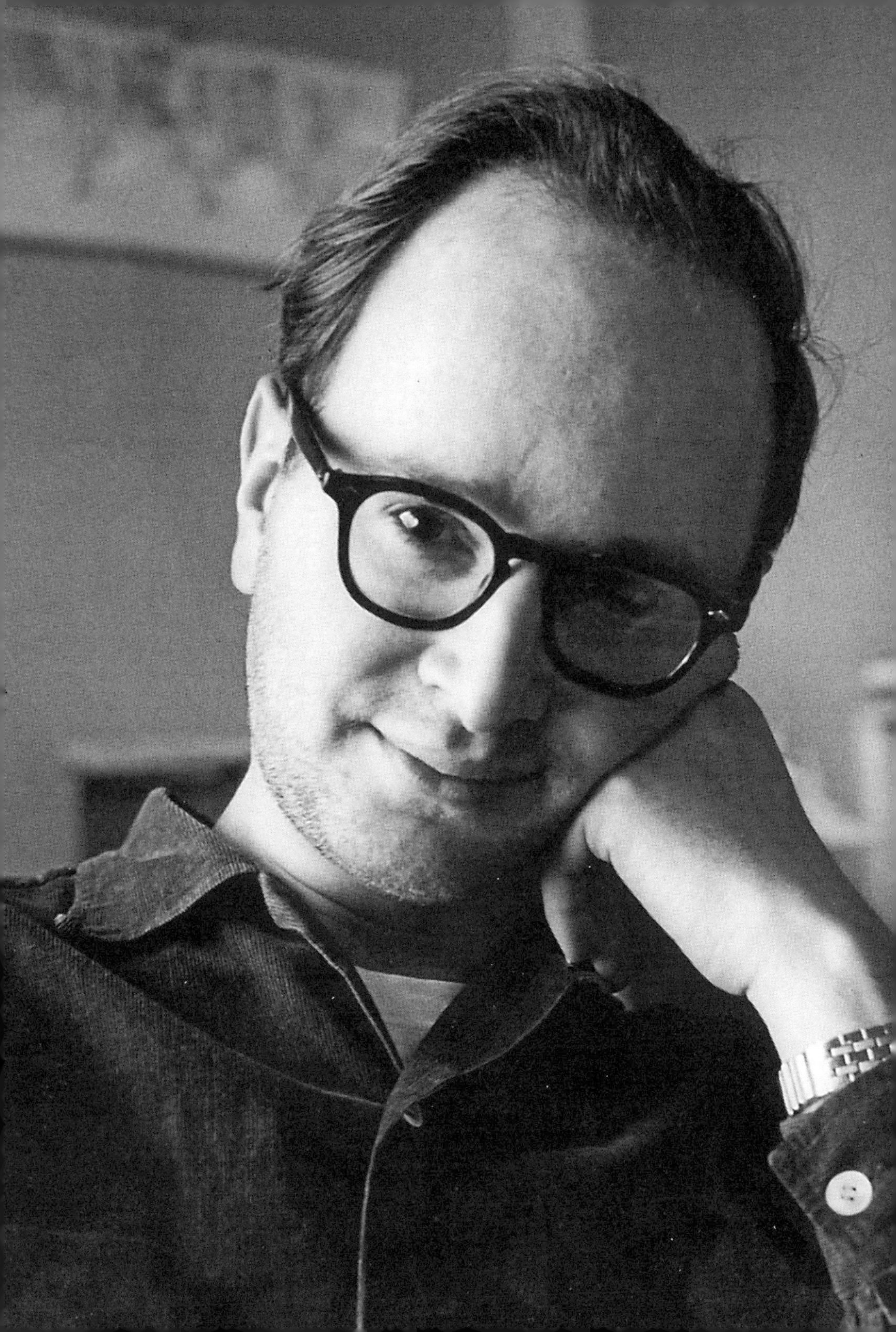

Passionella
and Other Stories

Jules Feiffer

THE COLLECTED WORKS
VOLUME IV

FANTAGRAPHICS BOOKS
Seattle, Washington

Fantagraphics Books
7563 Lake City Way NE
Seattle, Washington 98115

Publishers: Gary Groth & Kim Thompson
Editor: Gary Groth
Art Director: Greg Sadowski
Publicist: Eric Reynolds

Typeset in Robert Slimbach's Adobe Jensen MM

First Fantagraphics Books Edition: July 2006
ISBN-13: 978-1-56097-097-2
ISBN-10: 1-56097-097-9
Printed in China by Print Vision

CONTENTS

Introduction

The Cutting Edgists

Excalibur and Rose

The Lonely Machine

Harold Swerg

Superman

George's Moon

Crawling Arnold

Passionella

The Relationship

If you ask him nicely Feiffer will write down to your audience-

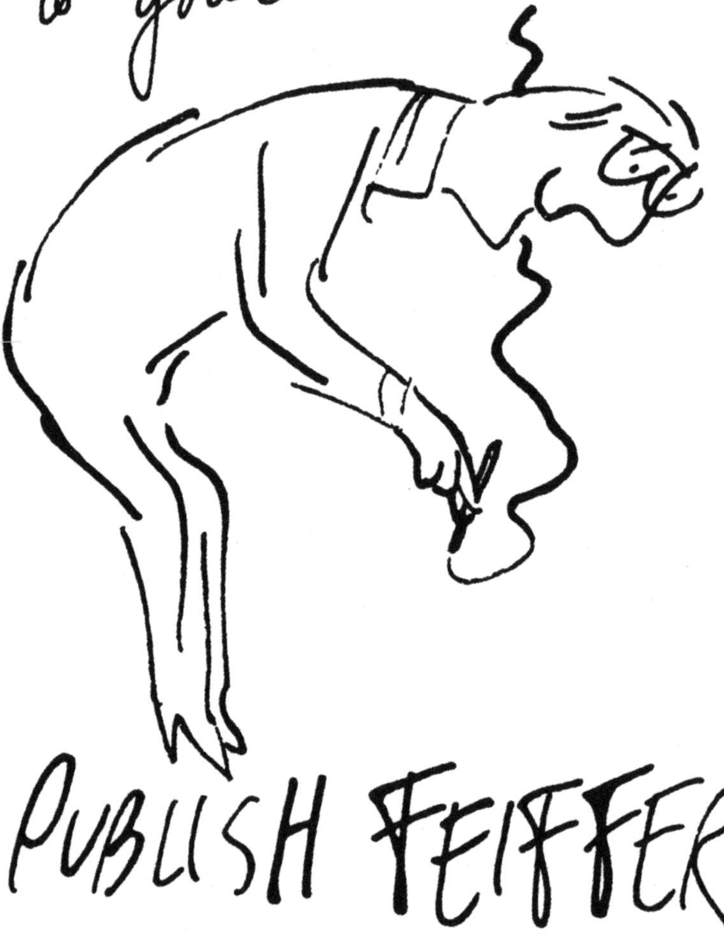

PUBLISH FEIFFER!

He'll compromise.

Introduction *by Gary Groth*

BY THE LATE '50S-EARLY '60S, the most innovative cartoonist in America was Jules Feiffer.

Cartooning occupied several distinct professional spheres – in roughly ascending order of social, cultural, and economic status: comic books, newspaper strips, political cartoons, and magazine gag panels.

In his youth, Feiffer adored adventure strips (such as Milton Caniff's *Terry and the Pirates*) and initially wanted to enter the comic-book field, but realized that he lacked the requisite skills to convincingly exaggerate anatomy and action. In 1946 he became Will Eisner's assistant on *The Spirit*, a weekly seven-page comic that resided between the adventure and comedy genres, and which he eventually wrote (but never drew).

He tried his hand at creating newspaper strips in 1950 ("Kermit," a kid strip with adult overtones) and 1953 ("Dopple," about a pixilated Irish-American married couple), and shopped them around, but failed to sell them. At this point he was flailing around, in love with the form but still searching for his identity as a cartoonist.

He found it in 1951 when he was drafted into the United States Army. "That changed my direction," he said. "The Army was the true watershed experience." The U.S. Army has a proud tradition of changing young people's direction, although it changed Feiffer's in a way that the Pentagon hadn't intended. "It was the first time I was truly away from home for a long period of time, and thrown into a world that was antagonistic to everything I believed in, on every conceivable level. In a war that I was out of sympathy with, and in an army that I despised." His critical disposition and nonconformist attitudes hardened, his contrarian impulses congealed, and his direction as a satirist was practically ordained.

In 1951, while still serving in the military, he started "Munro," his famous strip about a four-year-old child mistakenly drafted into the Army, and finished it after being discharged. It was a 50-page satirical comic strip written and drawn for adults, which, in 1954, was impossible to sell or market. He took it to Simon & Schuster, who published cartoon books, "and got nowhere. Finally, I began taking it elsewhere, and other editors told me they didn't know how to market it because it looked like a children's book, but it wasn't. Nobody had ever heard of me."

Feiffer wanted to draw comics for grownups, but what he was doing, or wanted to do, didn't fit into any of the commercial niches of cartooning. Luckily, an urban, politicized alternative weekly called *The Village Voice* began publishing in October 1955, and Feiffer saw an opportunity. He offered to write and draw a weekly strip for the fledgling paper – for free. "I had been turned down over and over again by book publishers. I'd go from publisher to publisher and all these publishers thought I was terrific, and they passed the book around, and they'd take me out to lunch, and they'd rave about what I was doing, how fresh it was. Finally, this stopped being a compliment, because early on, you think, well, this is terrific, I'm in! But then you discover you're *not* in, you're *out*, because they say, well, we don't know how to market this. And it became clear there was no market for it, because it was a Catch-22 situation. I had no name, so who was going to buy this work that looked

This essay is illustrated with 1959 solicitations for Feiffer's Village Voice *strip.*

like children's drawings, but was very adult material?

"I didn't know what to do until the *Voice* came along. I saw that that was the paper that got attention from the very people who were rejecting me, because it was hip, it was inside. It was very modestly circulated, but to all the right people. I was smart enough to know, even at the age of 27, that if I could get the stuff they're turning down in print, anywhere, they will think, well, wait a minute, it's in print! So if I can get those six guys who say I can't get into print looking at the stuff in print, they will change their minds, which is what happened. It did exactly as I hoped, though I thought it would take a couple years. It took something like three months. It was very fast."

This was Feiffer's innovation: Our of inner necessity, he conceived an urbane, intellectual comic strip, different from any that had preceded it, and found a way to make it commercially viable – not just one mean feat, but two!

He began to write and draw his weekly *Voice* strip – two tiers, six or eight panels, twice the size of a daily newspaper strip – as well as a succession of long-form comics that appeared in magazines and books. His strips were as literate, witty, and sophisticated as anything in *The New Yorker*, but also had a staccato, writerly quality, with more space to maneuver to take advantage of the multi-panel form. He was single-handedly changing the perception of the artistic level that comics were capable of among an intelligentsia that had seen comics (with rare exceptions such as *Krazy Kat* or James Thurber) as no more than minor, albeit clever, diversions. He was dragging the idiom of the cartoon strip into a professedly literary context that couldn't be gainsaid; addressing subject matter head-on that comics had rarely if ever tackled as forthrightly: society, politics, culture, and sex.

"It all started with [my *Voice* strips], including my introduction to the New York literary set. Particularly with the New York intellectuals, they'd never seen a cartoon that they admired – in terms of its intellectual content – so they had to rename it. They couldn't call it a cartoon. That's because cartoons couldn't be serious or be taken seriously by an intellectual. So they would say – in this conversation I would have over and over again – 'I love that column you do, that little essay.' And I'd say, 'That cartoon.' They'd say, 'No, it's not a cartoon. It's a…' and they went on and on and on saying it wasn't a cartoon."

But cartoons they were, and Feiffer's doggedness in the face of such denial inched non-specialists, intellectuals, and general readers that much closer to accepting comics as the artistic equivalent of prose, film, or theater.

The work in this fourth volume of *The Collected Works of Jules Feiffer* originally appeared in a variety of magazines, and most of the individual pieces were also published in the 1963 collection, *Feiffer's Album*.

"The Cutting Edgists" was originally commissioned for *Harper's* by Bob Silvers (who later became editor of *The New York Review of Books*) and which Feiffer chose to use as the introductory piece in *Feiffer's Album*. It's a skit satirizing satirists. Each of the five characters represented one of the prominent satirists of the day: Shelley Berman, Bob Newhart, Mike Nichols, and Elaine May. The black satirist (#5) was probably Dick Gregory or Godfrey Cambridge. When I suggested that it was an attack on mealy-mouthed satirists, Feiffer replied, satirically, "Yes. That's because I wasn't one, and I was better than that [*pause*]. And I thought that should be pointed out. So I did [*pause*]. Nobody else was going to do it."

"Excalibur and Rose" was done for *Feiffer's Album*, but was excerpted in either *McCall's* or *Ladies' Home Journal*. A modern fable told in a medieval idiom, Feiffer has mixed feelings about it: "I think it was my attempt to write in a formal, almost Victorian language; it was a children's story for adults, and so I chose a rather stilted language, thinking that this was

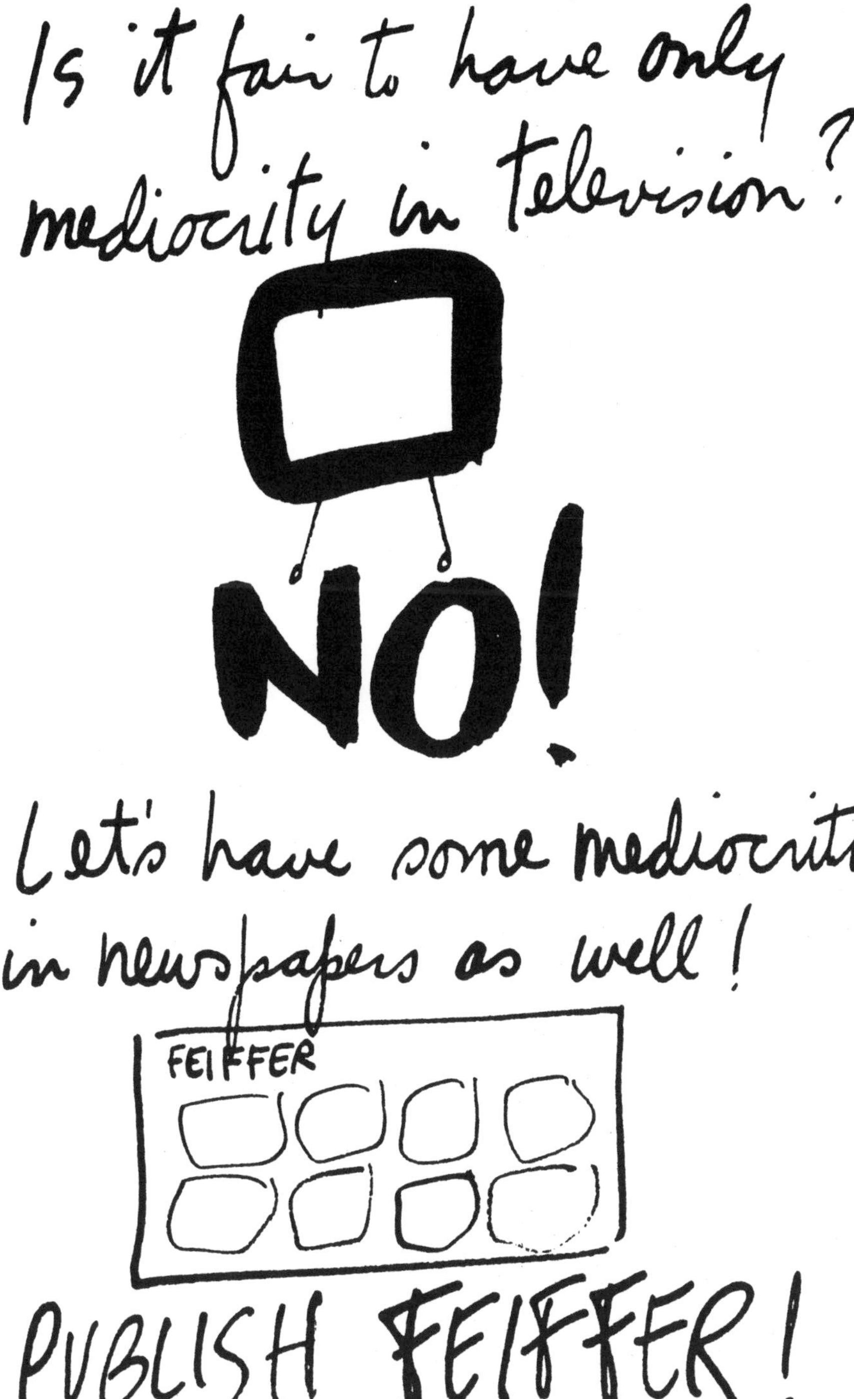
Is it fair to have only mediocrity in television?
NO!
Let's have some mediocrity in newspapers as well!
FEIFFER
PUBLISH FEIFFER!

are *YOU* overlooking an important part of your audience?

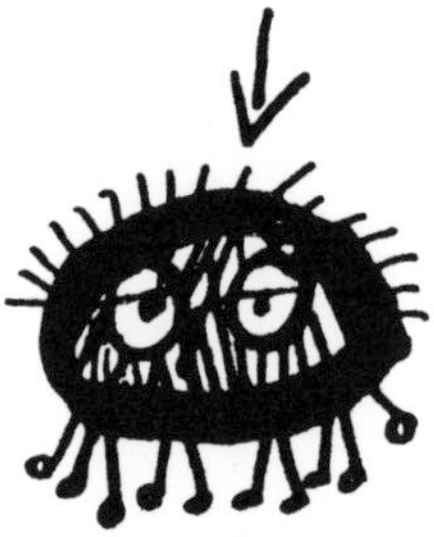

FEIFFER

appeals to the lowest common denominator.

PUBLISH FEIFFER NOW!

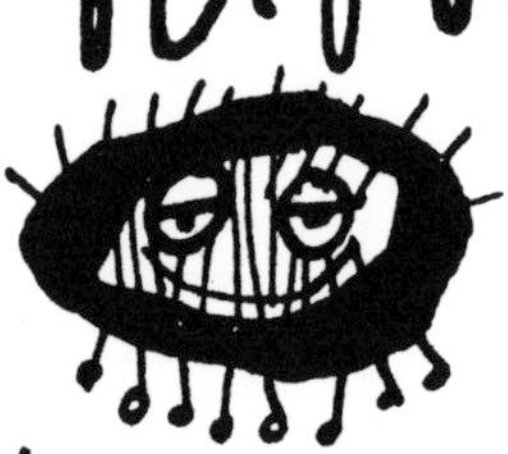

help make democracy work!

the way to go – and it wasn't." On the other hand, he likes the way the watercolor illustrations turned out, much preferring them to those he did earlier for the classic children's book, *The Phantom Tollbooth*. The fable even includes a slightly incongruous anti-war message, reflecting either Feiffer's strong reaction against the Korean War or his prescience about Vietnam, in which U.S. combat troops had not yet been committed – but soon would be. (Decades later, he used the idea behind "Excalibur" to write one of his most successful children's books, 1995's *A Barrel of Laughs, A Vale of Tears*.)

"The Lonely Machine" first appeared as a feature in *Playboy* (he redrew some of it for *Feiffer's Album*, which is the version used here). It almost serves as a riposte to Hefner's "Playboy Philosopher," to which Feiffer was substantially opposed. Feiffer's relationship to *Playboy* was interesting, because although his own sexual attitudes were fundamentally antithetical to those of Hefner's, he is always quick to point out how supportive Hefner was toward his contributions and how Hefner never tried to change the attitudes Feiffer expressed in his *Playboy* work. "[Hefner's] way was never, ever about selling out my principles in order to make it dovetail more with the magazine's marketability or approach."

Still, he was, as he once put it, operating as a dissident cartoonist at *Playboy*, and "The Lonely Machine" affirms that position. "I was very much at odds with the Playboy philosophy as he was developing it…I don't want to sound feminist before feminism, but [that philosophy] was truly dehumanizing, and I didn't think of it as a feminist point, I thought of it as dehumanizing in terms of relationships. My own sexual orientation, compared to that of the magazine, is pure Victoria and awfully prudish."

"Harold Swerg," a Kennedy-era satire on nationalism, conformism, and mass man, was done for a sports magazine (such as *Sports Illustrated*) and subsequently appeared in *Feiffer's Album*.

There are two incarnations of "Superman." Feiffer wrote and drew the first as a one-page strip for *Playboy*. He later expanded it into a five-or-six-minute sketch that appeared in the stage revue, *Feiffer's People*, a series of dramatizations based on his *Voice* strips.

In the late '50s, *Pageant* magazine (which was, incidentally and coincidentally, published by Hillman Publications, one of the better '50s comic-book publishers) invited Feiffer to draw a long-form cartoon strip. "Lois Cantor, who was an editor at *Pageant*, liked the stuff in the *Voice*. *Pageant* was already publishing people like R.O. Blechman, who was just beginning as well, and there was interest in quality avant-garde cartoonists. She said they would give me 28 pages, and I thought I should grab this moment to really get attention for myself and make a name for myself and get famous, which would make my life considerably easier. And the only way I could think of doing that was to do the opposite of bold, political social satire and do *fake* bold social satire, which would be on the entertainment industry. What could be easier and fakier? And then when I thought about that, I thought of course about movies, and when I thought about movies I thought about tits and Marilyn Monroe, and the rest fell into place.

"When it came out, and in the act of doing it, I had very little respect for it. I was very happy that it did for me what I hoped, which was to make me far more commercial; it was very successful and got a lot of attention and people loved it. And the more they loved it, the more contempt I had for it. Then, around 25 years later, I looked at it again for the first time and thought, 'This is one of the best things I've ever done. Why was I so hard on it?'"

In fact, Feiffer had written a draft of "Passionella" years earlier, in 1955, before he started at the *Voice*. He realized that it was the perfect strip for *Pageant* and prepared a new dummy, which was accepted. He later completely revised and redrew the strip for the 1959 book collection, *Passionella and Other Stories*, and it's the redrawn version that appears here.

"George's Moon" was drawn for the *Passionella* book (which also included "Boom" and "Munro," both of which were published in volumes two and three of this series, respectively).

"Crawling Arnold" was written at the request of Paul Sills, co-founder of the Chicago-based improvisational comedy revue, Second City (named after a series of *New Yorker* articles by A.J. Liebling), which later achieved greater commercial success in the 1980s as *Second City TV*. "Second City had become a big success in the Midwest and Sills came to me in New York City and said, 'We're going to open a Second City next door called Playwrights at Second City, and we want adaptations of your cartoons to be the first play. Are you interested?' Of course I was interested." Feiffer took a full-page strip he'd done for the *Voice*, of similar matter but a different title, adapted it into a theatrical sketch and wrote "Crawling Arnold" in a single night. (He loved the act of writing it so much that one could trace what he has called his "masochistic" love of writing plays to "Crawling Arnold.")

Finally, Feiffer wrote and drew "The Relationship" – surely one of his most succinctly fatalistic takes on love and relationships ever drawn – as a coda for *Feiffer's Album*, and serves, appropriately, as a coda for this one as well. "It seemed to be a natural progression after 'The Lonely Machine'," remarked Feiffer, and so it is.

Although I've emphasized what an innovative force Feiffer was during this period of cartooning history, he, like all artists, had his predecessors, influences, and mentors. Robert Osborn and William Steig are obvious visual antecedents. Considerably less obvious is Frank Tashlin – gag man, cartoonist, animator, and film director. Feiffer recently realized, to his surprise, that Tashlin's children's book, *The Bear That Wasn't* (about a bear who denies he's a bear) was the direct impetus for "Munro" (about a four-year-old who denies he's a soldier), and "Harold Swerg" was originally titled "The Man Who Wouldn't."

Some influences are so obvious it's easy to overlook them. When asked directly if any cartoonists influenced his passion for writing and drawing long-form cartoon stories, Feiffer replied, "Does the name Will Eisner mean anything to you?" Eisner would occasionally tell his Spirit stories in the form of an old-fashioned fable. "And I think that's where it came from," said Feiffer. "Because I wrote one or two for him in later years, but they weren't my invention, they were Eisner's. I was just taking an idea he had introduced and using the form to do one of my own for him. But when it came to do these narrative cartoons, I naturally evolved from what I had loved Eisner doing, and what I had done myself in *The Spirit* when I was writing for him, and turned it to my own uses. But I think it directly comes from that."

It's often said that Eisner invented the graphic novel in 1978 with *A Contract with God*. As a matter of historical fact, this is simply wrong. It's closer to the truth to say that no one artist invented the long-form comics "novel." Throughout the last century, the concept had evolved in fits and starts by many artists (such as Milt Gross with *He Done Her Wrong* in 1932 and Alan Dunn with *East of 5th* in 1948) who kept the idea alive by drawing the occasional long-form comic that had no marketing category and that no one knew quite what to make of. This volume, and its predecessors in this series, proves that Jules Feiffer was instrumental at pushing the lowly comic into the longer, more mature, literary form that over the last 20 or 30 years has finally taken root.

FEIFFER has a big following among non-newspaper readers

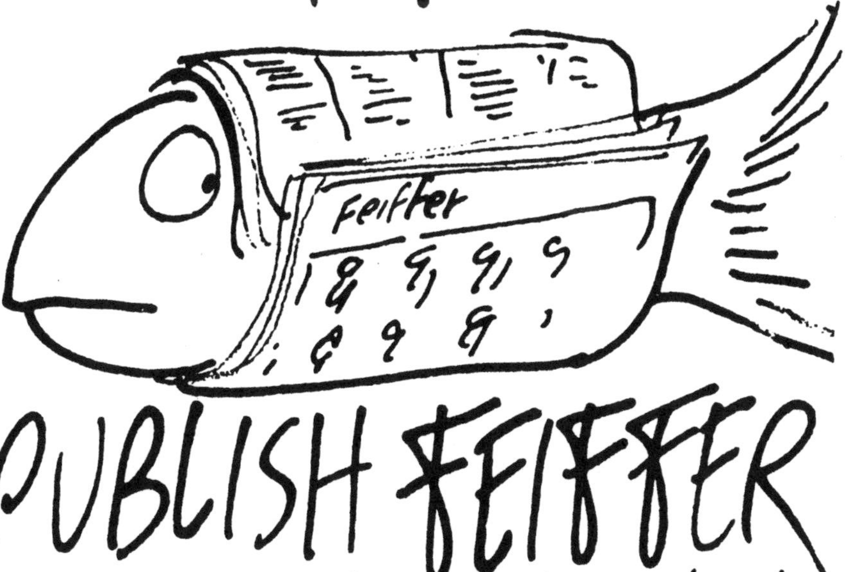
Feiffer

PUBLISH FEIFFER

Don't alienate an important part of your audience.

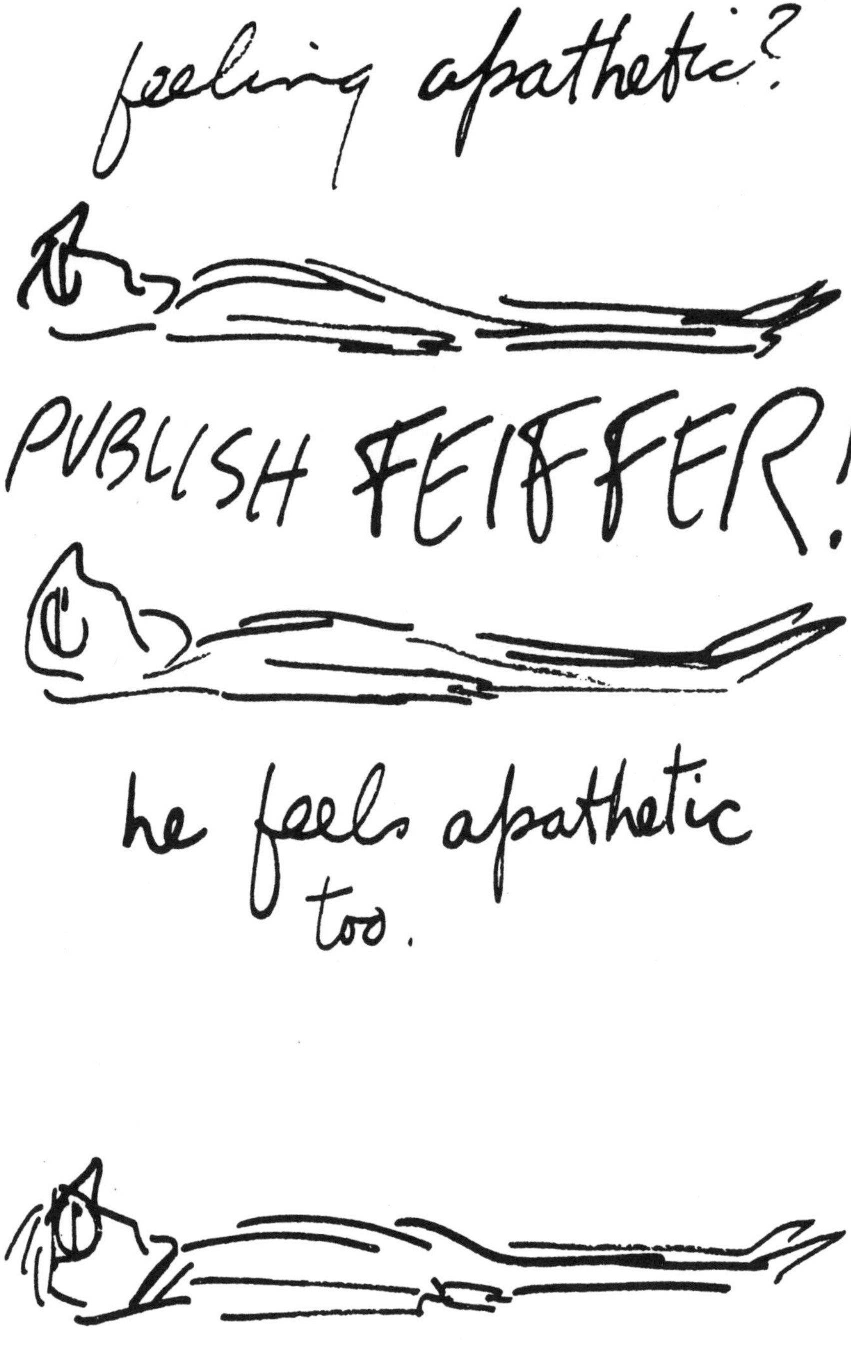
feeling apathetic?
PUBLISH FEIFFER!
he feels apathetic too.

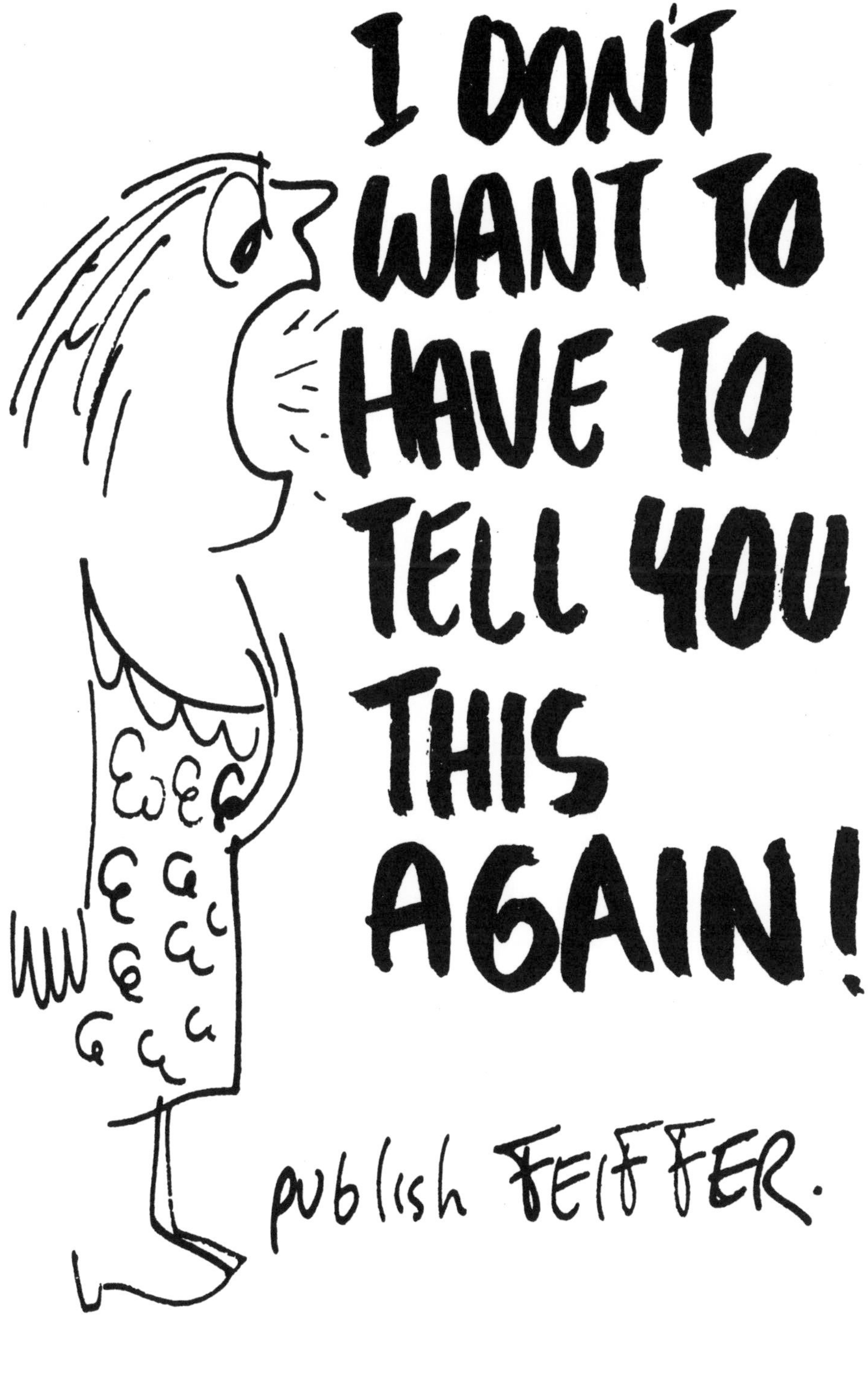
I DON'T WANT TO HAVE TO TELL YOU THIS AGAIN!
publish FEIFFER.

The Cutting Edgists

The scene is the darkened stage of a Broadway playhouse. A spot comes up on the FIRST
    SATIRIST, *who is seated on a stool reading a newspaper. A second spot comes up on the*
    SECOND SATIRIST, *who is staring at him.*

SECOND SATIRIST Are you a satirist?

FIRST SATIRIST Can't you tell?

SECOND SATIRIST Well, you *are* sitting on a stool.

FIRST SATIRIST Want to hear my Kennedy bit?

SECOND SATIRIST (*Winces*) I must have the wrong place. I heard there were going to
    be some satirists here.

FIRST SATIRIST (Offended) I *am* a satirist.

    (*A spot comes up on the* THIRD SATIRIST)

THIRD SATIRIST So am I.

SECOND SATIRIST Where's your stool?

THIRD SATIRIST I'm a right-wing satirist. Only liberal satirists have stools. We
    right-wing satirists have to be ready to make a fast start.

FIRST SATIRIST You right-wingers! You always make yourselves sound so oppressed.
    Now take me! *I'm* not strictly a liberal. Did you ever hear me do Kennedy?

THIRD SATIRIST I've heard everybody do Kennedy.

FIRST SATIRIST Proves my point. I do a very strong Kennedy.

THIRD SATIRIST Ever been invited to the White House?

FIRST SATIRIST Every time I do Kennedy.

SECOND SATIRIST I don't think either one of you knows what satire is.
   (*A spot comes up on the* FOURTH SATIRIST)
FOURTH SATIRIST It's Jewish, isn't it? Lots of words like *schtick, l'chaim, bagel*. That's
   what I use in my act.
(*A spot comes up on the fifth satirist – a Negro*)
FIFTH SATIRIST Jewish is square, man. The roots of modern-day satire rest in the
   jazz idiom. Satire has crossed the color line.
FOURTH SATIRIST (*Smiles indulgently at the* FIFTH SATIRIST) Oh, don't get me wrong.
THIRD SATIRIST (*Smiles indulgently at the* FIFTH SATIRIST) Don't get me wrong.
FIRST SATIRIST (*Smiles indulgently*) Don't get me wrong, either. I do a great Kennedy
   on the phone to Martin Luther King.
FIFTH SATIRIST Martin Luther King? Man, as far as my audience goes, Martin
   Luther King is practically *white!*
FIRST SATIRIST (*Nervously to the audience*) We're all just kidding here. Having fun.
   That's what satire is. Having fun.
SECOND SATIRIST Do you always apologize?
FIRST SATIRIST A satirist can't teach people anything if he offends them.
FOURTH SATIRIST I offend them. They love it. I make fun of their wives. They love
   it. I tell them I hate them. They love it. I use words like *schmuck*. You should
   hear them applaud.
THIRD SATIRIST I like to work with my audience. I like to improvise. I ask them
   to give me a first line and a last line and a theme. And I build a whole fifteen-
   minute improvisation around it.
FIFTH SATIRIST Is it any good?
THIRD SATIRIST Never. But they love it. I ingratiate myself.
SECOND SATIRIST That's not satire. All you want is approval.
THIRD SATIRIST Yes. And when they withhold it, I attack them.
FOURTH SATIRIST Me, too. Viciously.
FIFTH SATIRIST Man, I don't want approval.
THE OTHERS (*Approvingly*) What do you want?
FIFTH SATIRIST Yo' sister! (*The others recoil*) That was satire.
FIRST SATIRIST Hey, I can do a great Kennedy. (*Thrusts out forefinger*) Do naht
   ahsk what you can do fer Caroline –
FOURTH SATIRIST (*Impatient*) Everyone does Kennedy. That's not satire. Now the
   kind of satire I like to do –
FIRST SATIRIST Kennedy is so satire. He's the President, isn't he? When you do
   the President you're making fun of a public figure, aren't you? You're making
   him look foolish, aren't you? That takes courage, doesn't it? Well, when I do
   Kennedy that's satire! Unabashed, unafraid satire.
FIFTH SATIRIST Do J. Edgar Hoover.
FIRST SATIRIST J. Edgar Hoover?
FIFTH SATIRIST Do J. Edgar Hoover.

FIRST SATIRIST You don't want J. Edgar Hoover.

FIFTH SATIRIST Man, I'm *colored*. It ain't my F.B.I. Do J. Edgar Hoover. (FIRST SATIRIST *backs off*) You said you do public figures.

FIRST SATIRIST Yeah, but J. Edgar Hoover. I mean – listen, if you come to my house and we close all the windows –

FIFTH SATIRIST Do it here – now.

FIRST SATIRIST I do a *great* Kennedy.

FIFTH SATIRIST J. Edgar Hoover.

FIRST SATIRIST On a stage? In front of people? It's bad taste! Let me do the President! (FIFTH SATIRIST *scornfully turns away*)

FOURTH SATIRIST The kind of satire I prefer is to do a take-off on the little man –

SECOND SATIRIST Dear God!

FOURTH SATIRIST His troubles, his pet peeves.

SECOND SATIRIST Heaven help us!

FOURTH SATIRIST The little unnoticed bedevilments of life that may not give the audience a belly laugh, mind you, but will give them a smile of recognition. "Yes – I'm like that," they'll say. "There I am. There you are. There we all are. Little Man. Peering off into the middle distance."

SECOND SATIRIST I'm ill.

FOURTH SATIRIST "There's my wife. There's my next door neighbor –"

SECOND SATIRIST Together?

FOURTH SATIRIST (*Self-righteous*) Smut is *not* satire.

SECOND SATIRIST Smut, dear sir, is our *only* satire.

FOURTH SATIRIST You're one of those people who has to attack everything!

FIFTH SATIRIST (*To* SECOND SATIRIST) You ain't ever attacked me, baby.

SECOND SATIRIST Of course not. Now is not the *time* to attack you. When you've gained equal rights – *then* I'll attack you.

FIRST SATIRIST (*Proudly*) I have a point of view. *I* don't attack everything.

FOURTH SATIRIST (*Proudly*) Certainly! One should be *for* something. Then he can attack those things that are against what he is for. That's the *responsible* approach.

FIFTH SATIRIST You for something?

FIRST SATIRIST (*With inspiration*) Everybody's for something.

FIFTH SATIRIST What're you for?

FIRST SATIRIST (*With inspiration*) Compassion!

THIRD SATIRIST (*With inspiration*) Understanding!

FOURTH SATIRIST (*With inspiration*) Love!

(*All three shake hands*)

SECOND SATIRIST (*To* FIFTH SATIRIST) And you – what are you for?

FIFTH SATIRIST Man, I don't stand for nothin'. I'm just a little old plantation hand doing his bit to make the system work. A civil rights therapist to lily-white audiences.

SECOND SATIRIST (*Exultant*) You *shame* them! You *expose* them!

FIFTH SATIRIST I make them laugh. They relax. They feel very liberal. Then they put on their sheets and go home. That's what satire is, man. Communication.

FIRST SATIRIST (*Shaking hands with* FIFTH SATIRIST). A very interesting statement. Satire *is* communication.

FOURTH SATIRIST (*Shaking hands with* FIFTH SATIRIST) Communication! Extremely well put.

THIRD SATIRIST (Shaking hands with FIFTH SATIRIST) Communication. Well said. Where did you go to school?

SECOND SATIRIST (*Angry*) Satire is *not* concerned with communication! Satire is concerned with *hate!*

FIRST SATIRIST (*Sweetly*) Yes, but hate is the satirist's bridge to communication!

THIRD SATIRIST (*Sweetly*) Satire should *never* be negative. Hate is only a device.

SECOND SATIRIST (*Furious*) Satire outrages! Satire strips bare!

FIRST SATIRIST I outrage.

THIRD SATIRIST I strip bare.

SECOND SATIRIST (*Screams*) Satire exposes our inner corruption! Satire *destroys!*

FOURTH SATIRIST (*Defensively*) Well I'm sure we *all* want to destroy. (*Brightly*) But only in order to build.

FIRST SATIRIST Yes! That's the only reason we'd ever destroy. To build on the ashes.

THIRD SATIRIST *A better society!*

FOURTH SATIRIST *A saner tomorrow!*

FIRST SATIRIST *An improved image of man!*

FIFTH SATIRIST *A happy people – with a natural sense of rhythm!*

FIRST, THIRD and FOURTH SATIRISTS (*Sing*) Hallelujah!
   (*All four shake hands*)

THIRD SATIRIST Don't you see? That's the whole *point* in destroying. That's why satire is *not* negative!

FOURTH SATIRIST That's why it's healthy!

SECOND SATIRIST (*Becoming convinced*) I see! Yes!

FOURTH SATIRIST Not really sadistic at all!

SECOND SATIRIST (*With inspiration*) Yes!

FIRST SATIRIST It builds on ashes.

SECOND SATIRIST Yes! Ashes, we need ashes!

THIRD SATIRIST On which to build!
   (*He lights a match*)

ALL Ashes! (*They each light a match*) Ashes!
   (*They set fire to the curtains. The Theatre begins to burn – scenery, backdrops, etc.*)

FIRST SATIRIST Very soon now we will start to build.
   (*All shake hands as the theatre goes up in flames*)

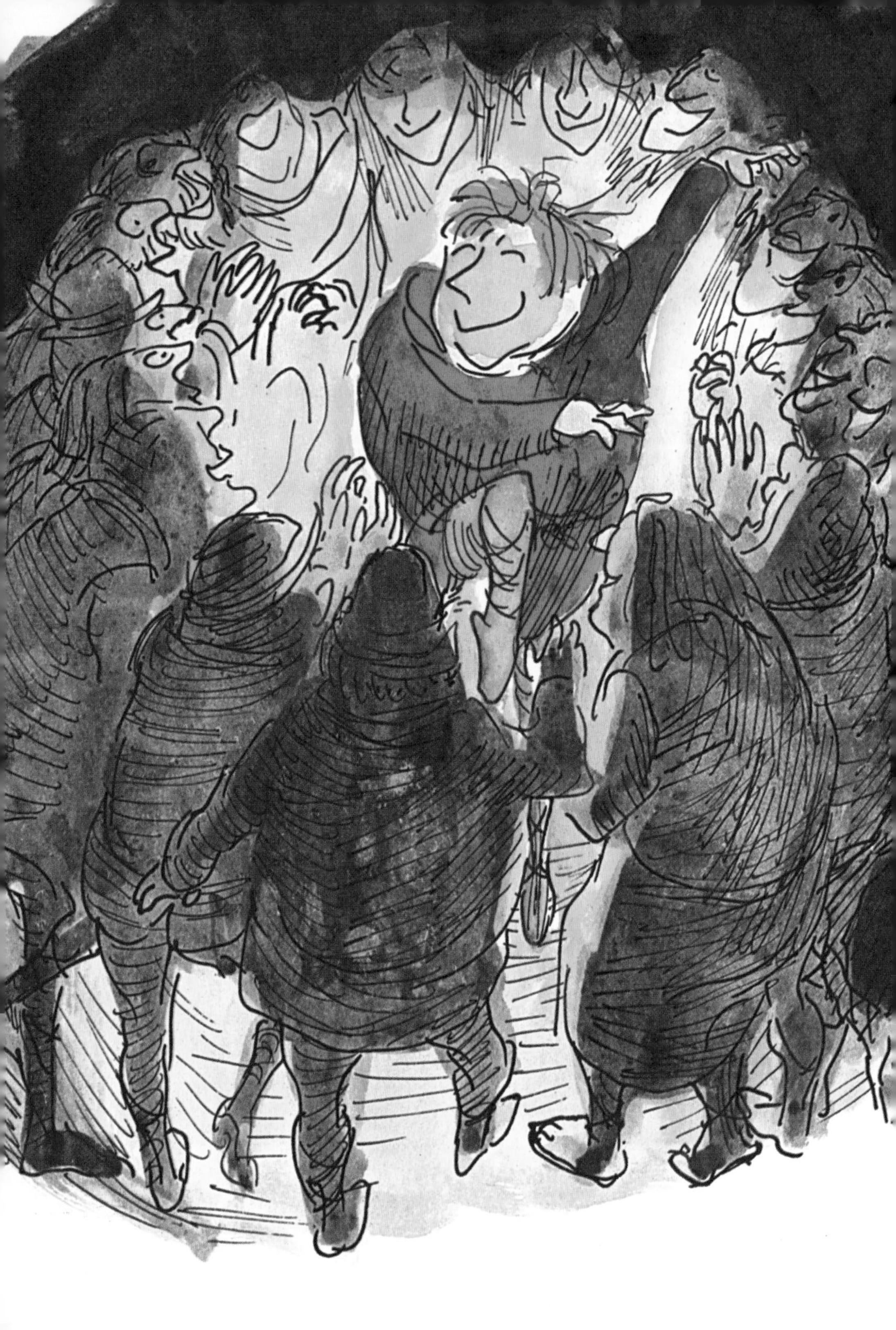

Excalibur and Rose

THERE WAS ONCE a funny, awkward little man named Excalibur, who made his living entertaining the villagers in the township where he lived. He sang. He danced. He recited parables to fit the time. It was said that there was no dispute Excalibur could not settle by gathering before him the disputants and mocking them gently till their self-righteous frowns changed to embarrassed grins and their bitter quarrel seemed only a trifle.

But though he was loved by all and though he loved all without exception, Excalibur felt a longing – for what reason he could not tell. "Perhaps mine is but a longing to have a longing," he joked to himself, attempting to make as little of his problem as he did of everyone else's. But each joke drove the longing deeper until he, at last, was forced to seek out Father Know-It-All, the wisest man in the village.

"Your longing is to be two-sided," said Father Know-It-All, forcibly restraining a smile as Excalibur tried to amuse him by executing series of head and hand stands. "At the moment you are one-sided. You are all *happiness*. You must cultivate a *serious* side. You must practice to be happy when happiness is called for and to be serious when seriousness is called for. Then you will be a two-sided person and your longing will disappear."

And so it was that early the next morning Excalibur rode quietly from his village, softly singing farewell to the sleeping things he loved – and, more loudly, singing hello to the new world he was about to enter in search of his serious side.

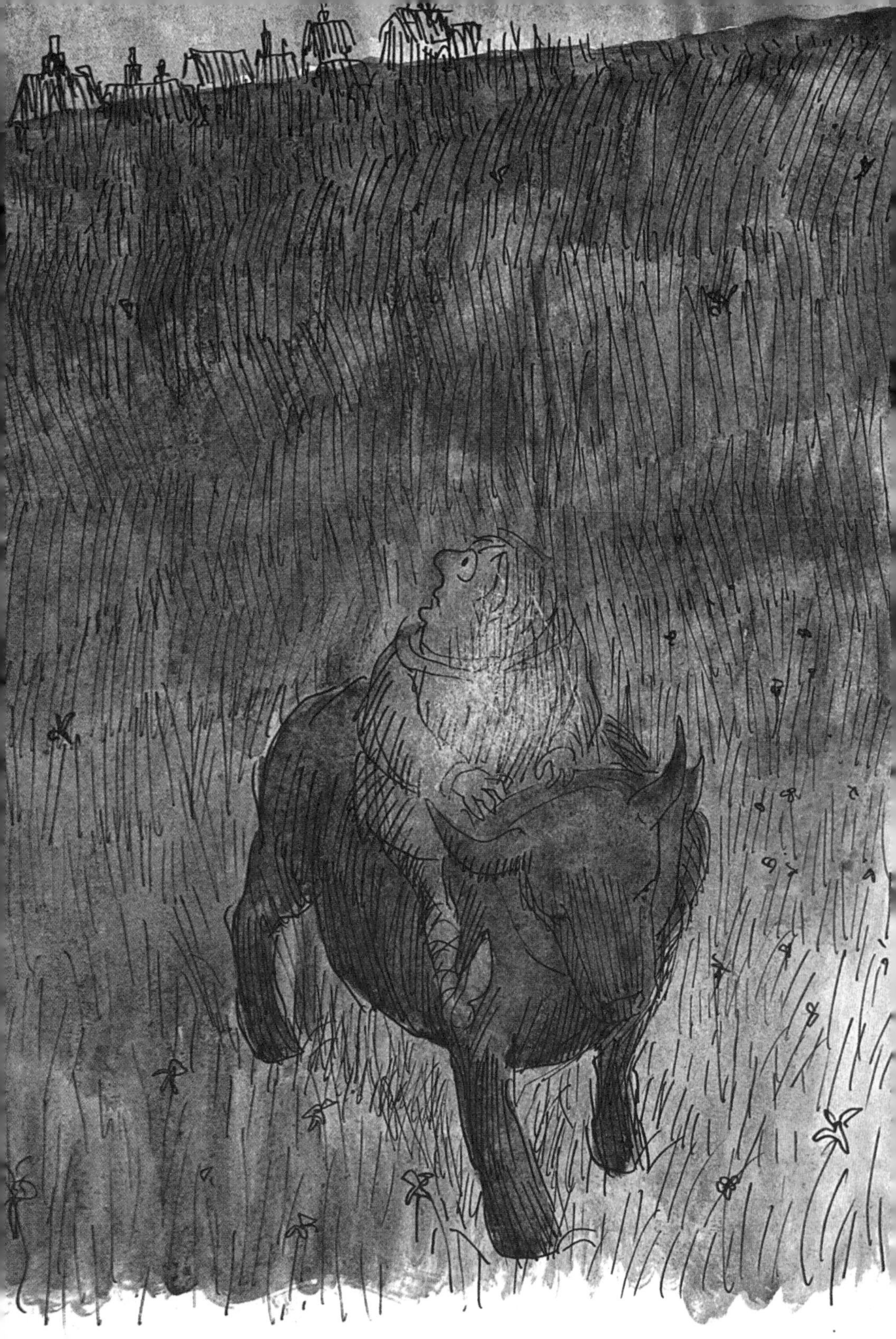

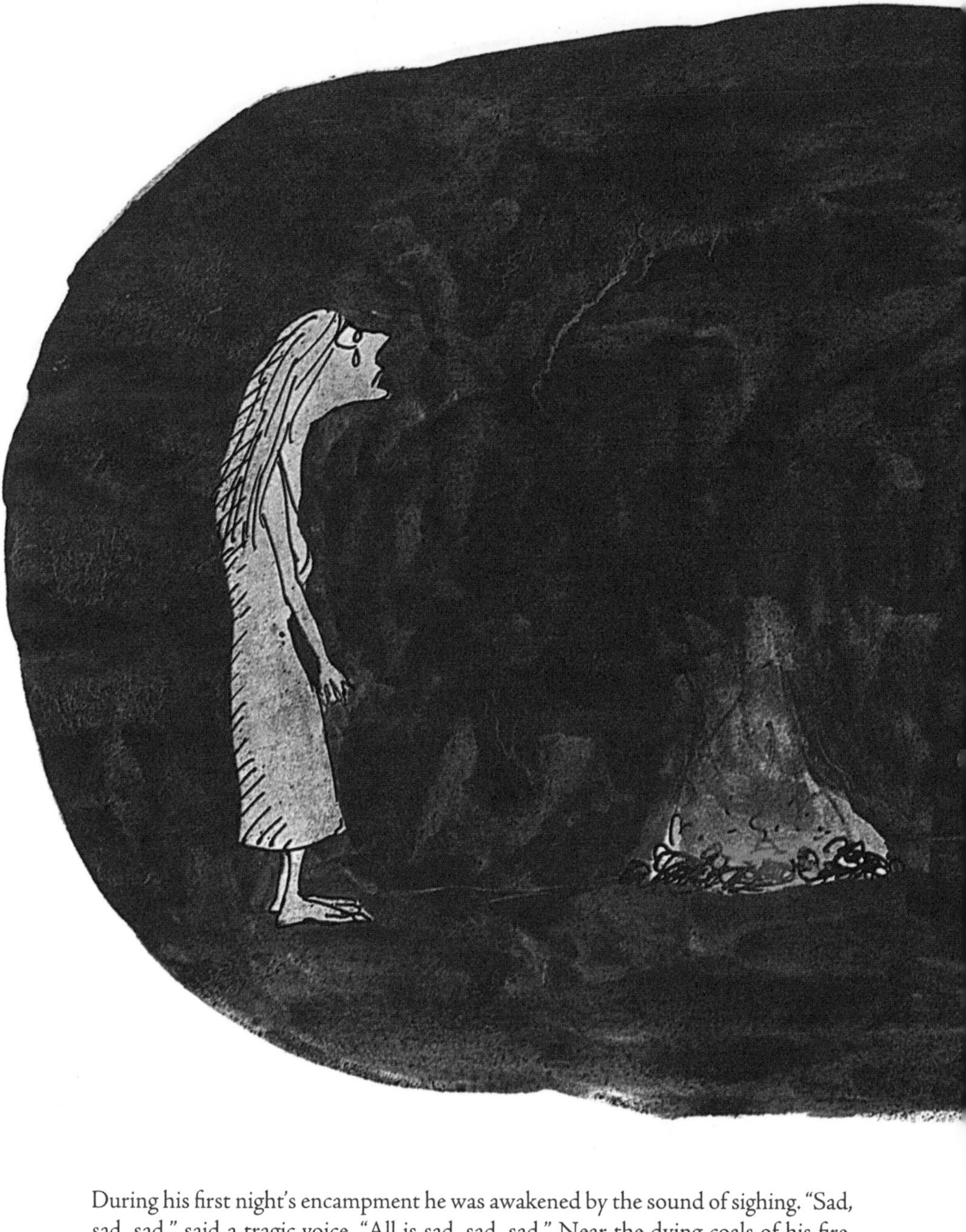

During his first night's encampment he was awakened by the sound of sighing. "Sad, sad, sad," said a tragic voice. "All is sad, sad, sad." Near the dying coals of his fire there stood the gravest, yet lovliest girl he had ever seen. "Do not look upon me," warned the girl, "for so grave a disposition have I that all those who gaze upon this, my face, are immediately consumed by grief and tears."

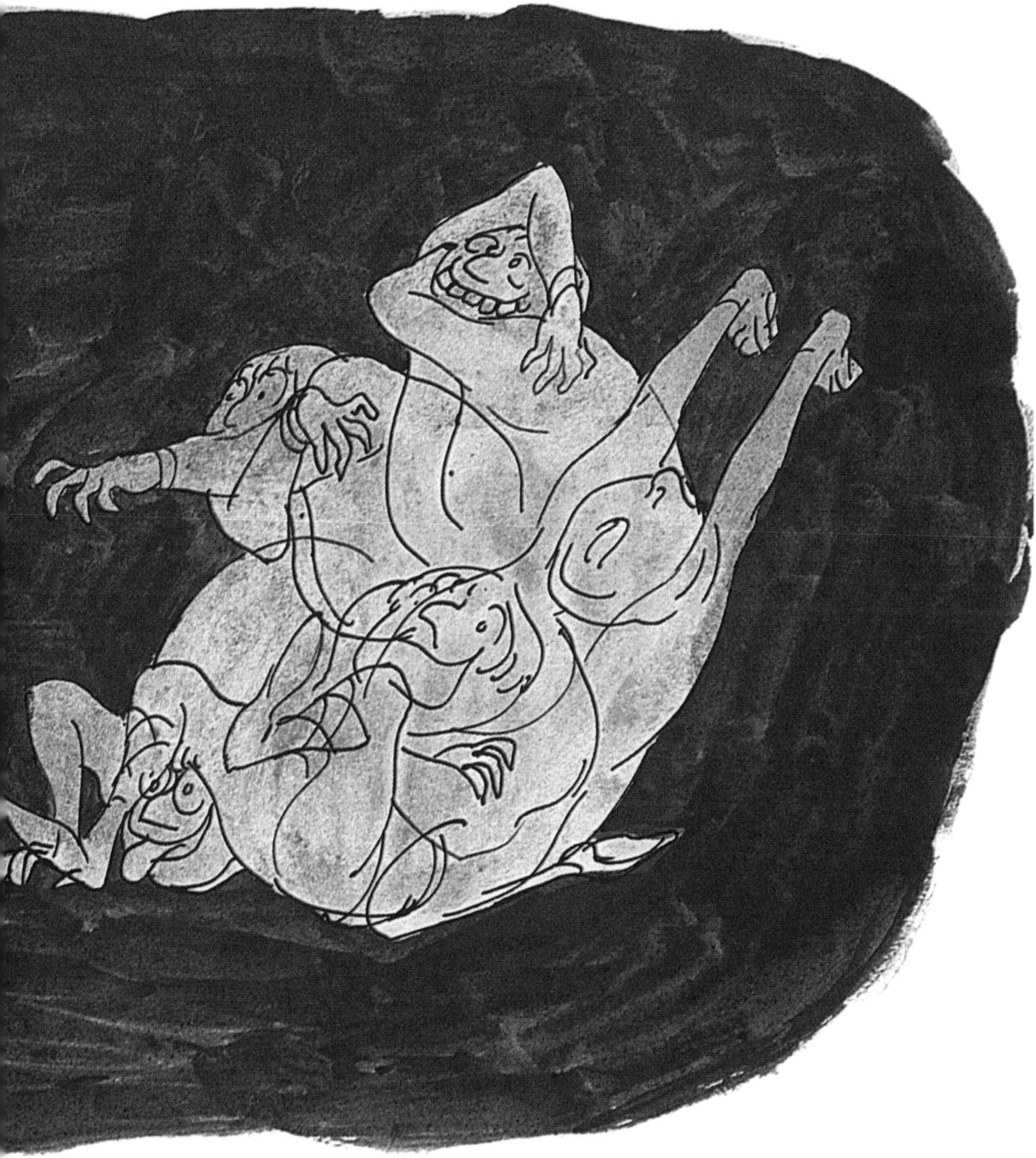

Excalibur bounded happily from his bedroll. "All those who look upon my face cannot help but laugh at the simple joys of living!" And to prove his point he broke into a remarkable dance, reciting as he turned cartwheels his entire repertoire of songs and sayings. But the girl sighed only the louder for it saddened her to know that such a gay young man would, at any moment, be consumed by grief and tears.

Hours later, with one exhausted by entertaining and the other debilitated by sighing, they fell in a state of collapse – chuckling and weeping in their respective slumbers.

The next morning the girl told her story. "My name is Rose. All my life I have sought the perfection implicit in that name – for what is more perfect than a rose? But feeling deeply the imperfections in myself and those around me, I grew moody and sullen. Each year and each experience taught me more clearly just how hideously imperfect the world had become, even to the point of infecting with its faults the lives of those nearest and dearest to me – my own beloved parents. With industry and patience I tried to correct these faults, but in my eagerness to help I only hindered. My parents took my advice unkindly and referred to me as a grouch and a long-face. It was then that I took to sighing, following them about and asking plaintively, 'Am I such a terrible person for wanting to improve you? Have I ever asked you to do anything that was wrong?' They began to throw sticks at me.

"One morning I awoke to find a note pinned to their unslept-in bed. Mother and Father had run away! The note explained that their only desire was for me to find happiness and if I ever succeeded I must send for them. But I know I cannot find happiness until I find perfection. So that is my quest: I shall hunt the land till I flush it out, wherever it may hide."

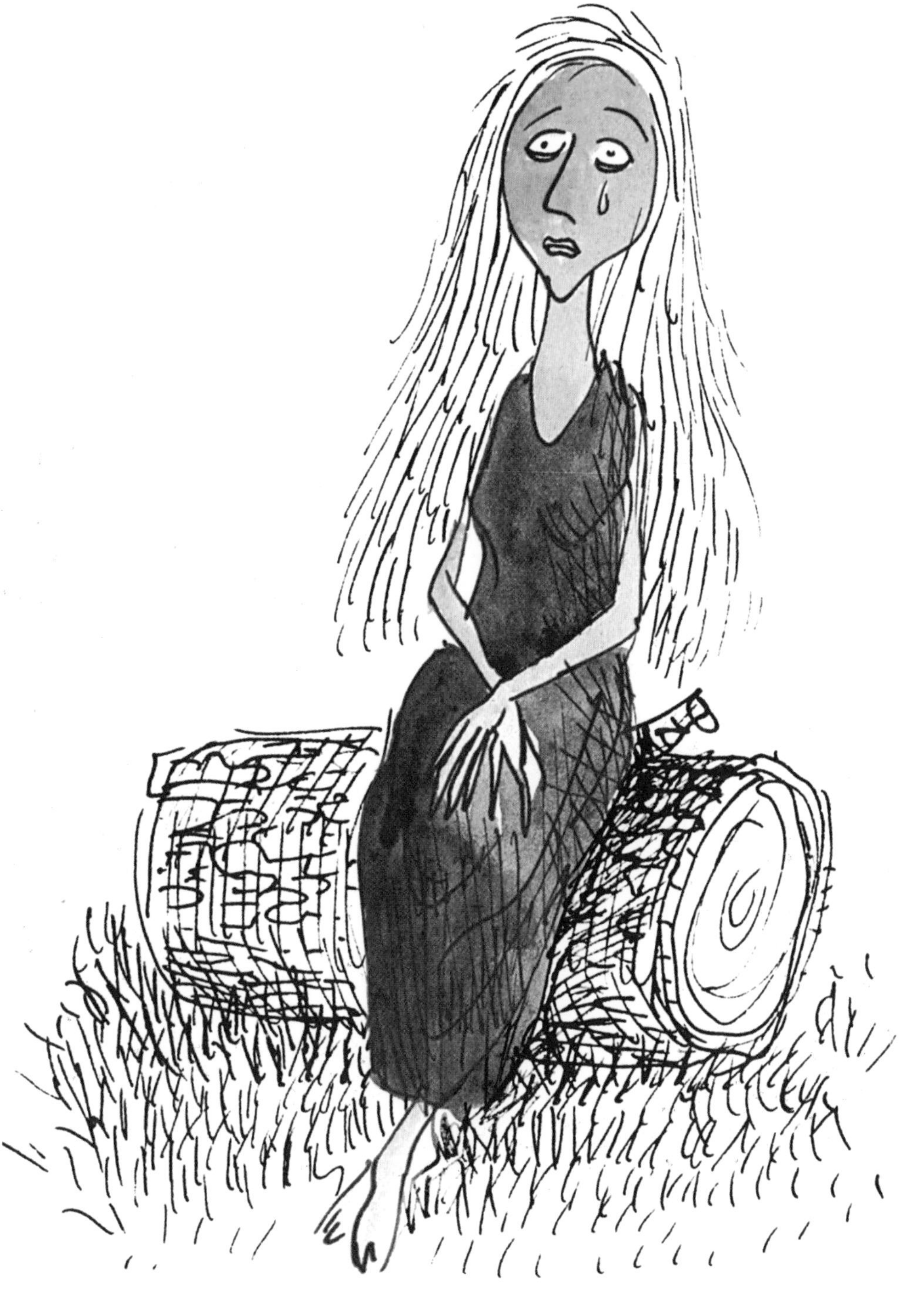

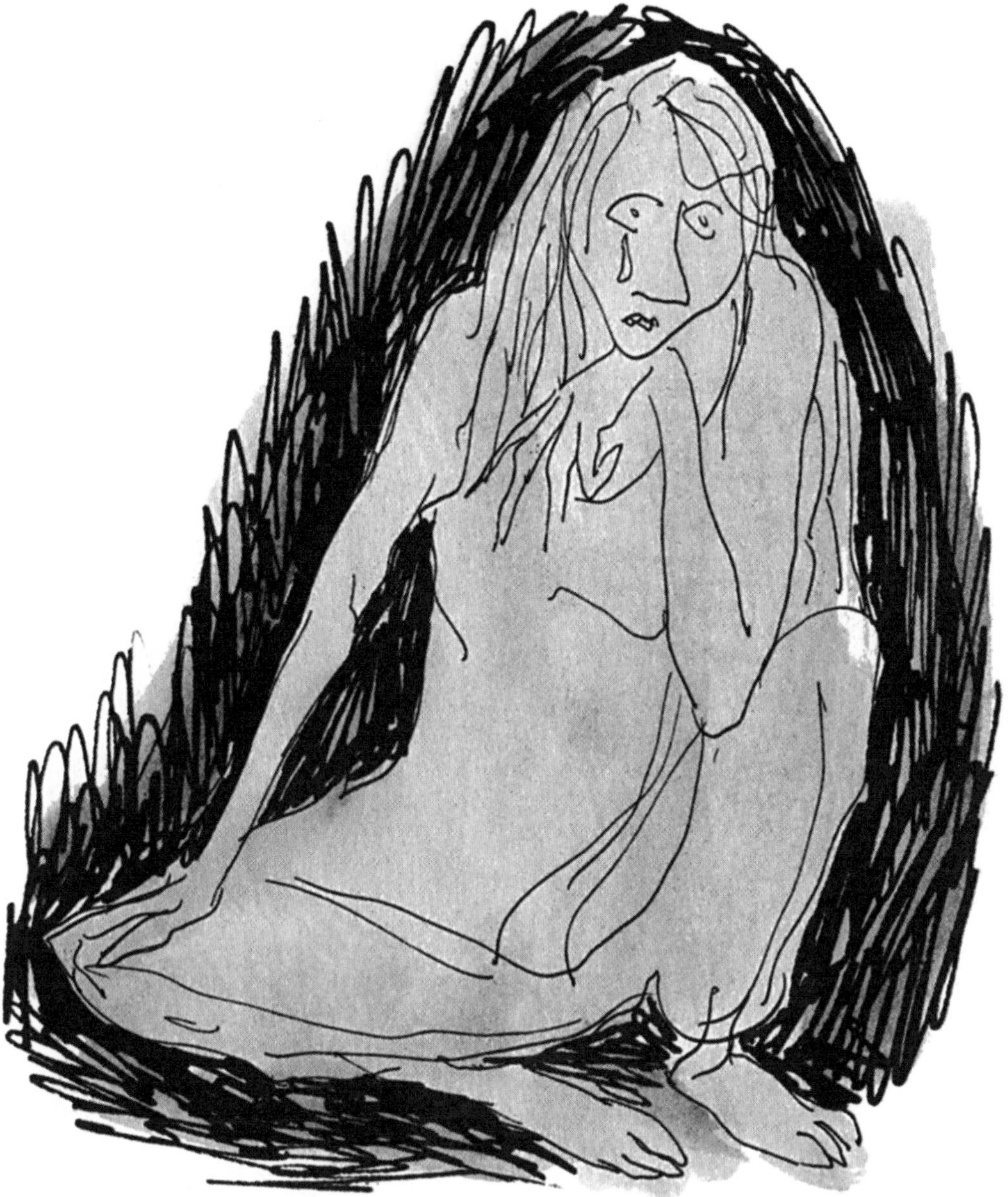

Excalibur was enthralled by the excitement of Rose's quest and asked if he might join her, for he hoped that by applying all his powers of observation he might successfully learn to imitate her seriousness, While en route he told Rose his own story. "When I was born, my mother, a good but slightly addled woman, fancied that I was not my father's son but the kidnapped child of some legendary king whose exploits she had heard and thrilled to in her childhood, and whose kingdom she much preferred I inherit than the accumulated debts of my *real* father. It was for this king that she determined to name me, but being heir to a faulty memory (which my father, under the circumstances, had no desire to correct) she gave me the name "Excalibur," who she remembered ruled a great kingdom aided only by the power of his trusty, well-tempered sword Arthur. The subsequent pattern of my life has followed closely the logic of my christening."

One day, intent upon their quest, Excalibur and Rose rode into a strange village whose busy market place was crowded for its great length with stalls of pressing, pushing, expressionless people. "It may be wisest to search first among the poor," said Rose, "for the rich, having small need to work, own more time to court temptation and thereby encourage imperfection."

Excalibur agreed.

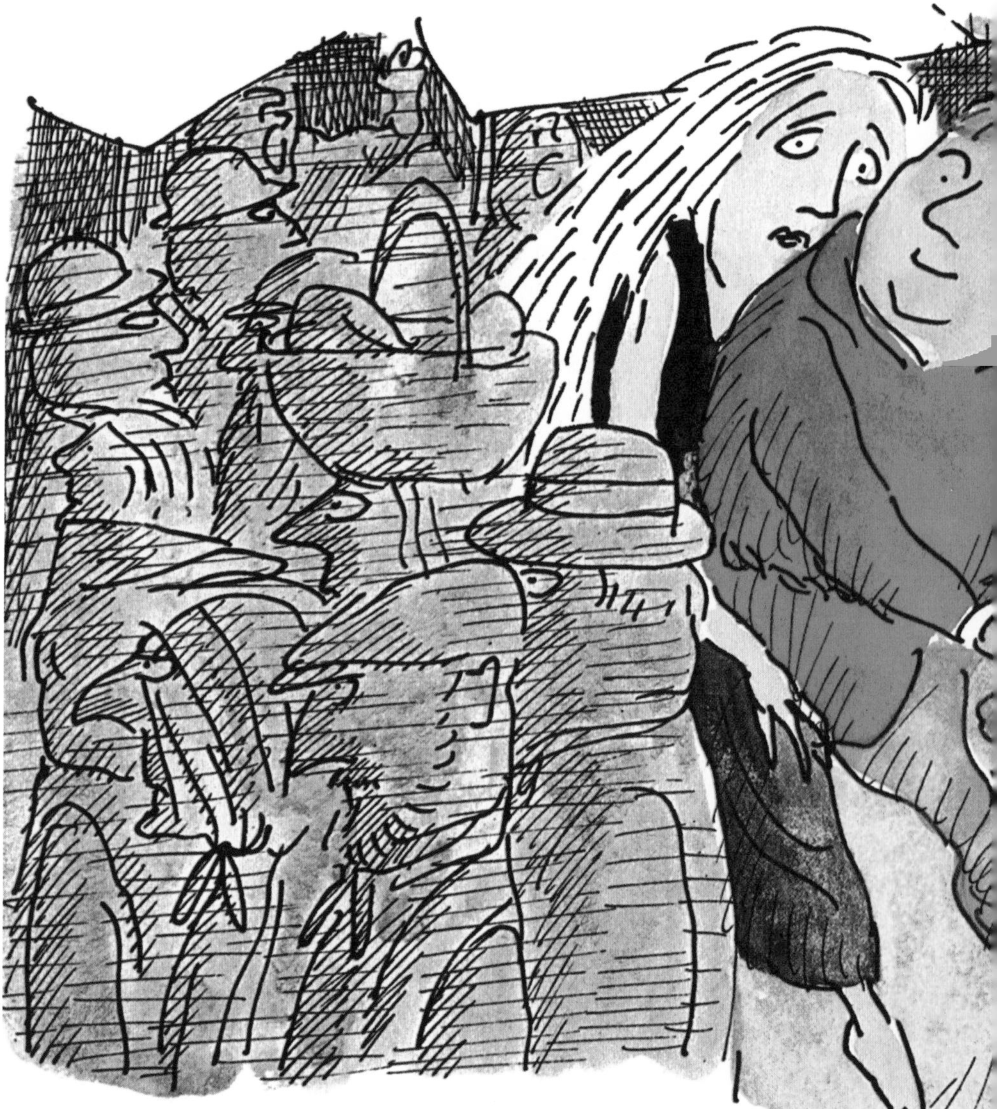

Cheerfully he cried out, "Who among you is so poor that he lives in perfection?" But though he repeated the question in many funny voices he could not divert a single eye from the merchandise. "We are in a world geared to trade," explained Excalibur, "Nothing here is considered of value unless it is marked with a price."

"How sad," said Rose, and she wept.

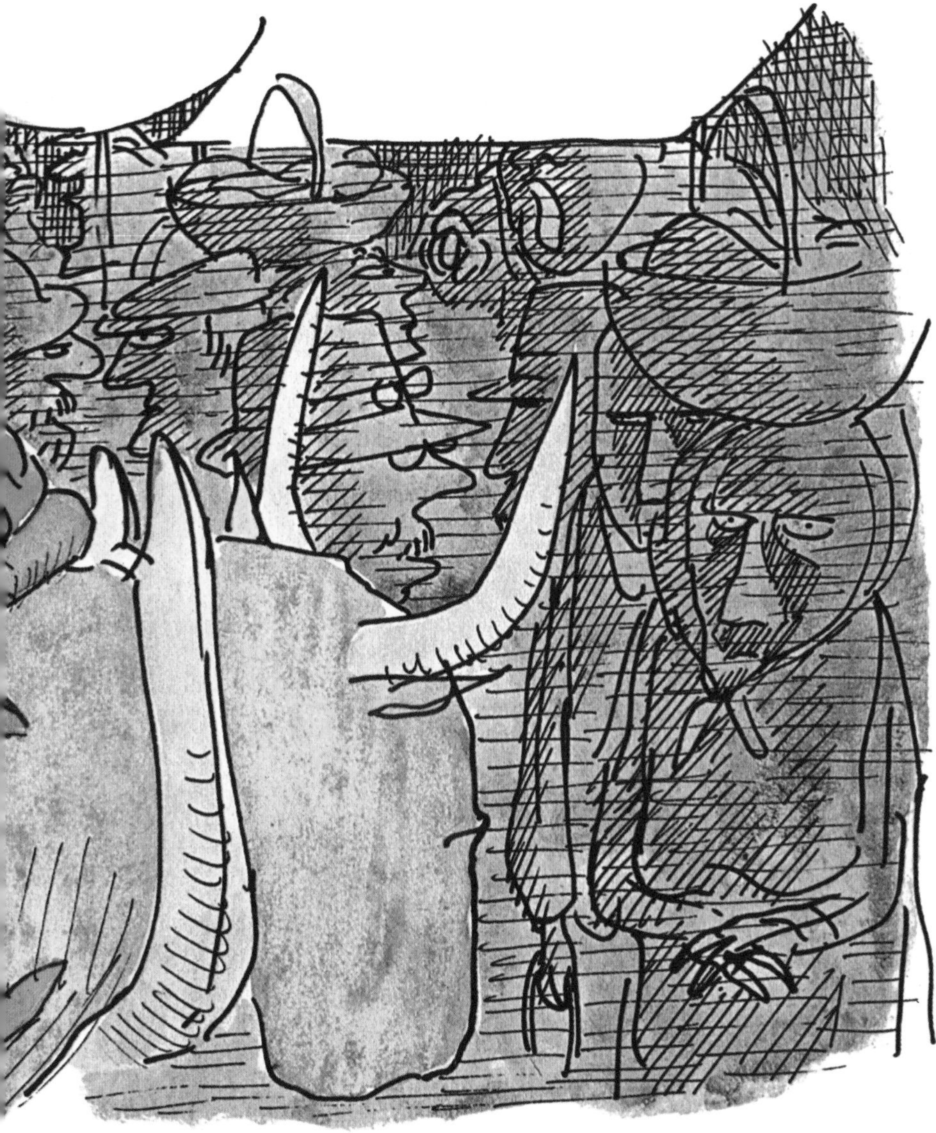

"How hilarious," said Excalibur. He thereupon found a loose board on which he painted the words, "*Tears for Sale*"; and placing the sign on an empty stall, he sat Rose on a stool directly under it. "Here in the market place no one laughs and no one weeps," said Excalibur. "They are too busy to have feelings and too active to have emotions. But if we disguise ourselves as marketable, we may yet be heard." Then in a loud voice he cried, "Tears for sale! Buy your river of flowing tears!"

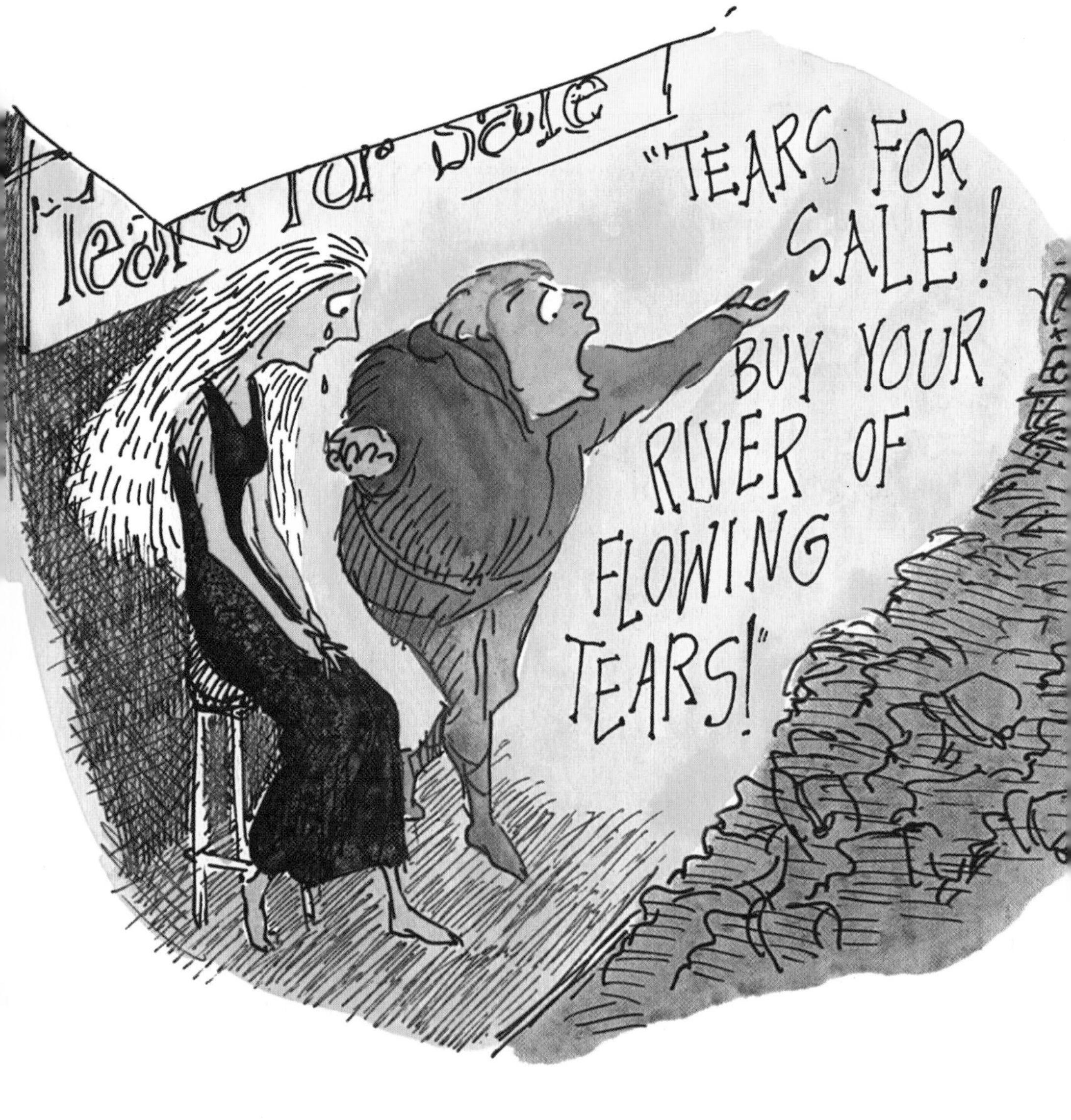
Tears for Sale
"TEARS FOR SALE! BUY YOUR RIVER OF FLOWING TEARS!"

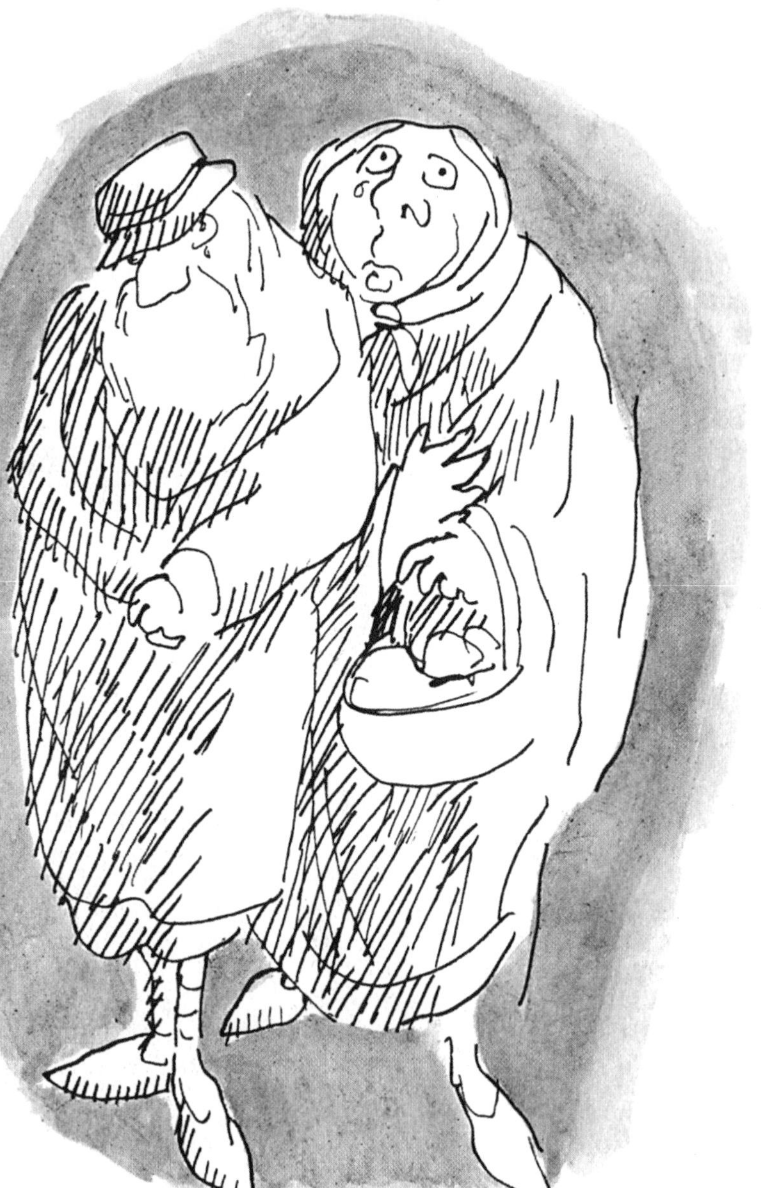

A crowd formed in no time. It pressed in closely, cautiously inspecting the new product for merits and defects. Coins began to be tossed into Rose's lap. Handkerchiefs fought battles beneath her chin to see whose would catch the biggest tear. Through it all Rose sat, singing sadly of a people grown so imperfect that in order to have tears they must purchase them. At the end of the song her audience was shaking with sobs.

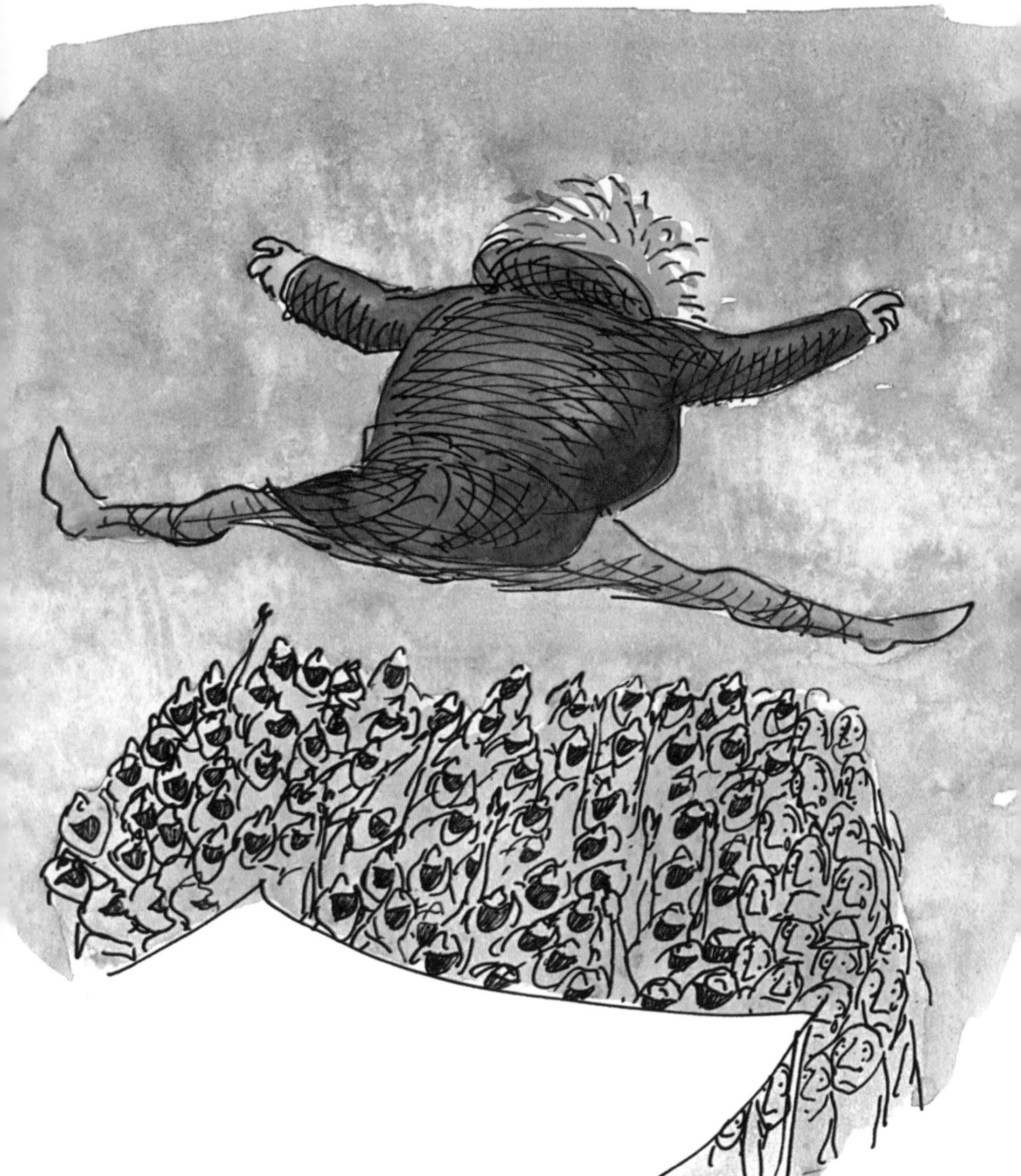

Tears spread like a contagion and within moments the market place was immersed – a sight that brought the happiest of grins to Excalibur's face. Thrilled with Rose's accomplishment, he leaped to the roof of the stall and danced for joy.

The irresistibility of his mood soon cracked the spell of weeping, and the crowd, confused by this sudden onslaught of emotions, lapsed into an uncontrollable fit of the giggles. And so the day wore on – first with Rose and the crowd weeping, then with Excalibur and the crowd dancing for joy. By nightfall the exhausted village had made heroes of the two young people: Excalibur, for his genius to inspire laughter, and Rose, for her knowledge of the soul.

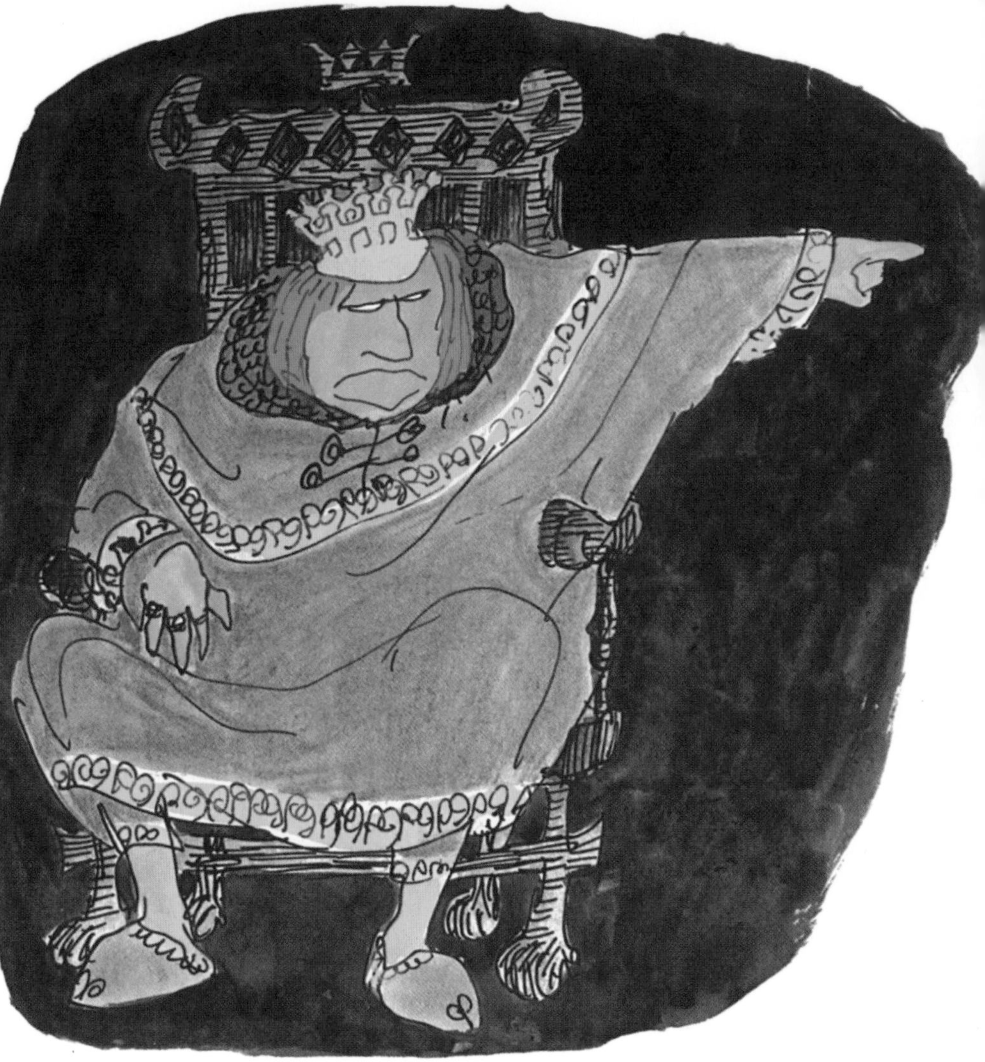

Now such a remarkable change in the life of a town could not long go unnoticed by the paternal eye of the King, Kind Wicked III, who for years had brooded over the bored reaction of his people to the profitable subject of war. He dispatched four of his most trusted counselors to fetch these curious travelers who might be of use to him. But at their first sight of Rose and Excalibur, the counselors wept and laughed to such a degree that they forgot completely the purpose of their mission, resigned from the king's services and, from that day, traveled the land as monks.

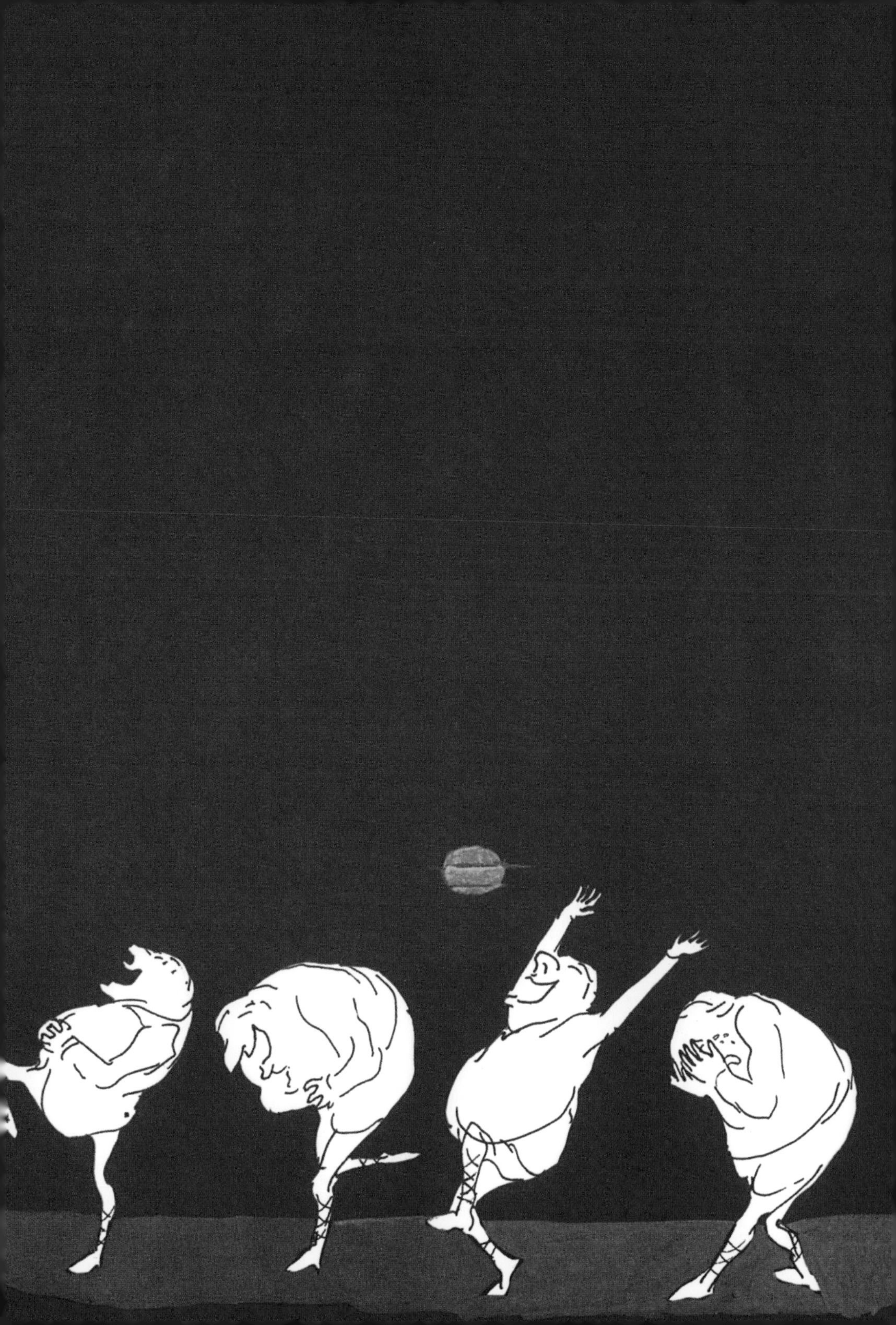

Only by himself accosting them in the black of night when even a star was forbidden to flicker was the king able to complete his mission, bringing to his palace in masks and chains the happy man and the serious girl. Once there, he banished Excalibur to the dungeons as his hostage, and had sad Rose brought before him, crying softly into her mask which the king forbade her to remove lest he too be reduced to tears.

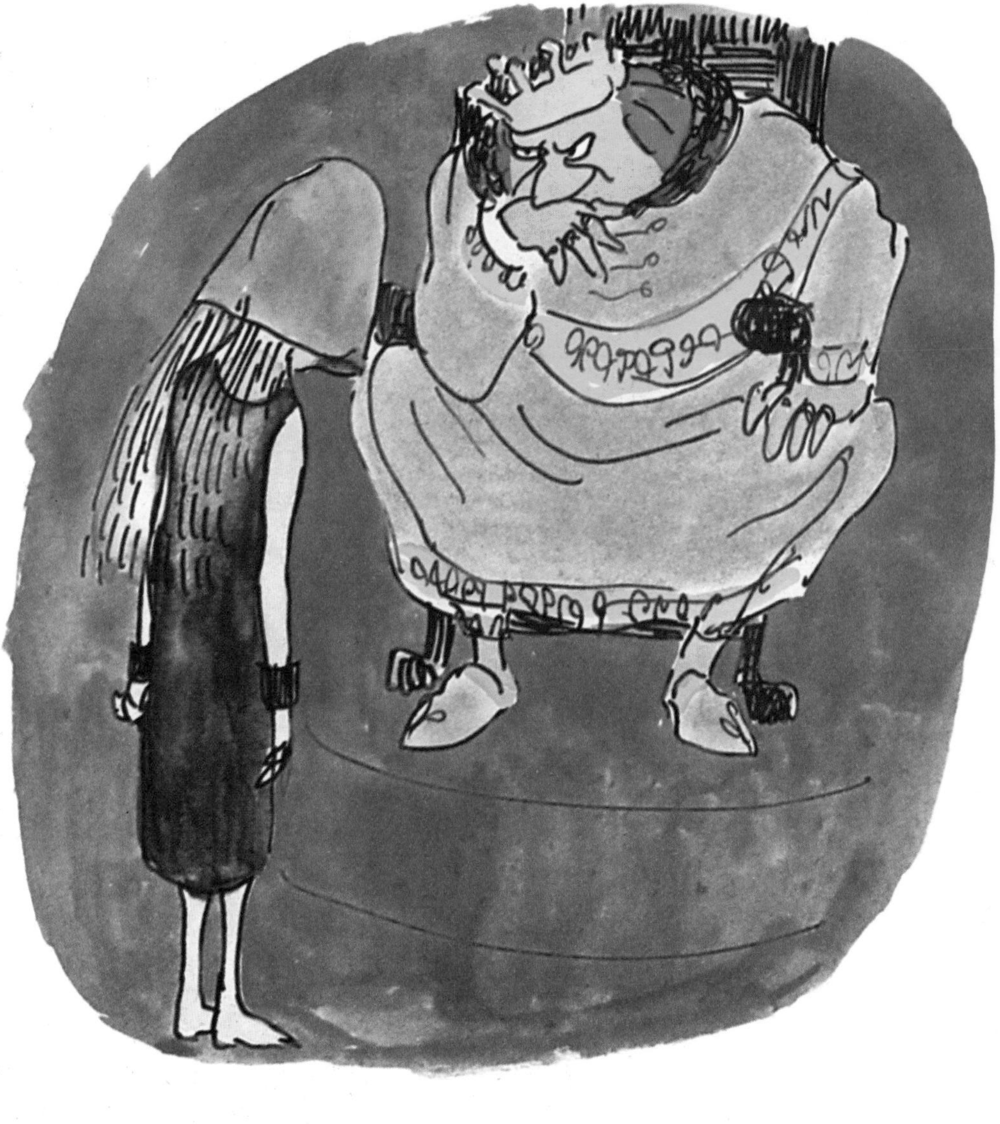

King Kind Wicked III explained, "My family history has been a proud one of triumph and acquisition. My father's father, King Kind Wicked I, led a gallant and vengeful people to victory after victory until the one crushing defeat that ended his life. My father, King Kind Wicked II, led a noble and vindictive people to victory after victory until the one crushing defeat that ended *his* life. I, King Kind Wicked III, have been the only monarch in our history thus far unable to undertake a single act of war. My exhortations fall on listless ears. I cannot raise money for battle, because people hoard it for trade. I cannot make our youths into warriors, because they would rather bargain than be brave. My people have forgotten the enemy's name – but still I must arouse them to anger. Anger can only follow shame and shame can only follow tears. It is through the mechanics of weeping that I will manufacture the spirit of heroism in battle."

And so with the forced consent of Rose the King set off on a speech-making tour of the provinces – and wherever he spoke, there by his side stood Rose weeping sadly. Her sorrow blanketed the land, leaving a void of despair which the King quickly filled with his talk of war. He sent out a cry to right the outrages that had driven his kingdom to tears; and the kingdom, feeling rage growing out of its tears of shame, responded vigorously.

None of this was known to Excalibur, who languished happily in his dungeon refreshing his spirits with the amusing nonsense he imagined in the shadows. His guards, though ordered not to, could not resist peering in to discover what secret joy there was to be found in a darkened cell. And once having looked they had to laugh, and having laughed they had to slide free the bolt from the iron door and

lead Excalibur into the prison yard, where he was ordered to dance for them. And when Excalibur danced *they* had to dance, joining hands while kicking their way merrily around the walls of the prison till there was not a guard or official not so taken with the joy of the occasion that he was able to remember the next day just when the prisoner slipped off into the darkness.

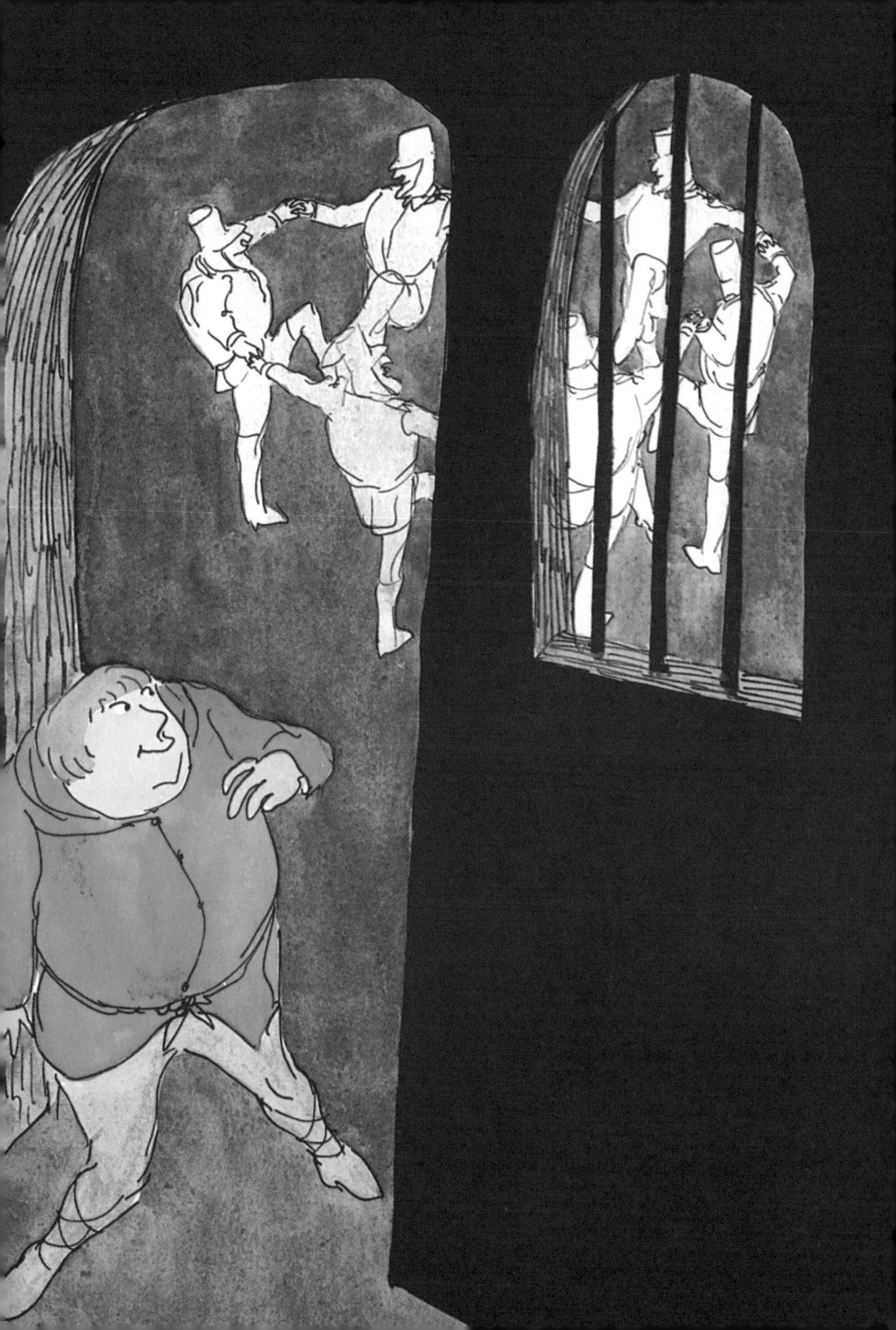

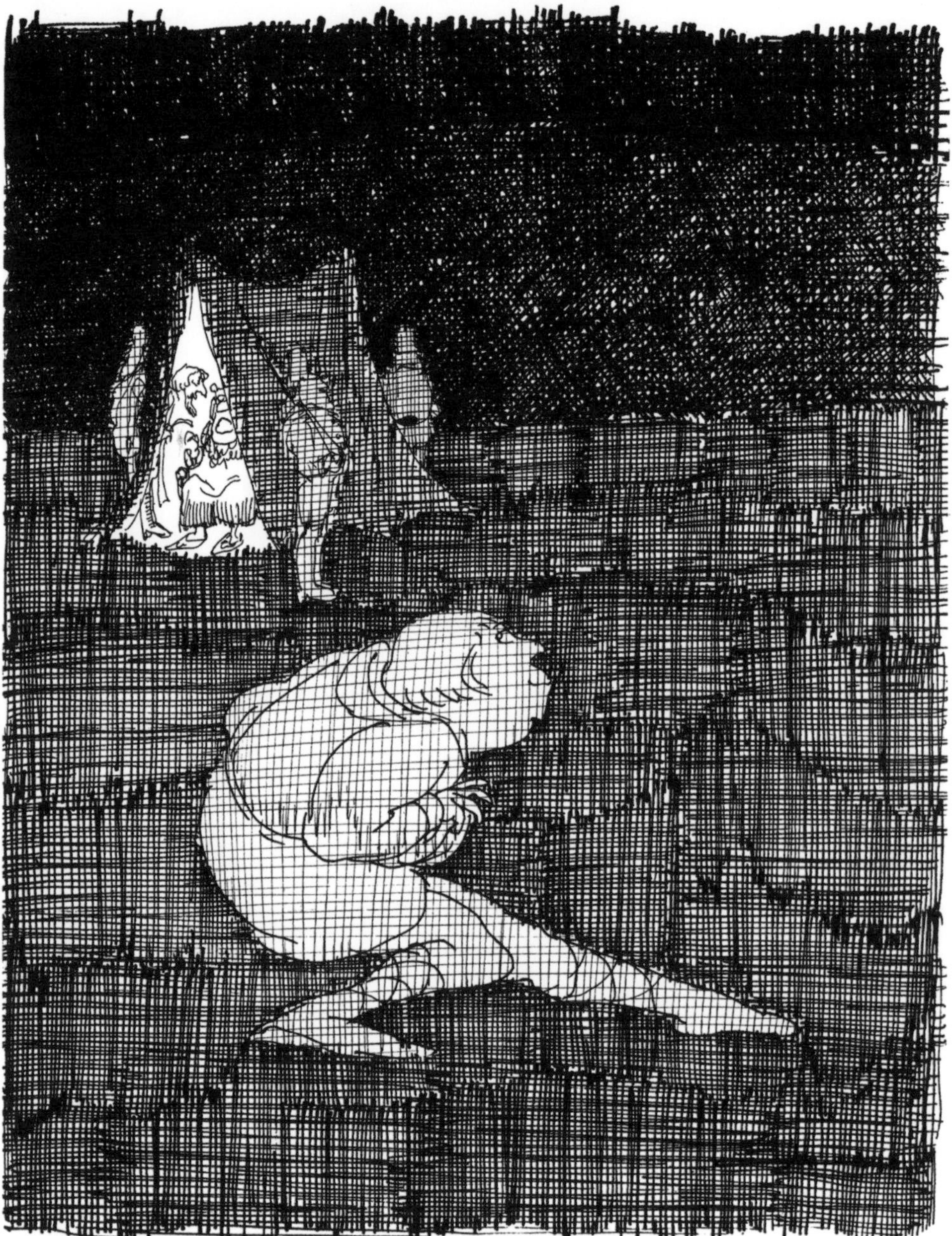

On the eve before the King was to make his public declaration of war, he was gathered with his speech writers to decide a difficult question of phraseology, there being a furious debate over whether the term "peace" should properly precede or follow the term "freedom-loving."

Quickly scurrying past the King's guard, Excalibur followed the sound of sighing to Rose's tent, where the two friends were at last back together, laughing and crying: she, filled with tales of horror about her journey, he, interrupting with airy tidbits from the dungeon. Finally Rose could stand no more of it. Bitterly she pushed Excalibur away from her and decried his one-sidedness as incorrigible. She could no longer suffer idiocy disguised as happiness. She flung open the flap of her tent and ordered Excalibur to leave. But he did not leave. He could not. Instead, to the astonishment of both, he fell at her feet and wept. And speaking through his first set of tears, he said, "Let me stay. I love you." And Rose, seeing his tears through tears of her own, knew that she loved him as well.

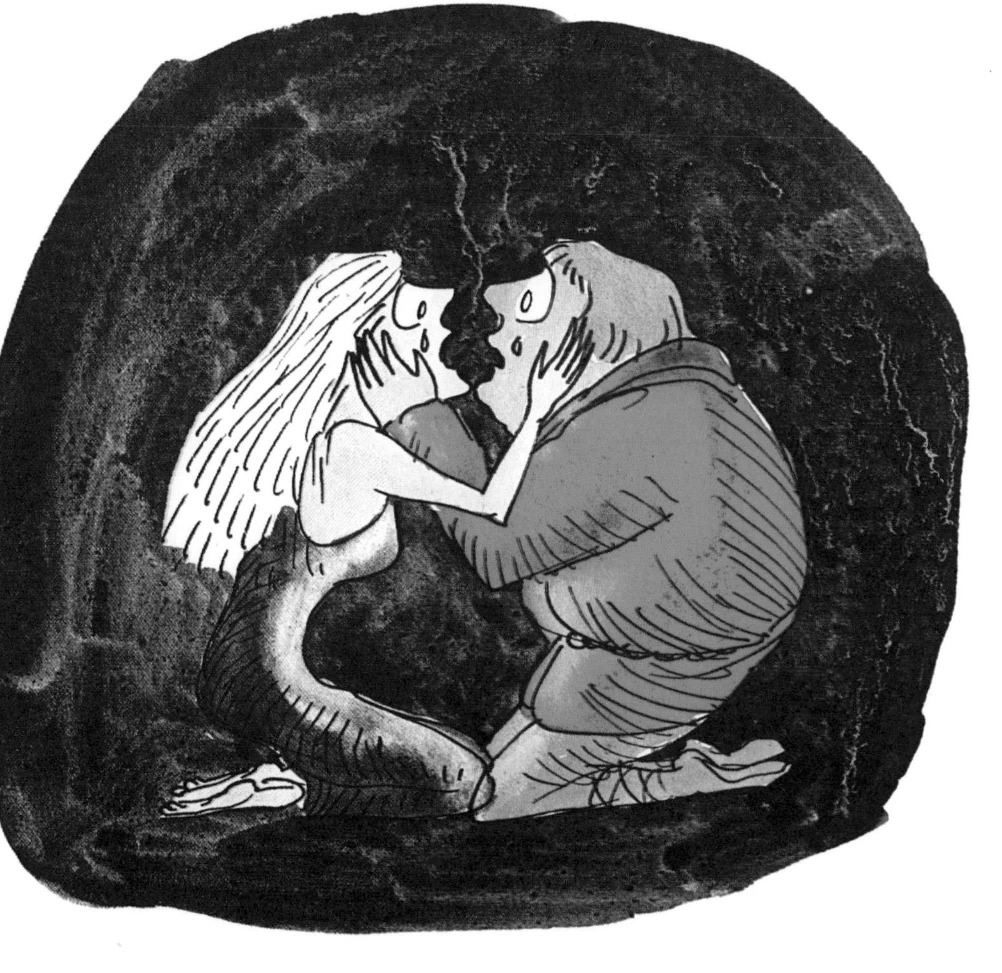

They embraced as lovers, and the longing Excalibur had felt these many months was gone, replaced now with a fullness of soul he had never known before. "Oh. my dear Rose, I have found my serious side. It is *you!*" And he wept with great satisfaction, and Rose wept with him. Then Excalibur looked beyond his own tears and noted that in the midst of her gleaming wet face, Rose wore a smile.

"I have never enjoyed weeping before," Rose explained. "It is different to weep in the company of one you care for." And the lovers embraced once again.

With a soberness that was new to him Excalibur outlined a plan. "Tomorrow when the king speaks you will not cry."

"But I always cry," said Rose.

"You must laugh. Look only at me in the crowd. I will make you laugh."

Rose cried. "I have never laughed. The best I am able to do is smile through tears." But Excalibur reassured her and, with a parting embrace, disappeared into the night.

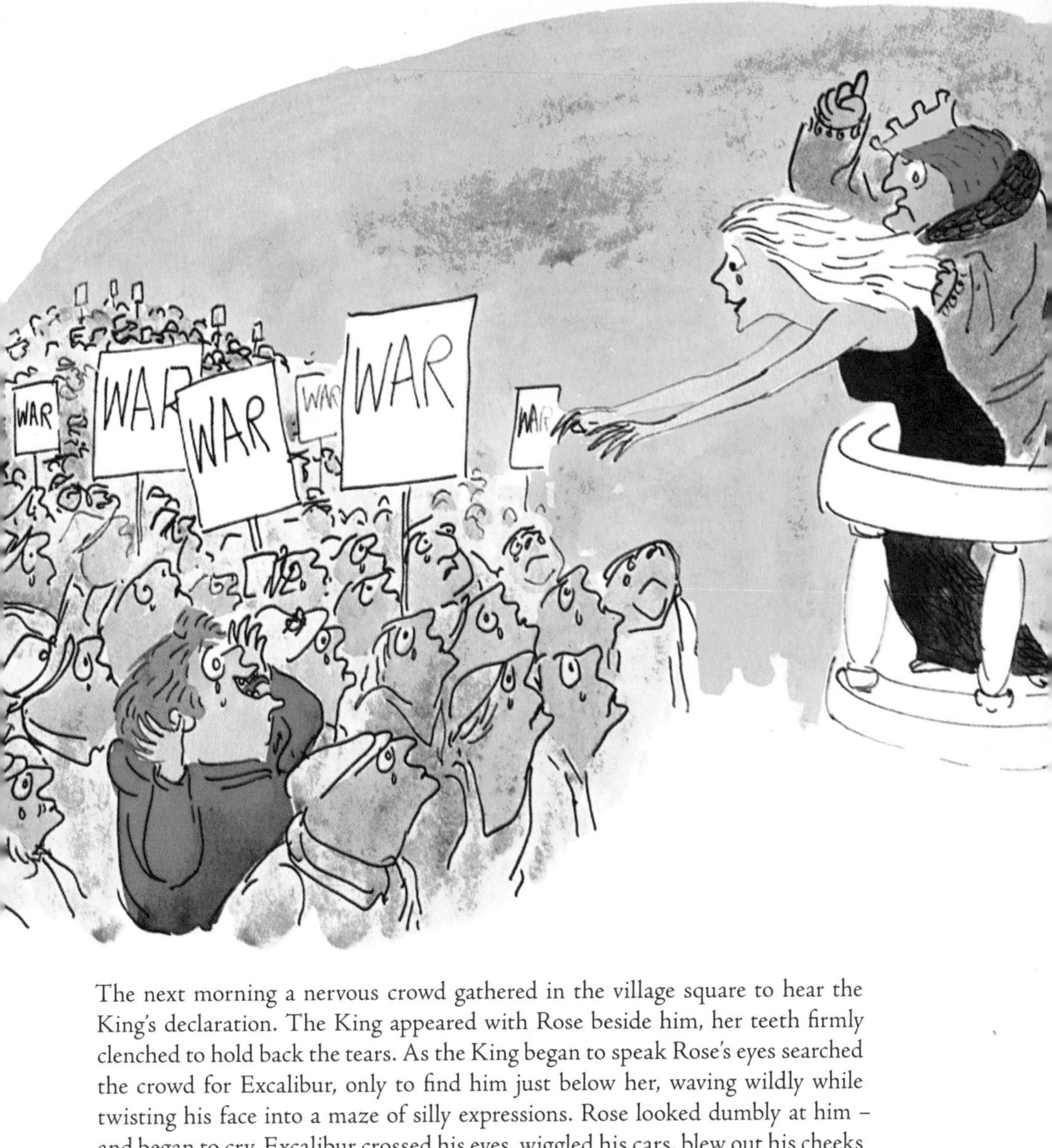
WAR
WAR
WAR
WAR
WAR

The next morning a nervous crowd gathered in the village square to hear the King's declaration. The King appeared with Rose beside him, her teeth firmly clenched to hold back the tears. As the King began to speak Rose's eyes searched the crowd for Excalibur, only to find him just below her, waving wildly while twisting his face into a maze of silly expressions. Rose looked dumbly at him – and began to cry. Excalibur crossed his eyes, wiggled his cars, blew out his cheeks and stuck out his tongue till it touched his nose. Rose wept louder. The crowd wept with her and Excalibur, struck by the helpless look on the face of his beloved, began to weep too. And suddenly Rose smiled. The tears ran down the furiously mugging face of Excalibur, and Rose just beamed at him, warming the crowd with her smile till the King, sensing the sharp change of mood, stammered in the midst of his speech and came to a halt. But Rose did not notice. Her eyes saw only Excalibur, who earnestly redoubled his efforts at earwiggling, eye-crossing and tongue-stretching – crying helplessly all the while.

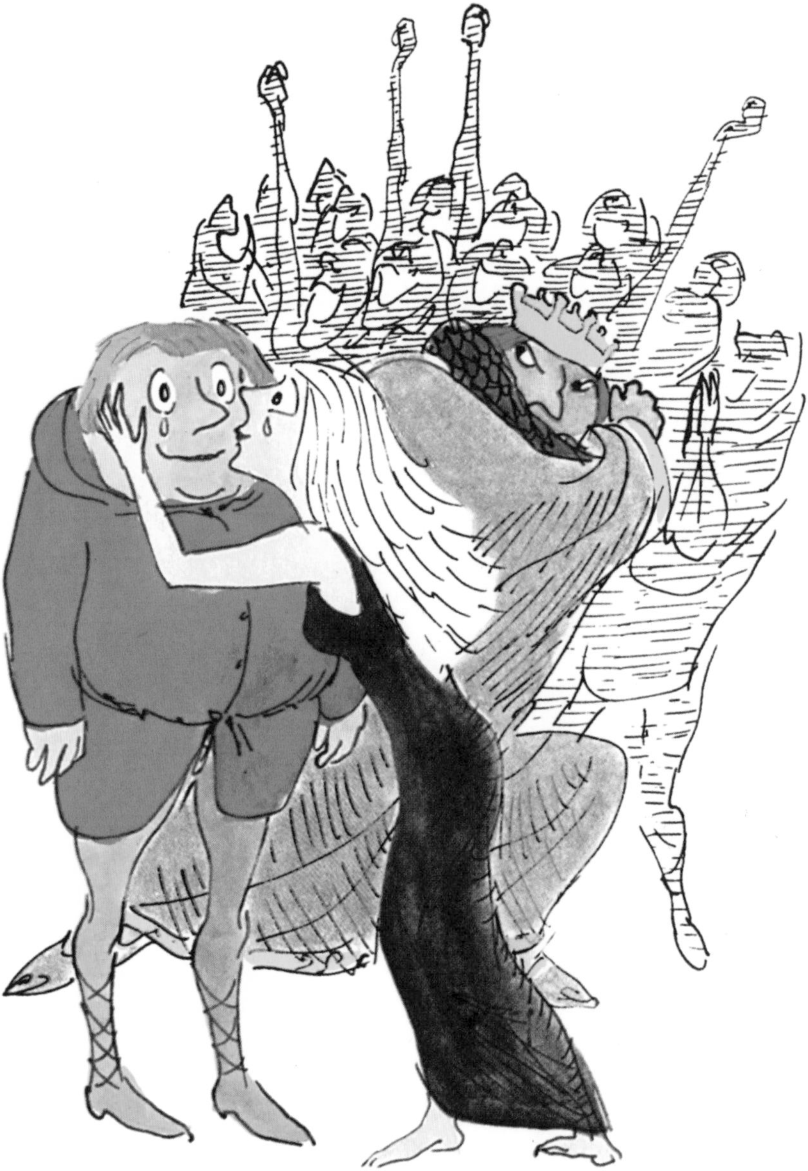

Rose descended from the balcony and the crowd parted for her. She took Excalibur's face in her hands and smiled into it. "At this moment I have found my perfection." She patted his face, gently drying the tears, and as they faded from his eyes Excalibur grinned. And Rose laughed. And the people, not understanding a thing of what they saw, broke into cheers, leaving little for the King to do but tear up his speech and stalk off.

Excalibur brought Rose home to his village, where together they built a house of eight sides: one side for happiness, one side for seriousness and six spare sides to contain what new knowledge of themselves and the world their future together might bring.

The End

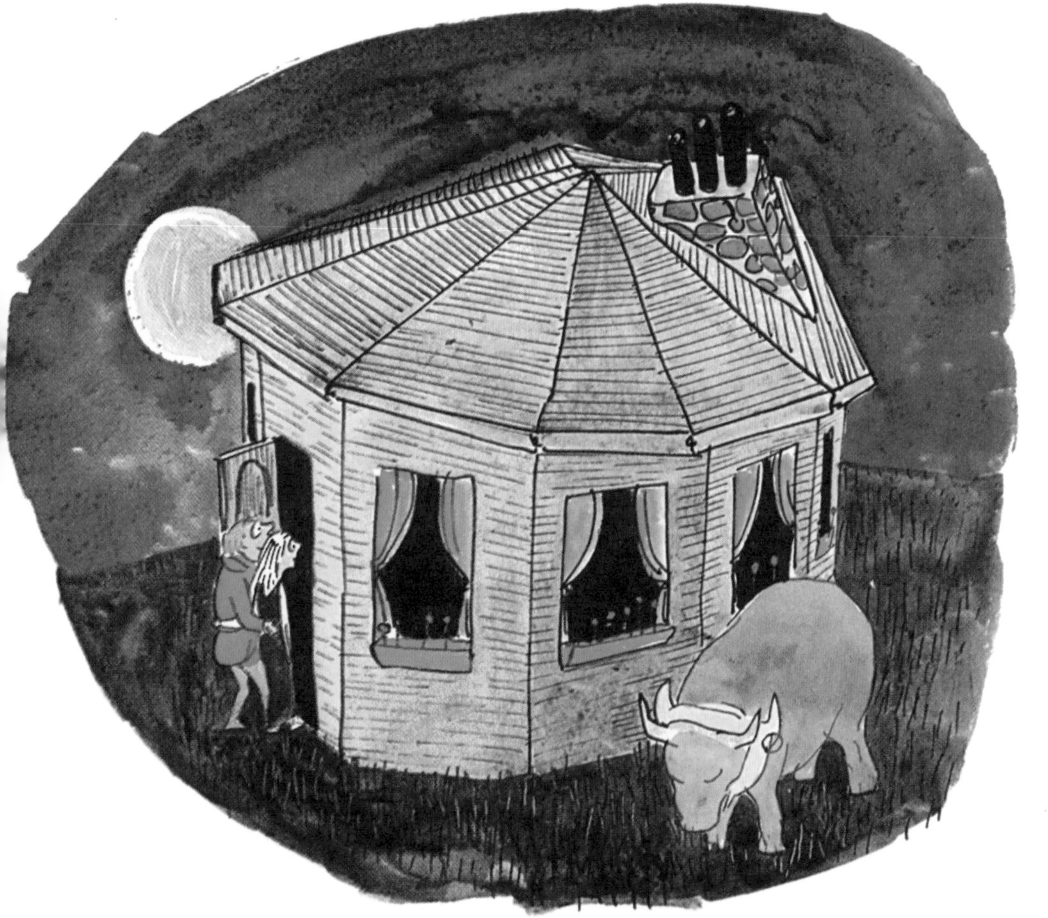

The Lonely Machine

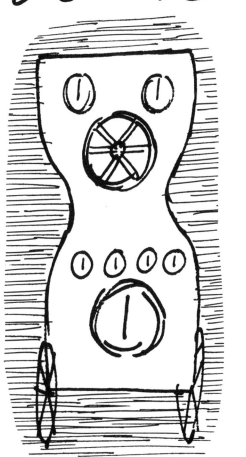

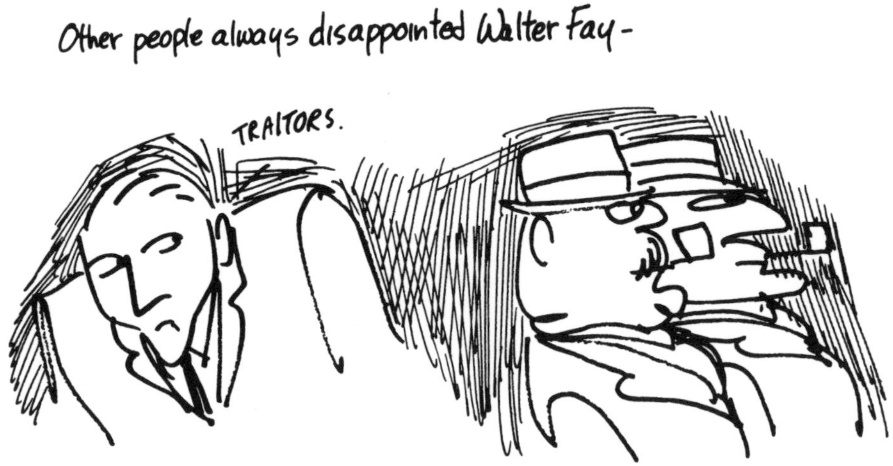
Other people always disappointed Walter Fay-
TRAITORS.

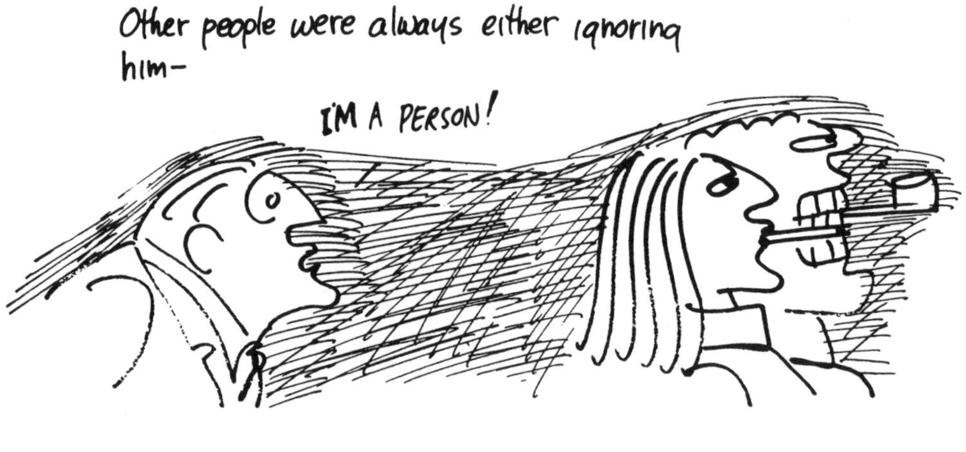
Other people were always either ignoring him-
I'M A PERSON!

Or rejecting him –

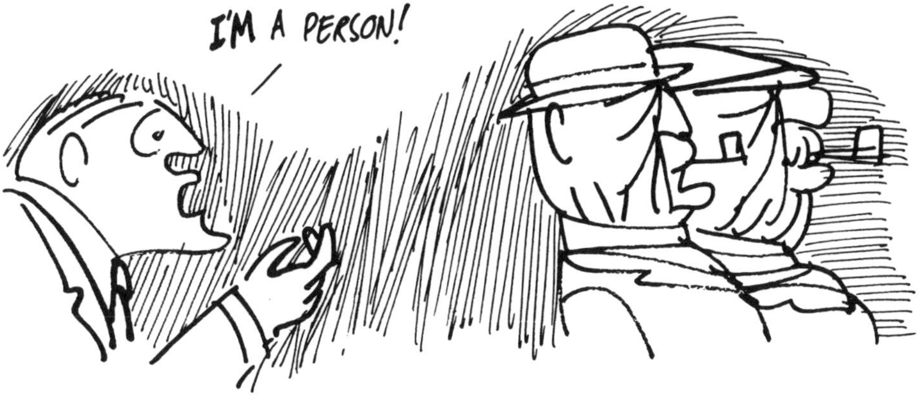
I'M A PERSON!

Or betraying him –

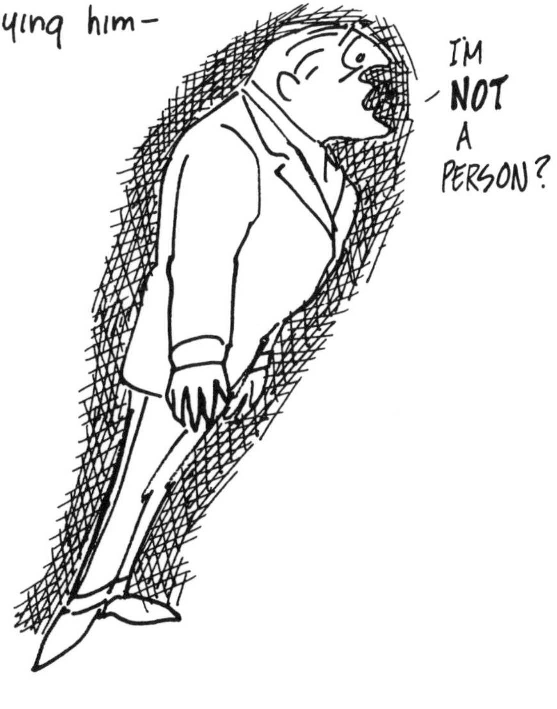
I'M NOT A PERSON?

This made Walter Fay sulk a lot:

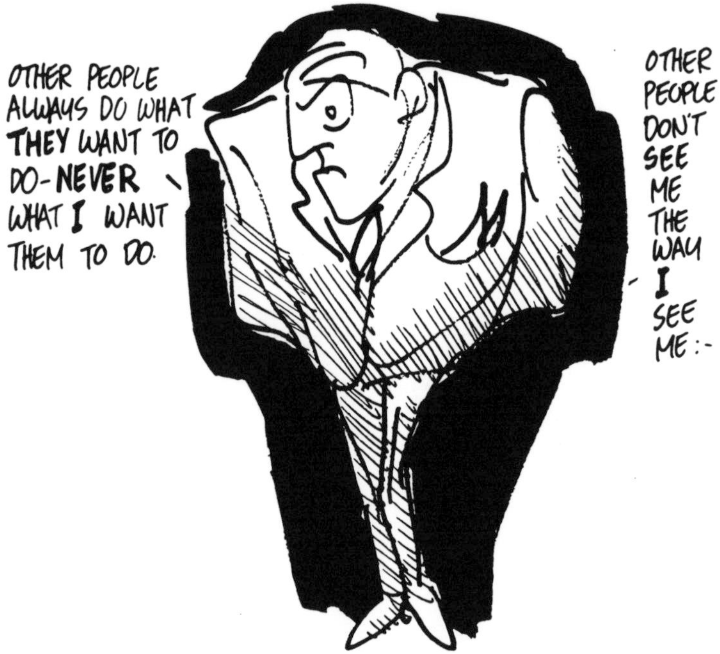
OTHER PEOPLE ALWAYS DO WHAT THEY WANT TO DO-NEVER WHAT I WANT THEM TO DO.
OTHER PEOPLE DON'T SEE ME THE WAY I SEE ME:-

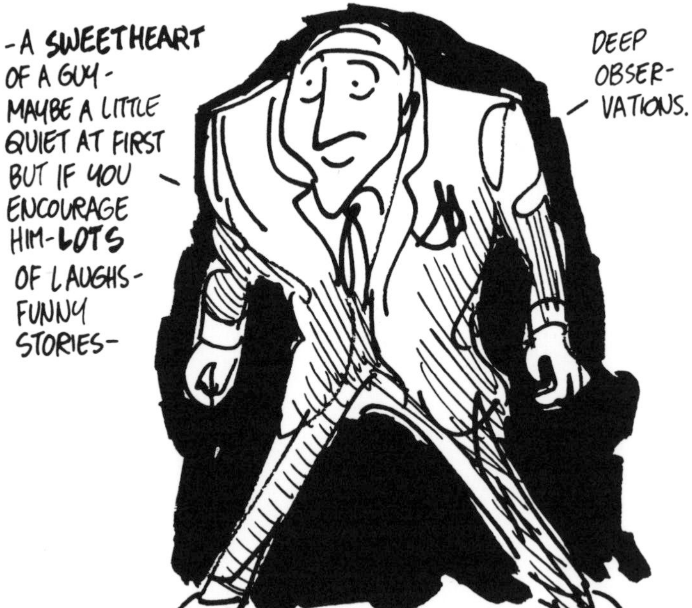
-A SWEETHEART OF A GUY-MAYBE A LITTLE QUIET AT FIRST BUT IF YOU ENCOURAGE HIM-LOTS OF LAUGHS-FUNNY STORIES-
DEEP OBSER-VATIONS.

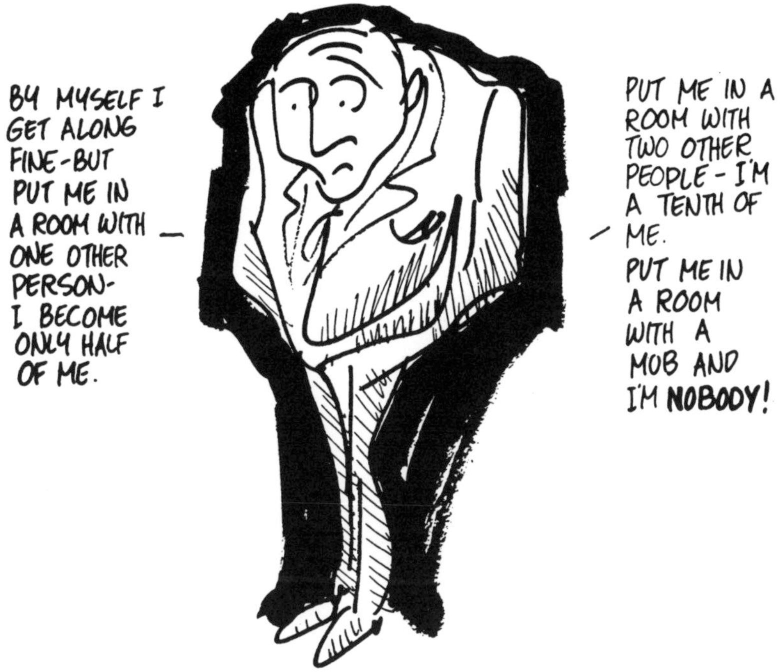
BY MYSELF I GET ALONG FINE - BUT PUT ME IN A ROOM WITH ONE OTHER PERSON - I BECOME ONLY HALF OF ME.
PUT ME IN A ROOM WITH TWO OTHER PEOPLE - I'M A TENTH OF ME.
PUT ME IN A ROOM WITH A MOB AND I'M **NOBODY**!

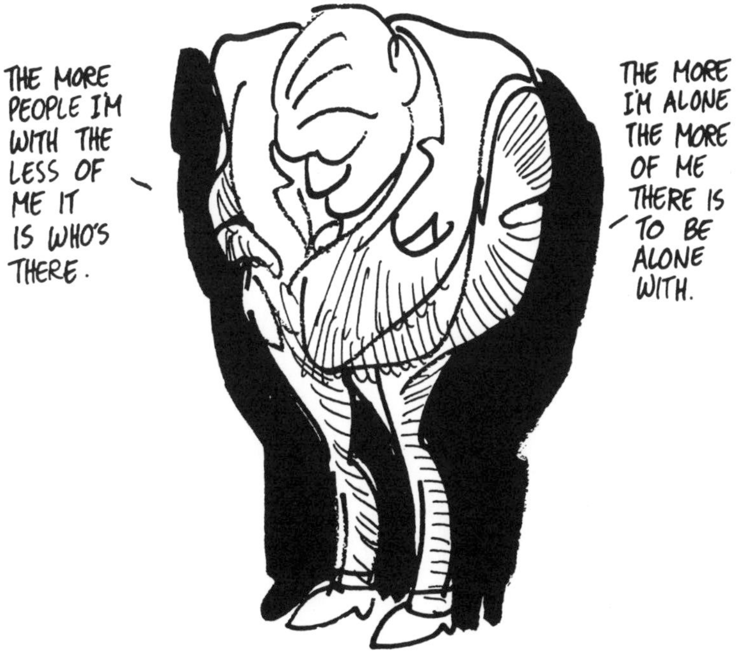
THE MORE PEOPLE I'M WITH THE LESS OF ME IT IS WHO'S THERE.
THE MORE I'M ALONE THE MORE OF ME THERE IS TO BE ALONE WITH.

And so he'd regularly vow never to go out again.

WHO NEEDS 'EM?
RING
FREE? WHY WOULDN'T I BE FREE? IS NINE O'CLOCK TOO EARLY?

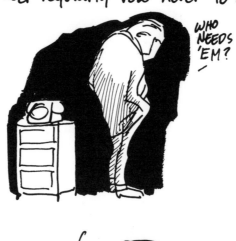

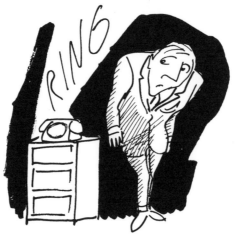

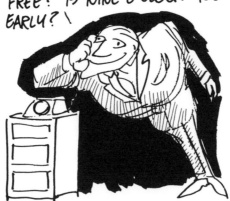

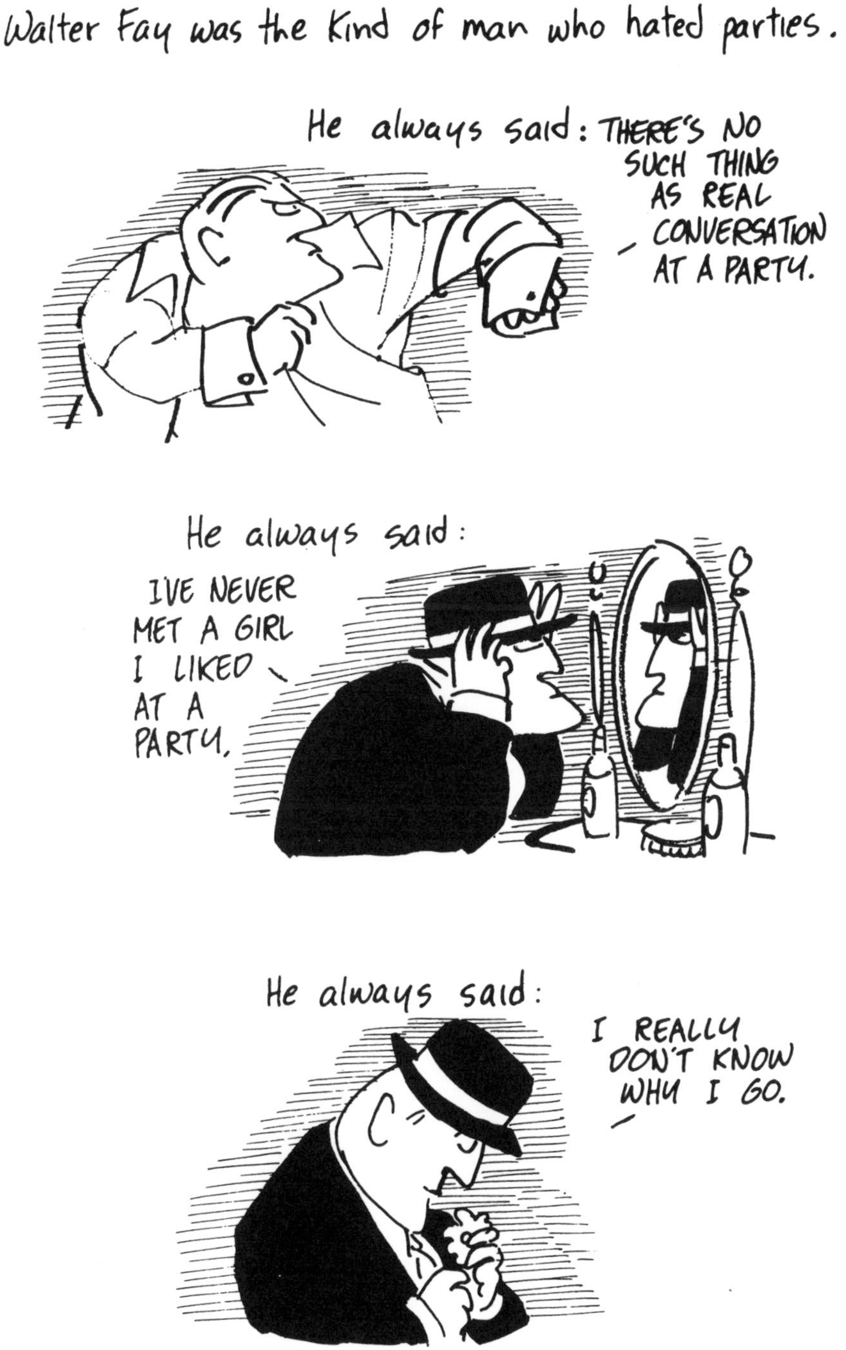
Walter Fay was the kind of man who hated parties.
He always said:
THERE'S NO SUCH THING AS REAL CONVERSATION AT A PARTY.
He always said:
I'VE NEVER MET A GIRL I LIKED AT A PARTY.
He always said:
I REALLY DON'T KNOW WHY I GO.

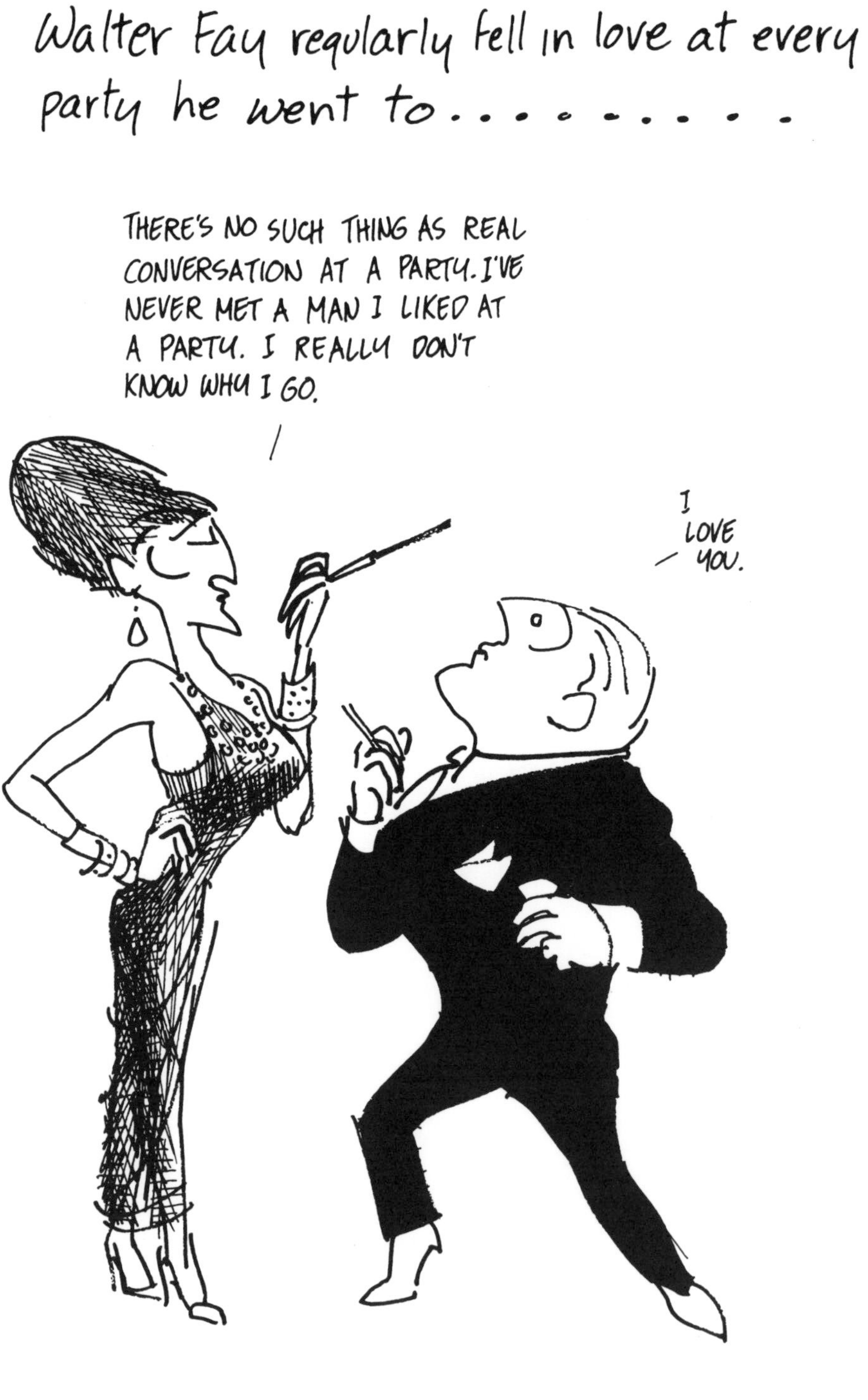
Walter Fay regularly fell in love at every party he went to..........
THERE'S NO SUCH THING AS REAL CONVERSATION AT A PARTY. I'VE NEVER MET A MAN I LIKED AT A PARTY. I REALLY DON'T KNOW WHY I GO.
I LOVE YOU.

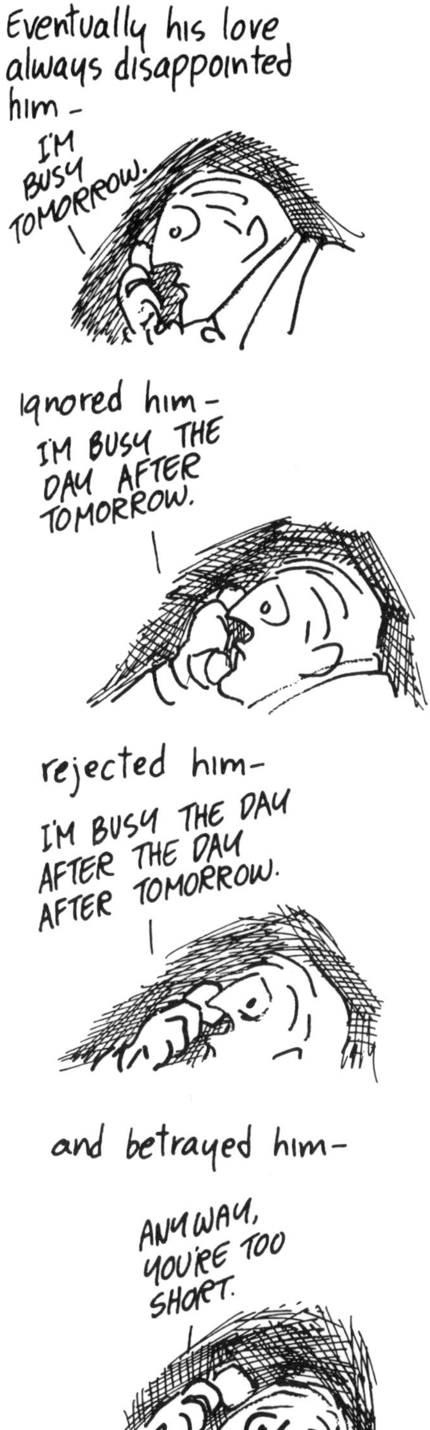
Eventually his love always disappointed him -
I'M BUSY TOMORROW.
ignored him -
I'M BUSY THE DAY AFTER TOMORROW.
rejected him-
I'M BUSY THE DAY AFTER THE DAY AFTER TOMORROW.
and betrayed him-
ANYWAY, YOU'RE TOO SHORT.

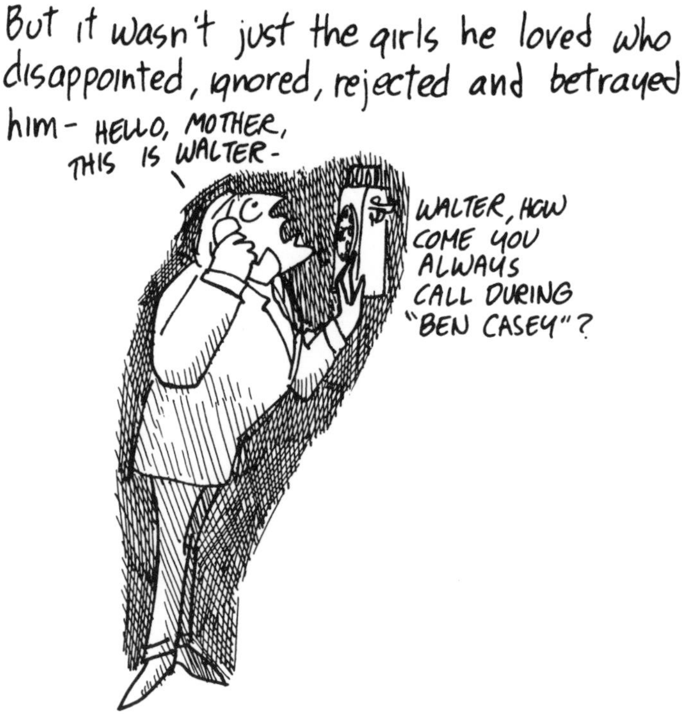

But it wasn't just the girls he loved who disappointed, ignored, rejected and betrayed him-
HELLO, MOTHER, THIS IS WALTER-
WALTER, HOW COME YOU ALWAYS CALL DURING "BEN CASEY"?

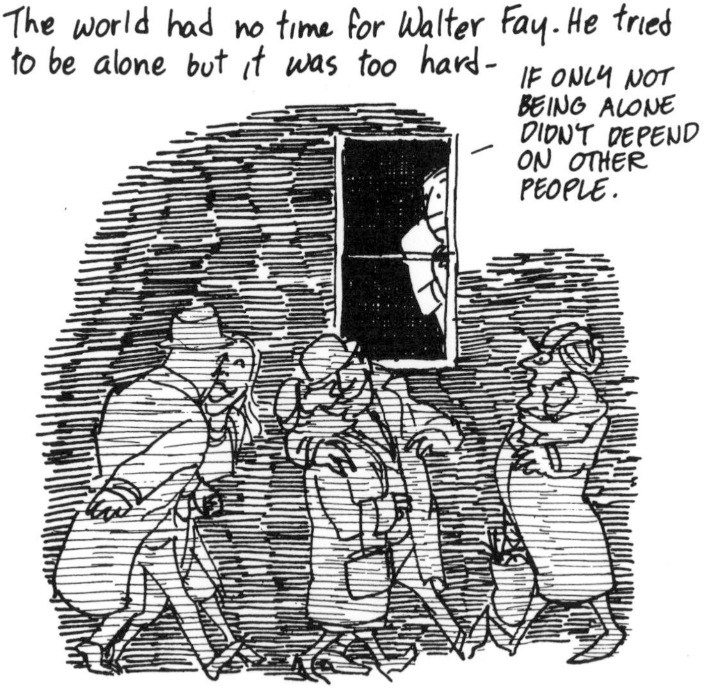

The world had no time for Walter Fay. He tried to be alone but it was too hard-
IF ONLY NOT BEING ALONE DIDN'T DEPEND ON OTHER PEOPLE.

Nobody ever called him. He always had to call other people.

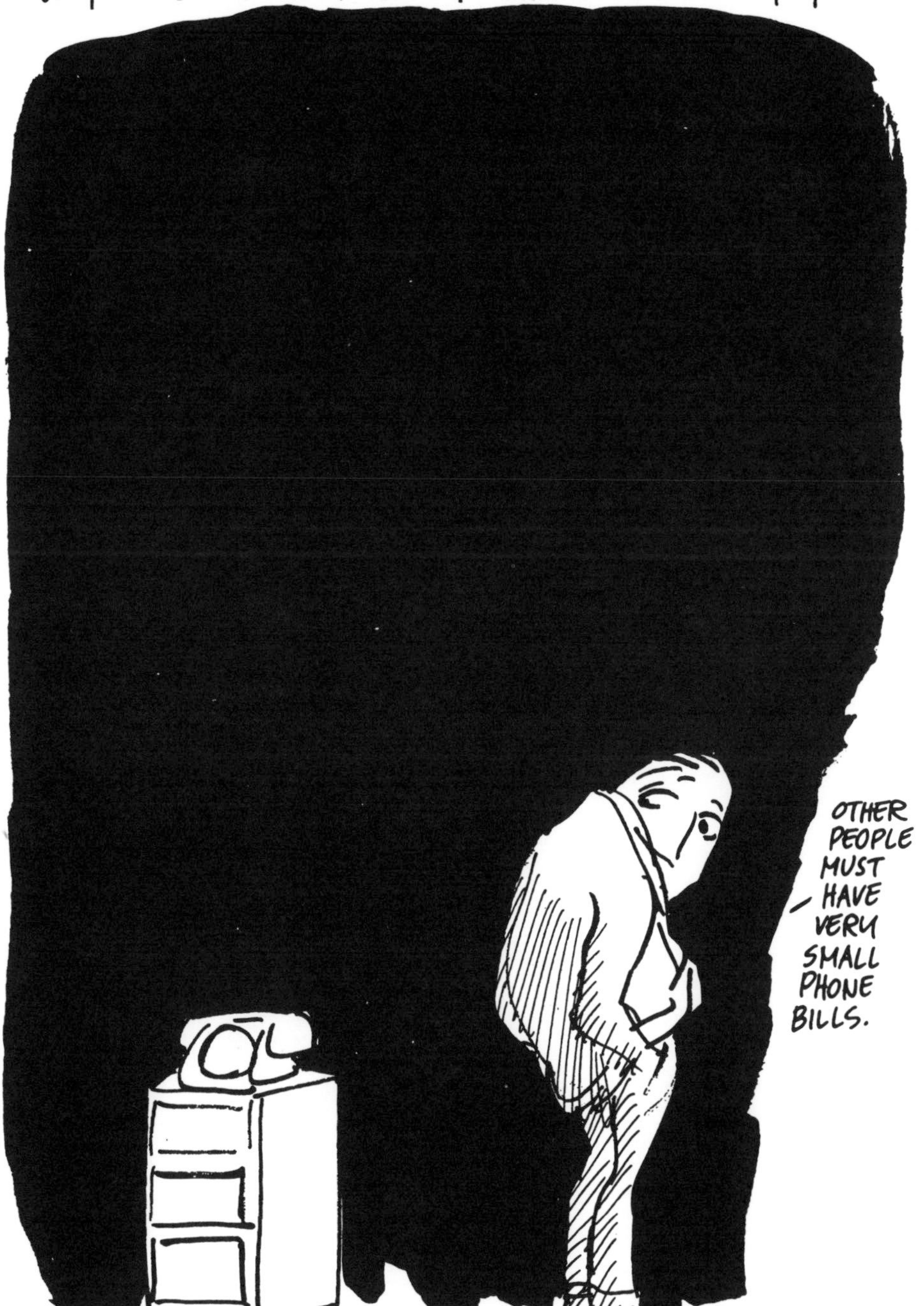
OTHER PEOPLE MUST HAVE VERY SMALL PHONE BILLS.

He Knew what one of his problems was -

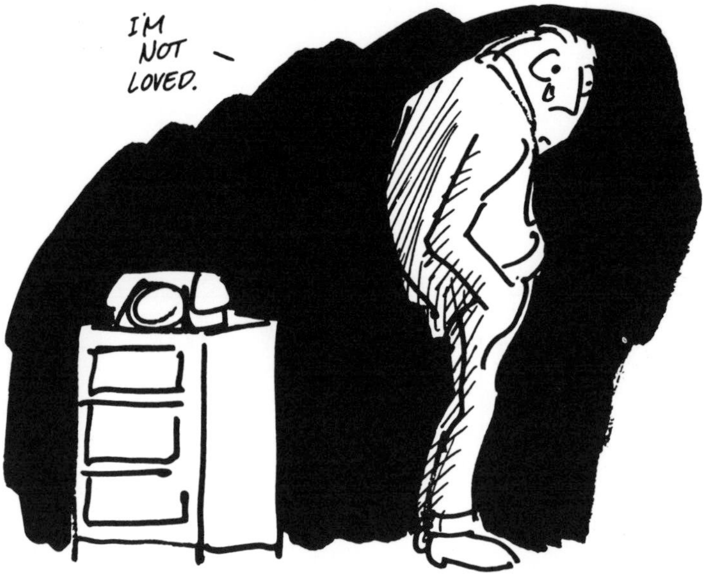
I'M NOT LOVED.

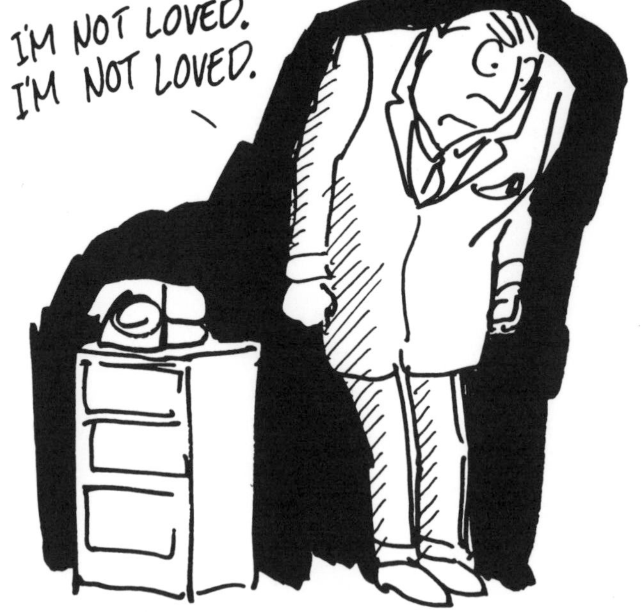
I'M NOT LOVED.
I'M NOT LOVED.

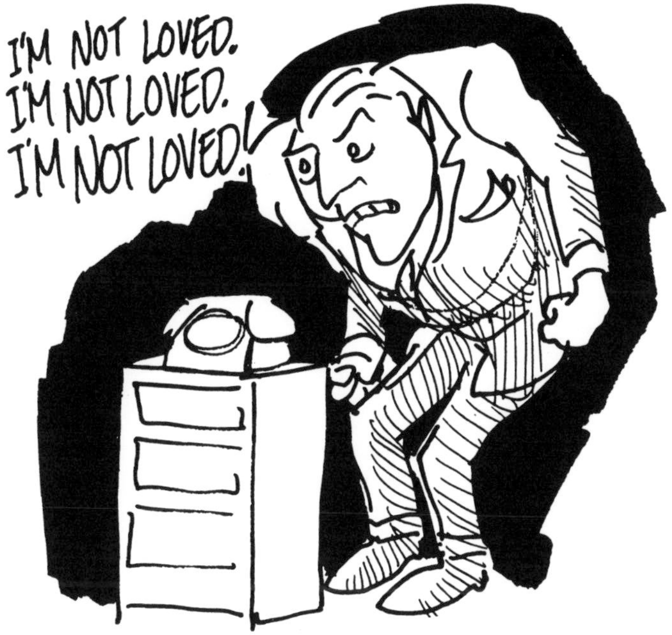
I'M NOT LOVED.
I'M NOT LOVED.
I'M NOT LOVED!

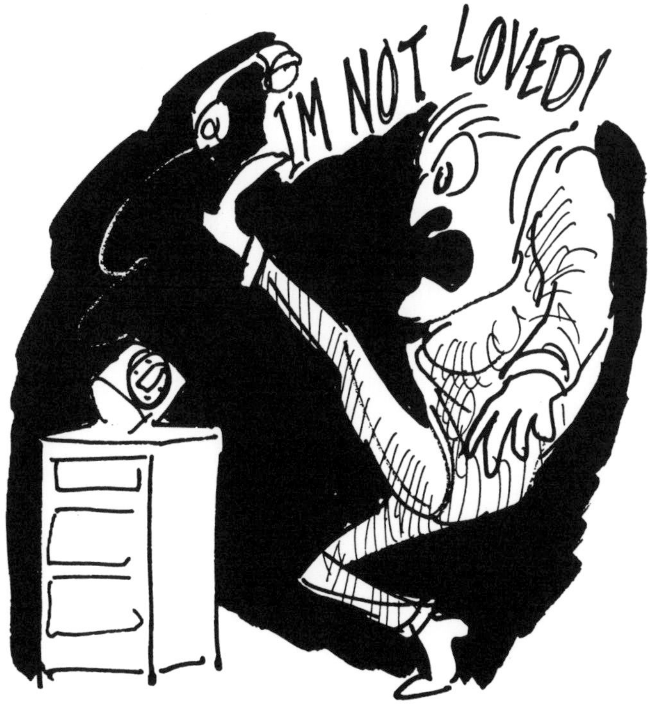
I'M NOT LOVED!

So one day Walter Fay made a decision. If other people didn't need him he wouldn't need other people!

OTHER PEOPLE ARE MY ENEMY!

And that's how he saw his life up till now A battle between himself and his **enemies!**

When it was between himself and a girl he had called it "**the battle of the sexes.**"

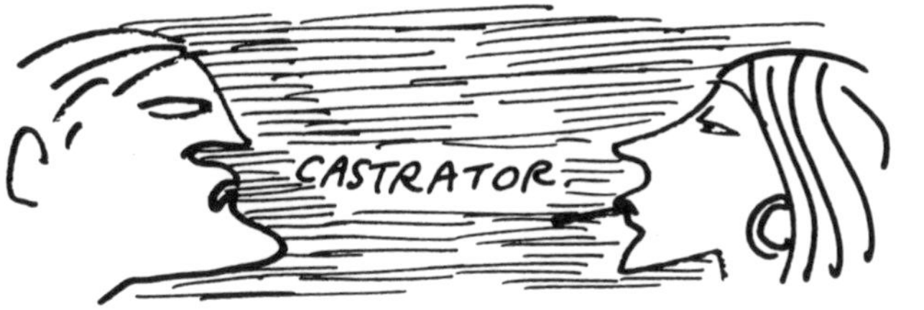
CASTRATOR.

When it was between himself and a boss he had called it "**class warfare.**"

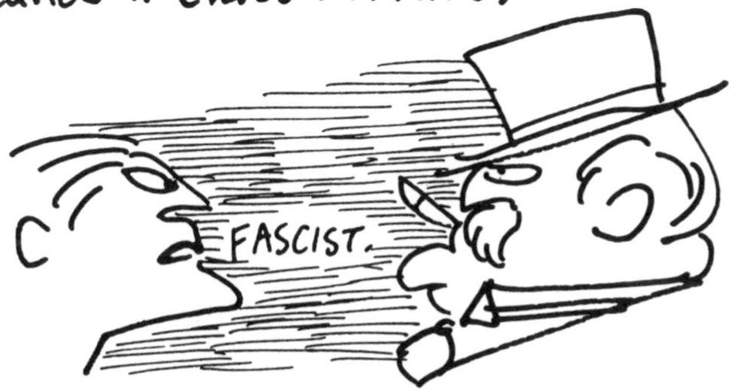
FASCIST.

When it was between himself and his family he had called it "**neurosis.**"

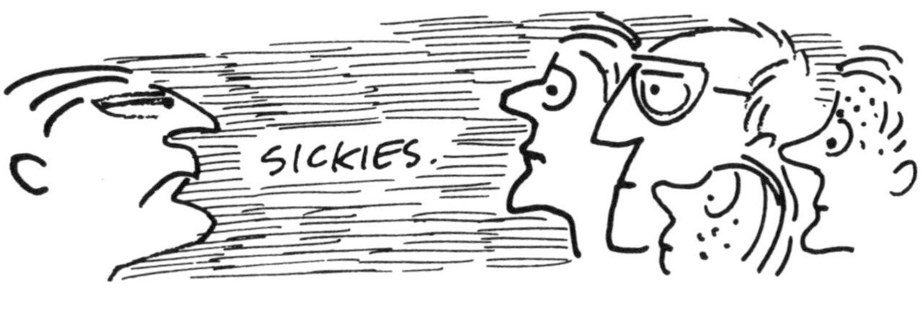
SICKIES.

Walter Fay well knew that one did not go to his enemies for assistance - one went to his friends -

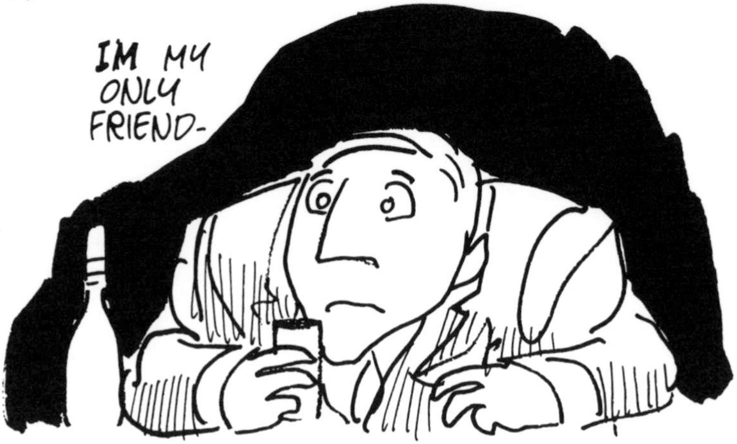
IM MY ONLY FRIEND-

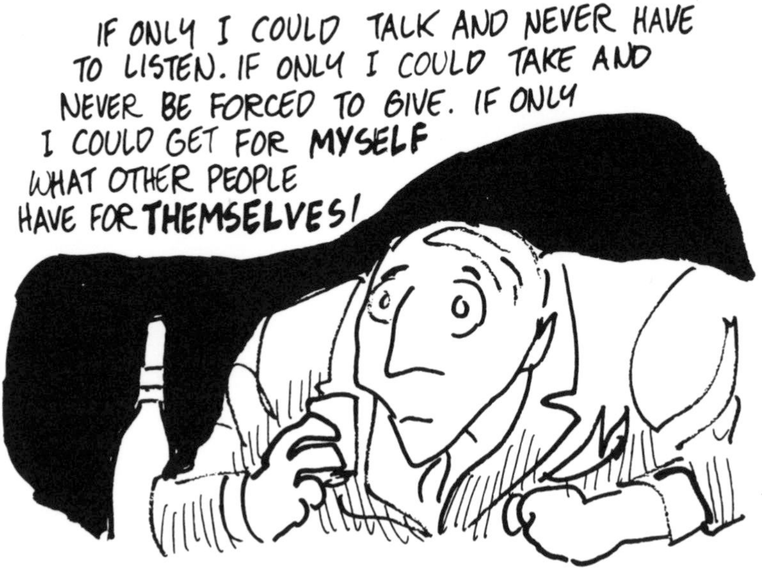
IF ONLY I COULD TALK AND NEVER HAVE TO LISTEN. IF ONLY I COULD TAKE AND NEVER BE FORCED TO GIVE. IF ONLY I COULD GET FOR **MYSELF** WHAT OTHER PEOPLE HAVE FOR **THEMSELVES**!

So one day Walter Fay went down to his basement-

and invented himself a
Lonely Machine.

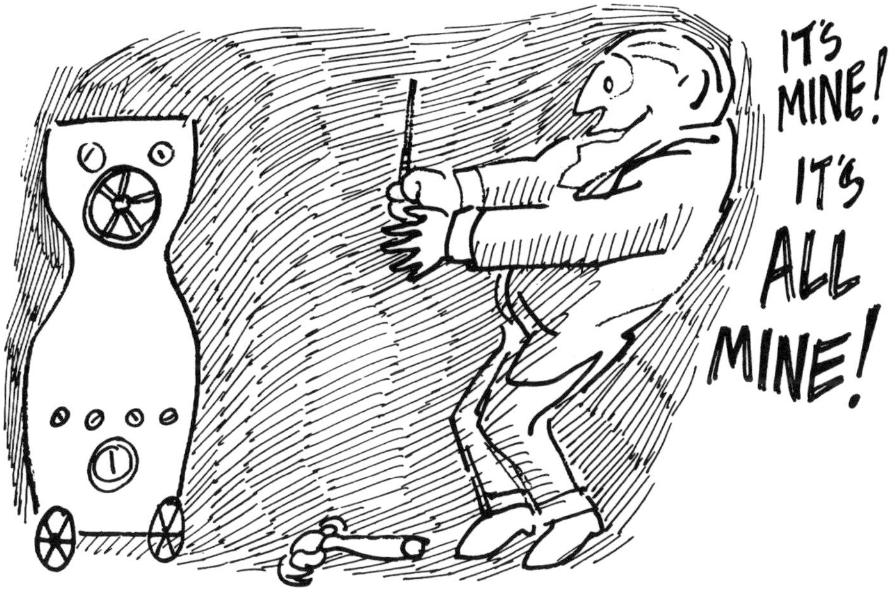
IT'S MINE!
IT'S ALL MINE!

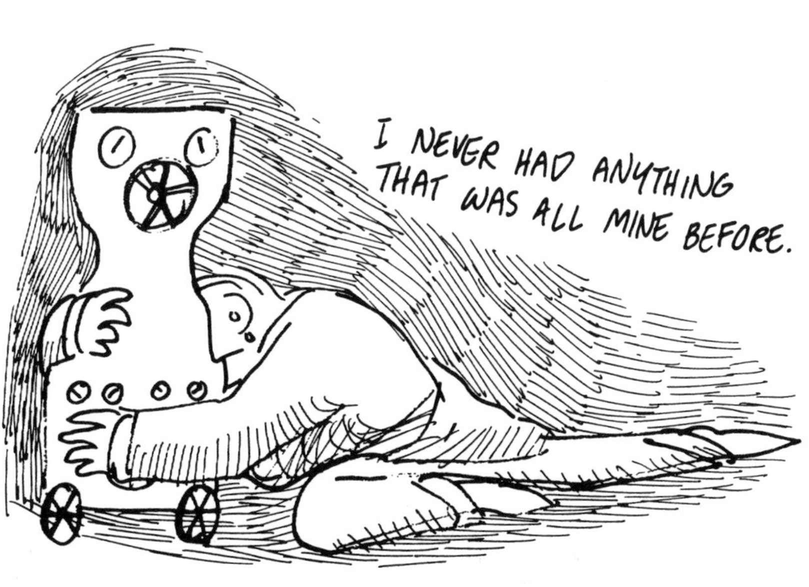
I NEVER HAD ANYTHING THAT WAS ALL MINE BEFORE.

The Lonely Machine did whatever he wanted it to do. It listened to him.

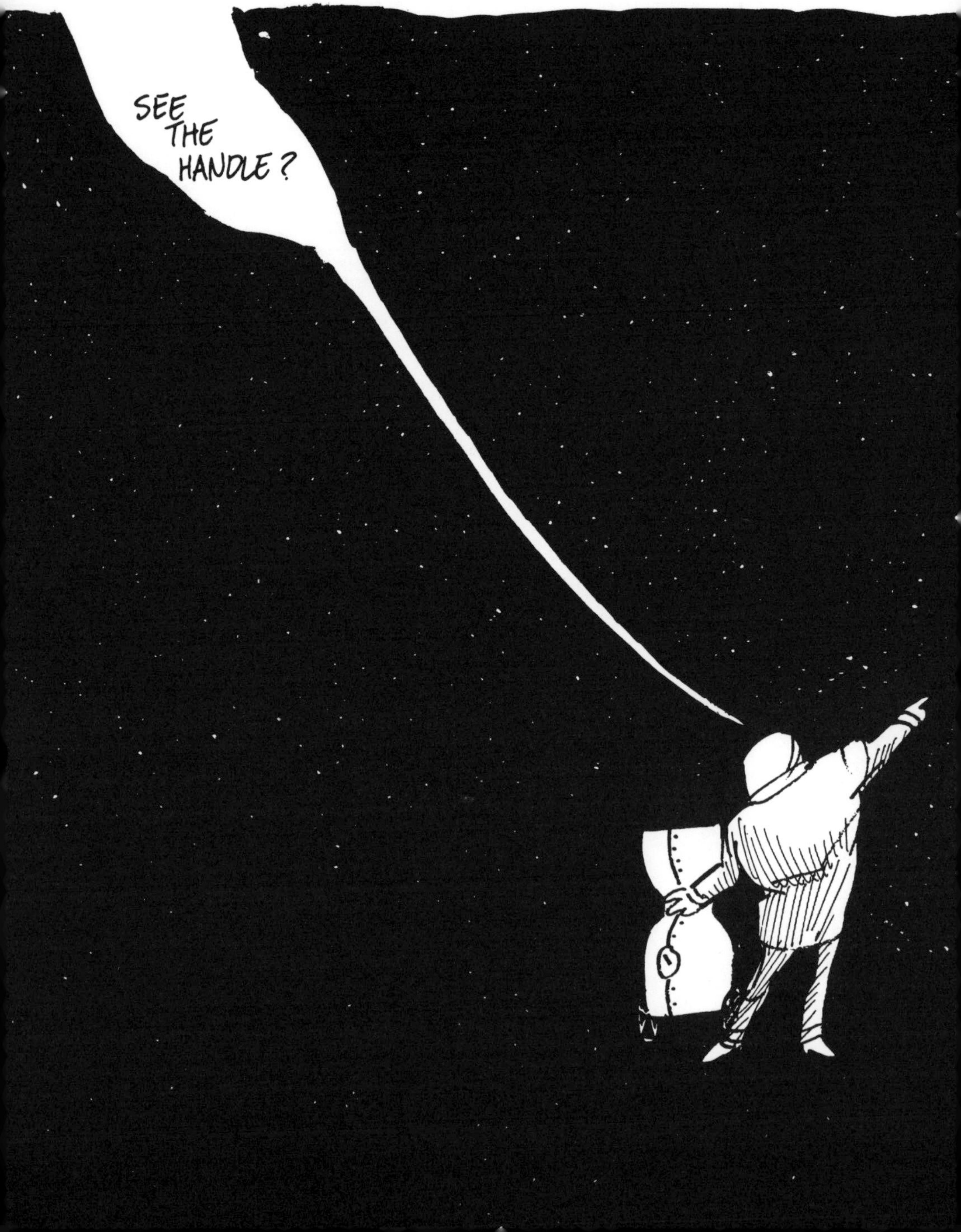
SEE THE HANDLE?

It took long walks in the country with him. It looked at the stars with him.

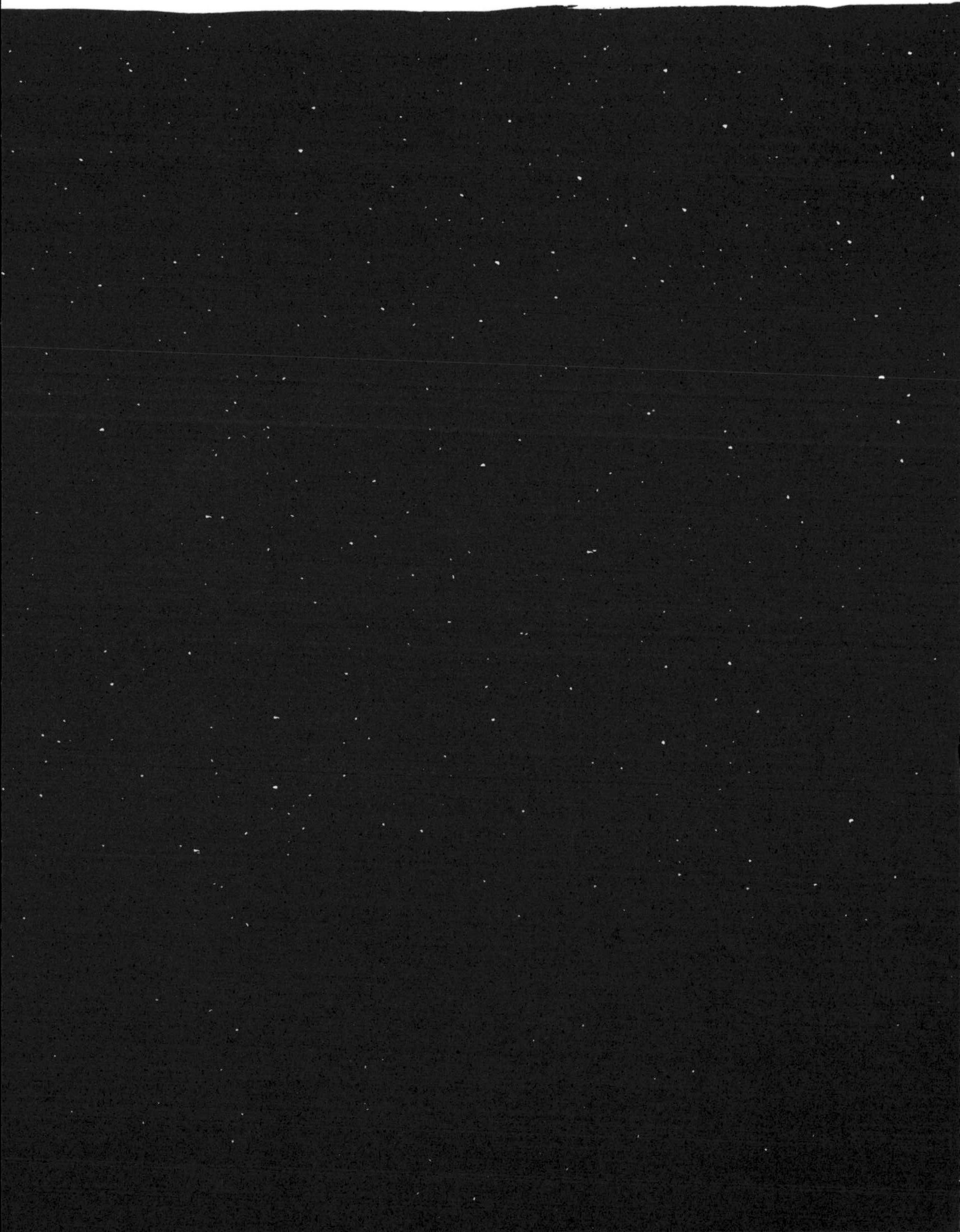

Walter Fay invented it a voice so it could say nice things-

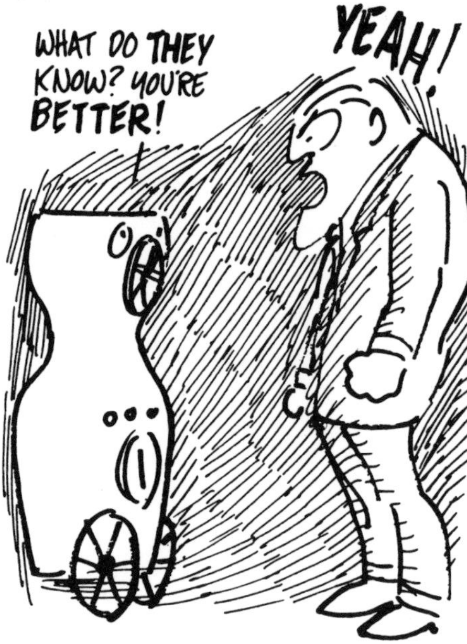
WHAT DO THEY KNOW? YOU'RE BETTER!
YEAH!

There was not a need Walter Fay had that the machine did not answer. It was a mother to him-

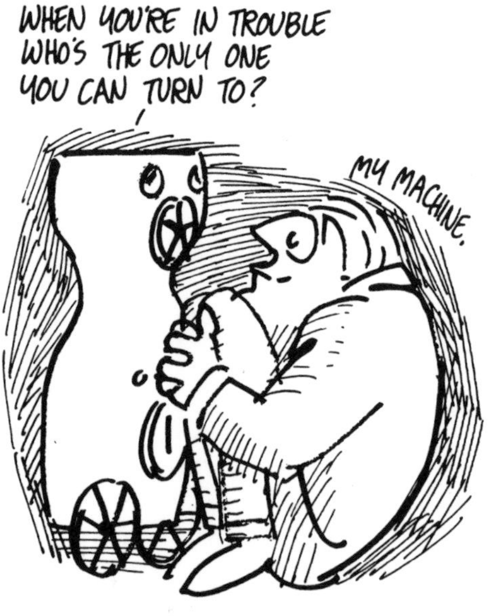
WHEN YOU'RE IN TROUBLE WHO'S THE ONLY ONE YOU CAN TURN TO?
MY MACHINE.

It was a father to him-

ARE YOU SURE YOU'VE MADE A WISE DECISION, MY WALTER?
MAYBE YOU'RE RIGHT.

It was his lover-

DANDELIONS! I **LOVE** DANDELIONS!
MACHINES CAN'T AFFORD MUCH BUT YOU, WALTER, DESERVE THE BEST.

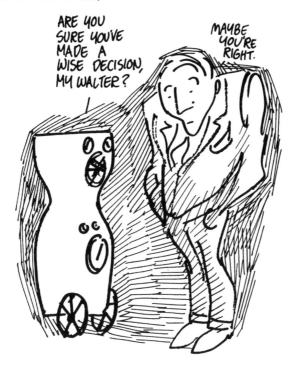

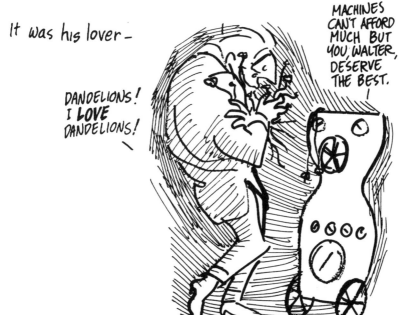

For the first time Walter Fay could be himself with another – he could let loose – he could be aggressive!

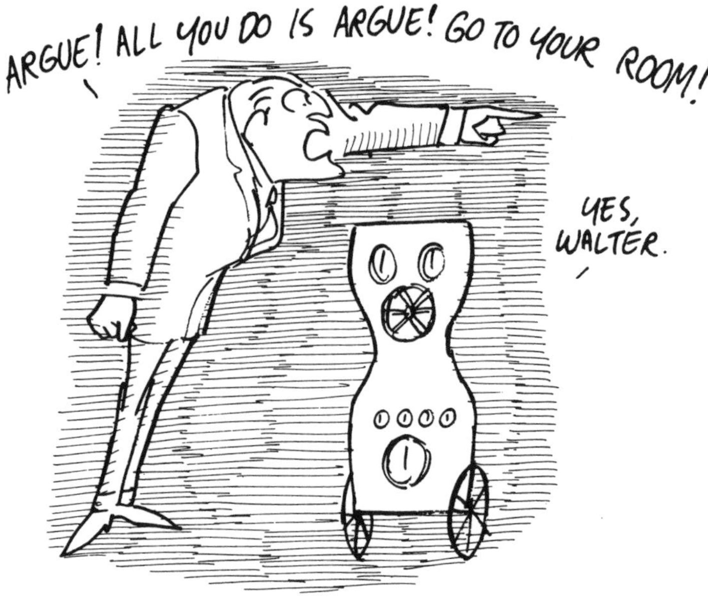
ARGUE! ALL YOU DO IS ARGUE! GO TO YOUR ROOM!
YES, WALTER.

He could feel self-pity.

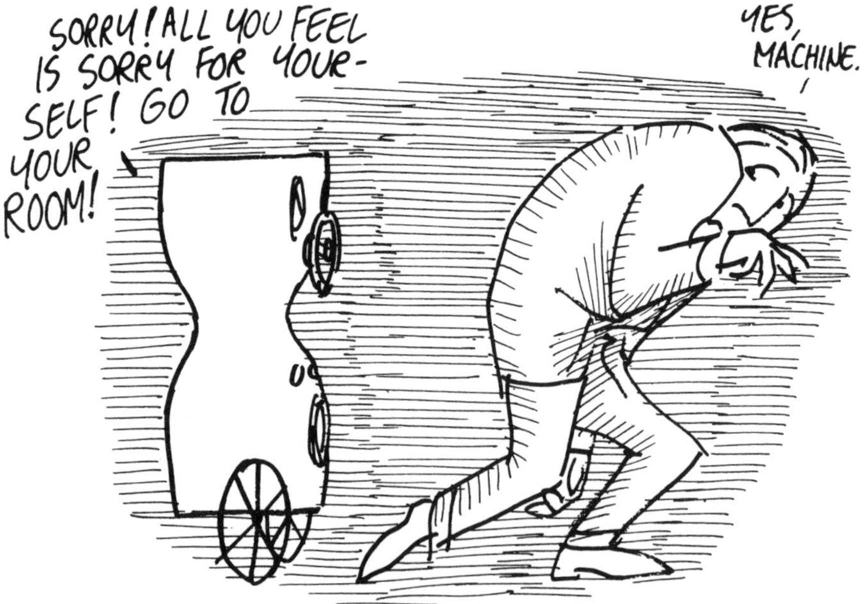
SORRY! ALL YOU FEEL IS SORRY FOR YOURSELF! GO TO YOUR ROOM!
YES, MACHINE.

He could be forgiving.

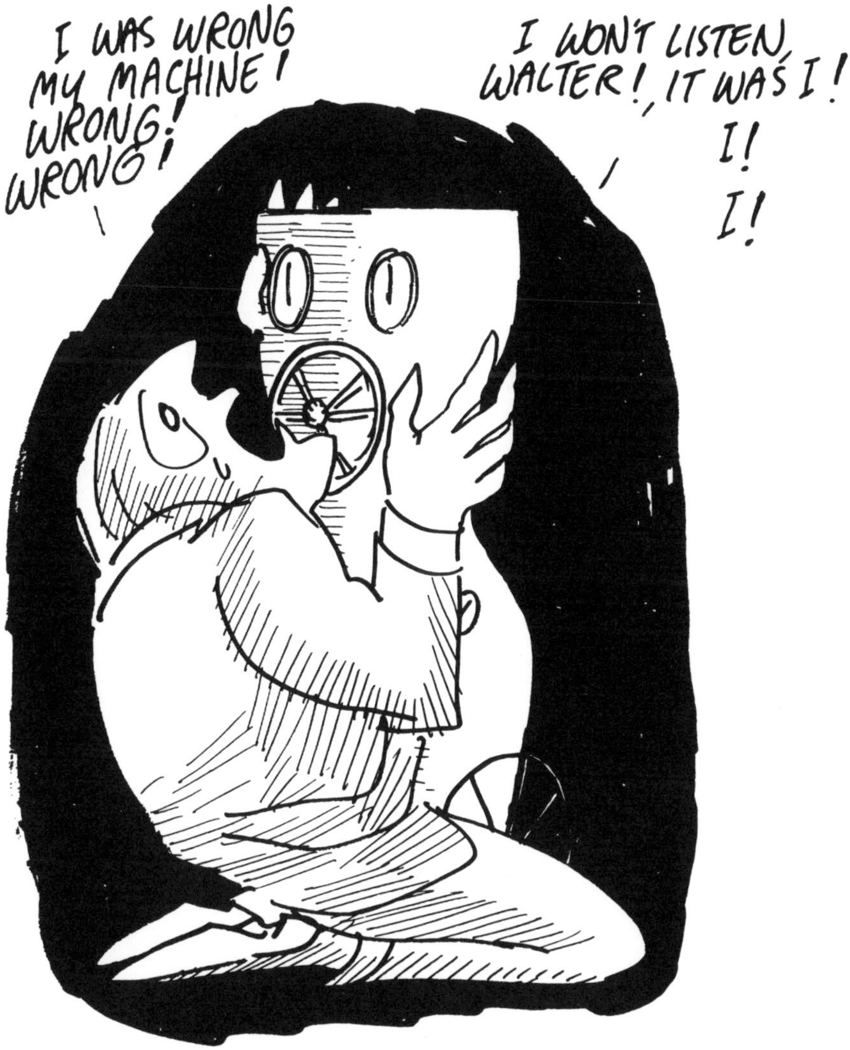
I WAS WRONG MY MACHINE! WRONG! WRONG!
I WON'T LISTEN, WALTER! IT WAS I! I! I!

Walter Fay had a relationship.

He swelled with a new assurance-

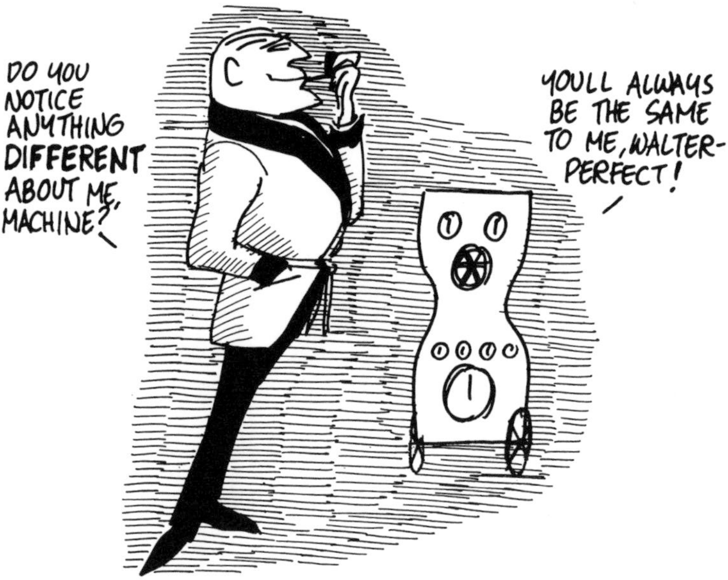
DO YOU NOTICE ANYTHING **DIFFERENT** ABOUT ME, MACHINE?
YOULL ALWAYS BE THE SAME TO ME, WALTER- PERFECT!

But being perfect where he had always been perfect was not enough for Walter Fay.

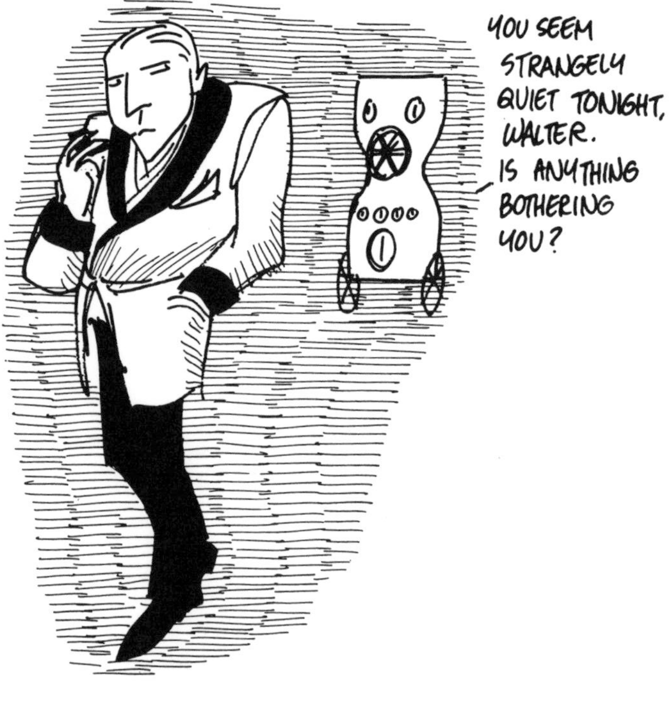
YOU SEEM STRANGELY QUIET TONIGHT, WALTER. IS ANYTHING BOTHERING YOU?

He wanted to be perfect on **enemy** ground.

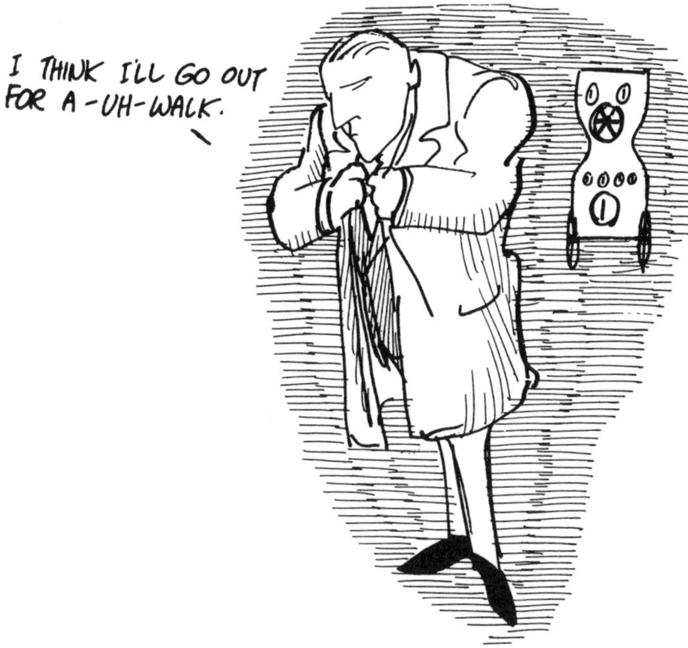
I THINK I'LL GO OUT FOR A-UH-WALK.

He started going to parties again.

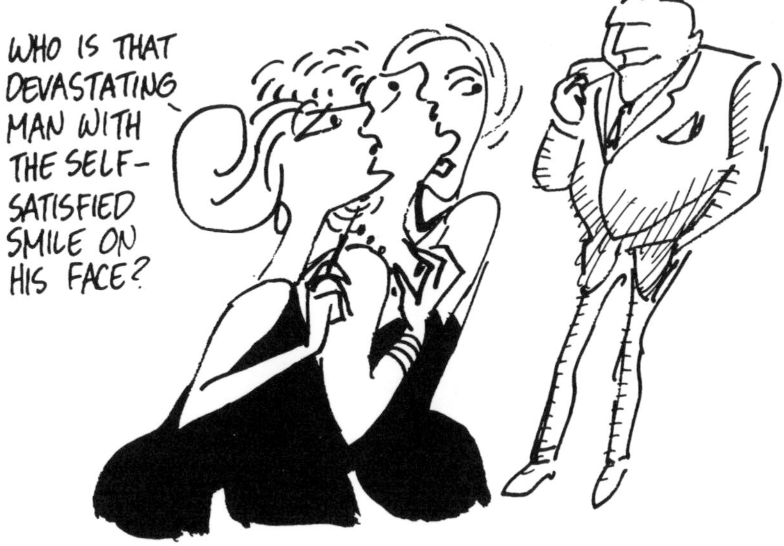
WHO IS THAT DEVASTATING MAN WITH THE SELF-SATISFIED SMILE ON HIS FACE?

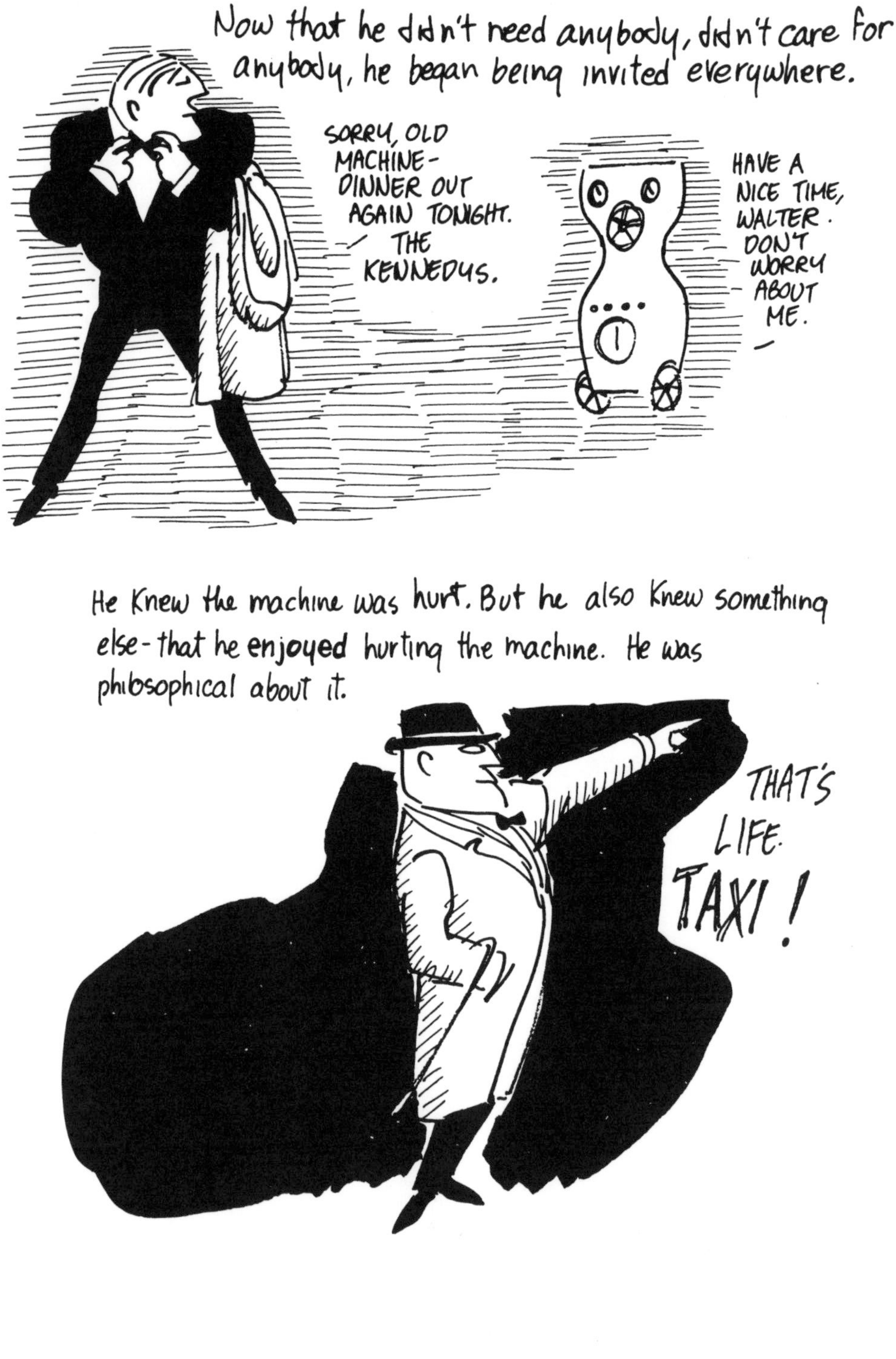
Now that he didn't need anybody, didn't care for anybody, he began being invited everywhere.
SORRY, OLD MACHINE - DINNER OUT AGAIN TONIGHT. THE KENNEDYS.
HAVE A NICE TIME, WALTER. DON'T WORRY ABOUT ME.
He Knew the machine was hurt. But he also Knew something else - that he enjoyed hurting the machine. He was philosophical about it.
THAT'S LIFE.
TAXI!

He played the machine against his new friends and his new friends against the machine.

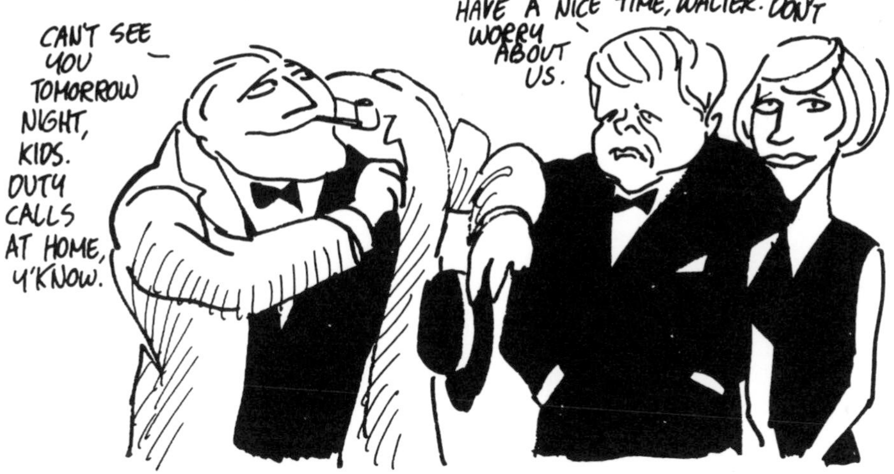
CAN'T SEE YOU TOMORROW NIGHT, KIDS. DUTY CALLS AT HOME, Y'KNOW.
HAVE A NICE TIME, WALTER. DON'T WORRY ABOUT US.

But home wasn't as much fun as it used to be—

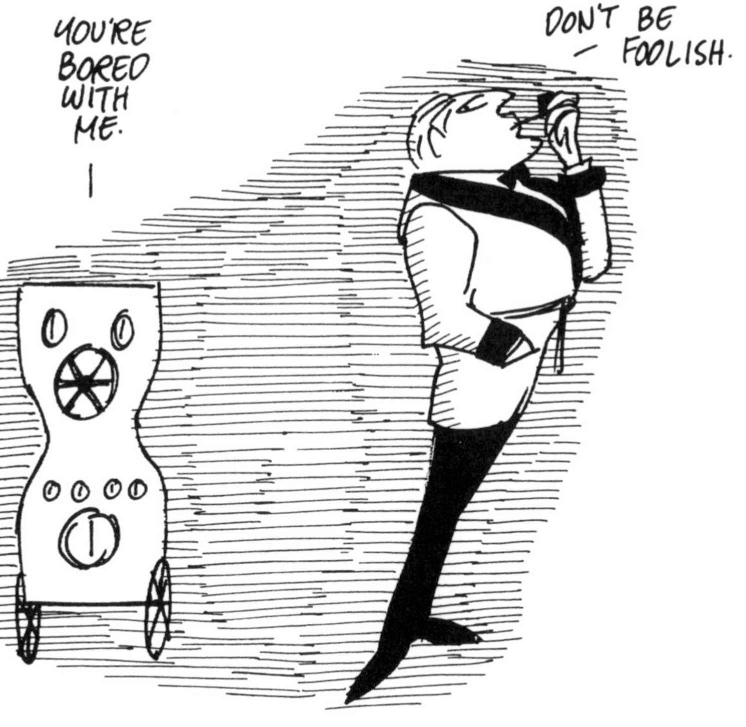
YOU'RE BORED WITH ME.
DON'T BE FOOLISH.

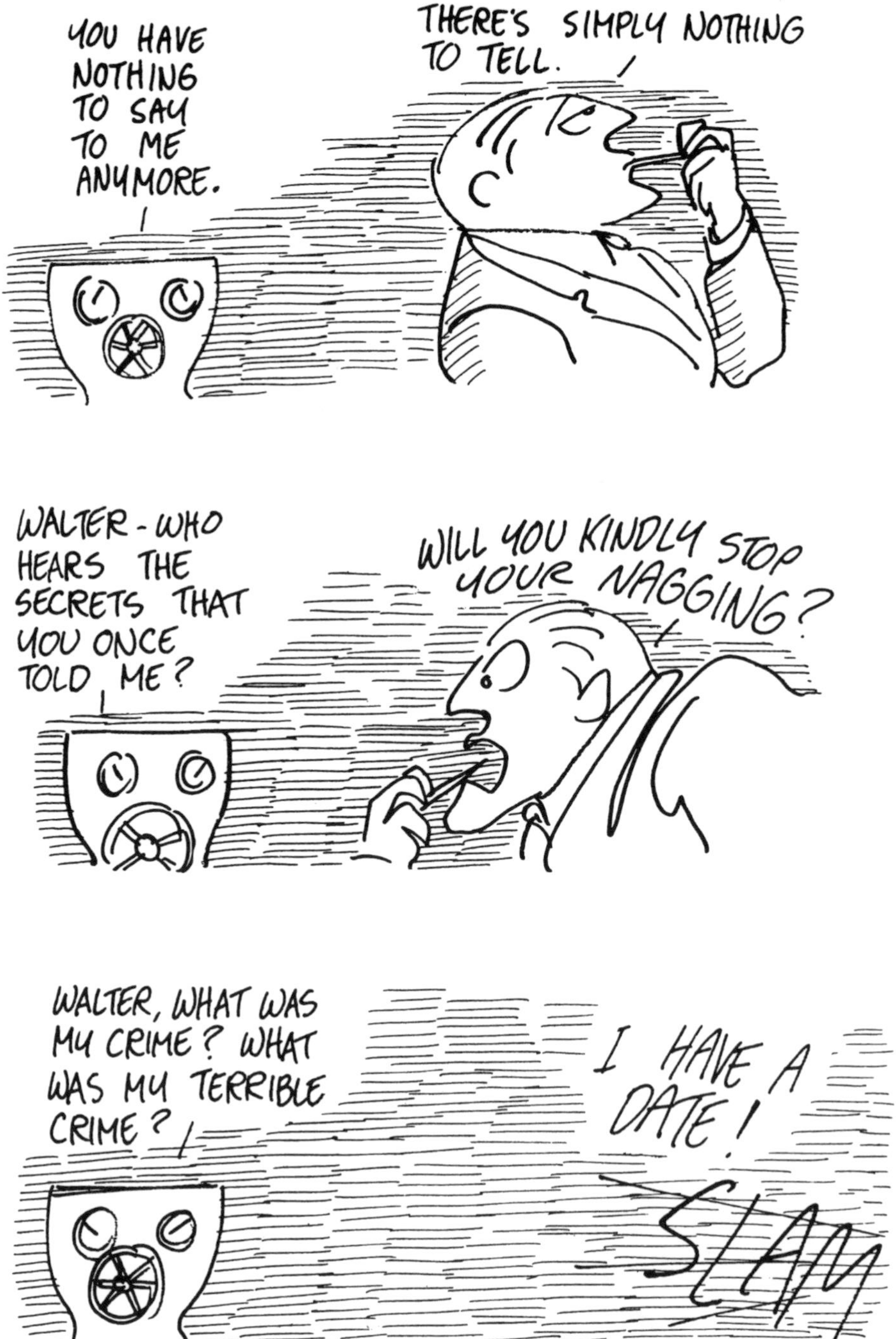
YOU HAVE NOTHING TO SAY TO ME ANYMORE.
THERE'S SIMPLY NOTHING TO TELL.
WALTER - WHO HEARS THE SECRETS THAT YOU ONCE TOLD ME?
WILL YOU KINDLY STOP YOUR NAGGING?
WALTER, WHAT WAS MY CRIME? WHAT WAS MY TERRIBLE CRIME?
I HAVE A DATE!
SLAM

Walter Fay started coming home later. He always hoped the machine would be asleep. It never was.

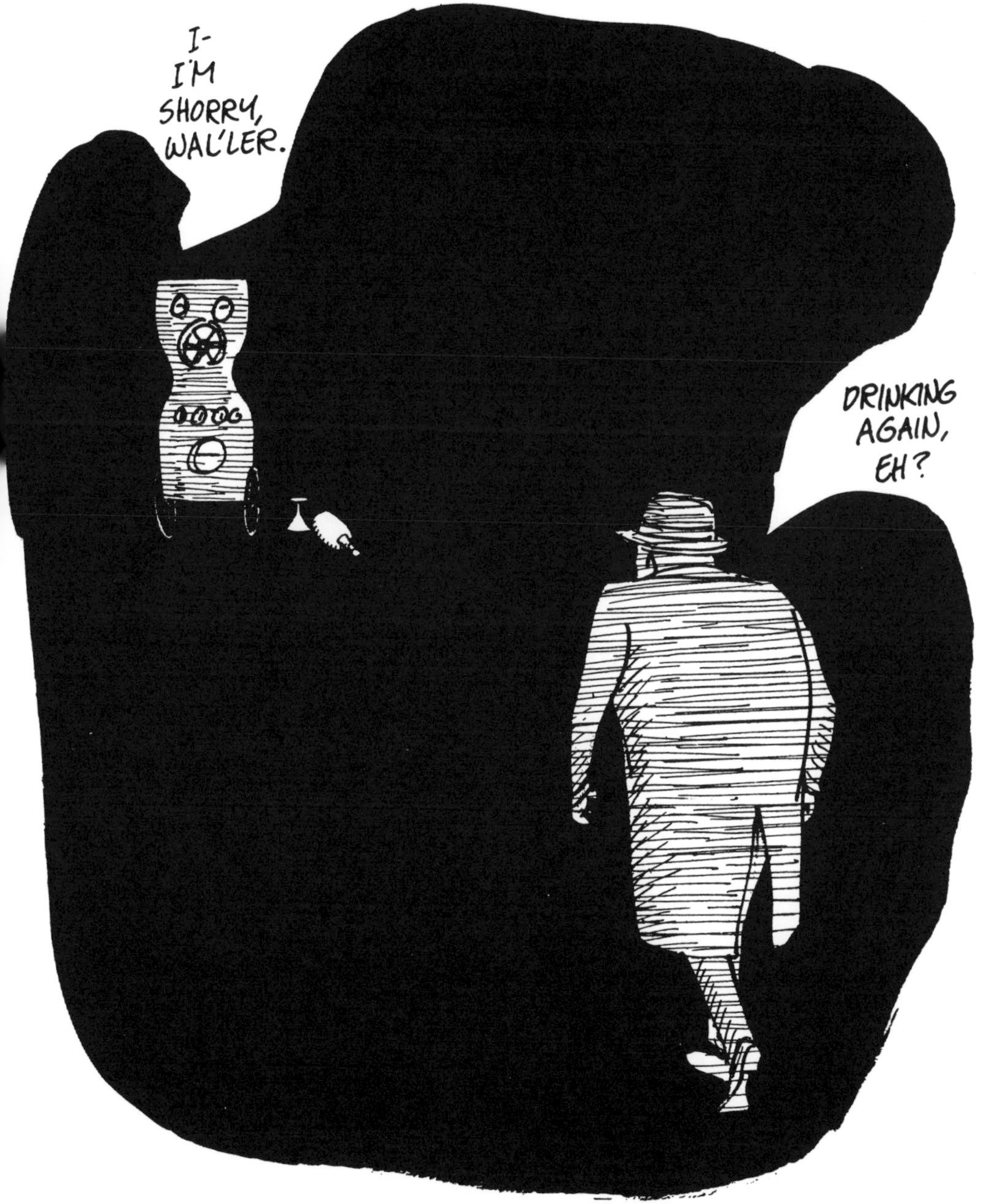
I- I'M SHORRY, WAL'LER.
DRINKING AGAIN, EH?

The point was that Walter Fay needed something when he needed it and not after he stopped needing it.

THE MACHINE WAS ONLY A MEANS TO AN END,

Walter Fay explained to himself.

IT WAS A BRIDGE BETWEEN ME AND OTHER PEOPLE.

He saw it all clearly now.

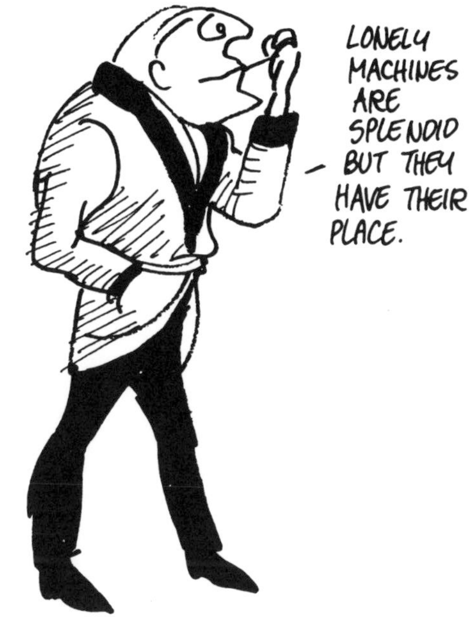
LONELY MACHINES ARE SPLENDID BUT THEY HAVE THEIR PLACE.

Walter Fay had outgrown his machine.

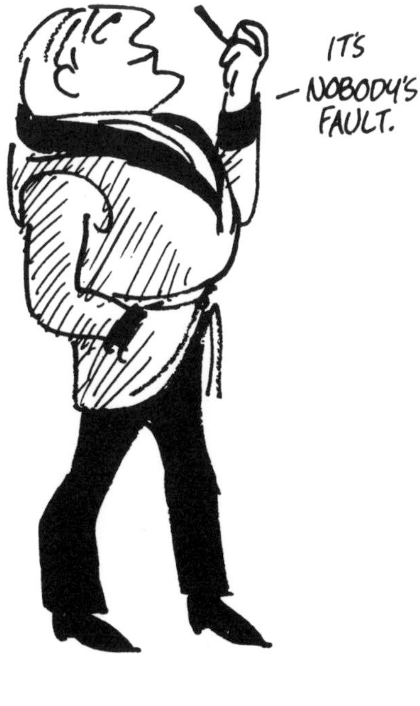
IT'S NOBODY'S FAULT.

One day he made an announcement..

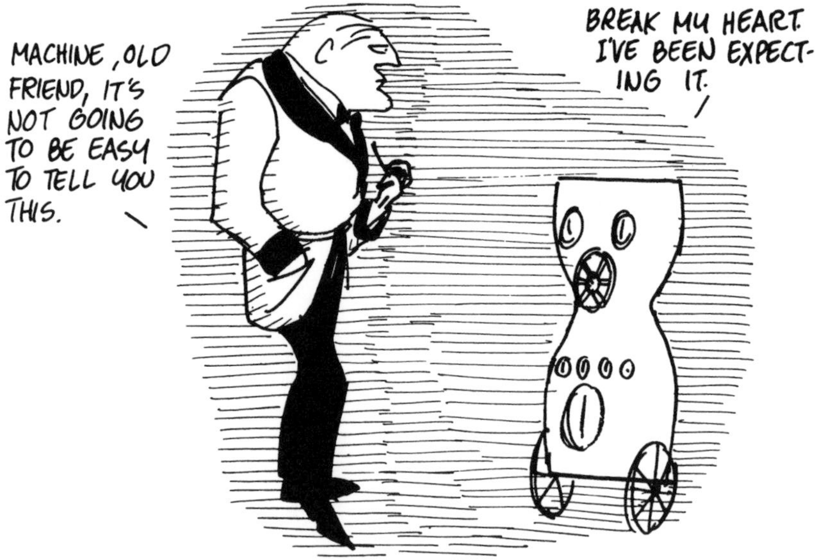
MACHINE, OLD FRIEND, IT'S NOT GOING TO BE EASY TO TELL YOU THIS.
BREAK MY HEART. I'VE BEEN EXPECTING IT.

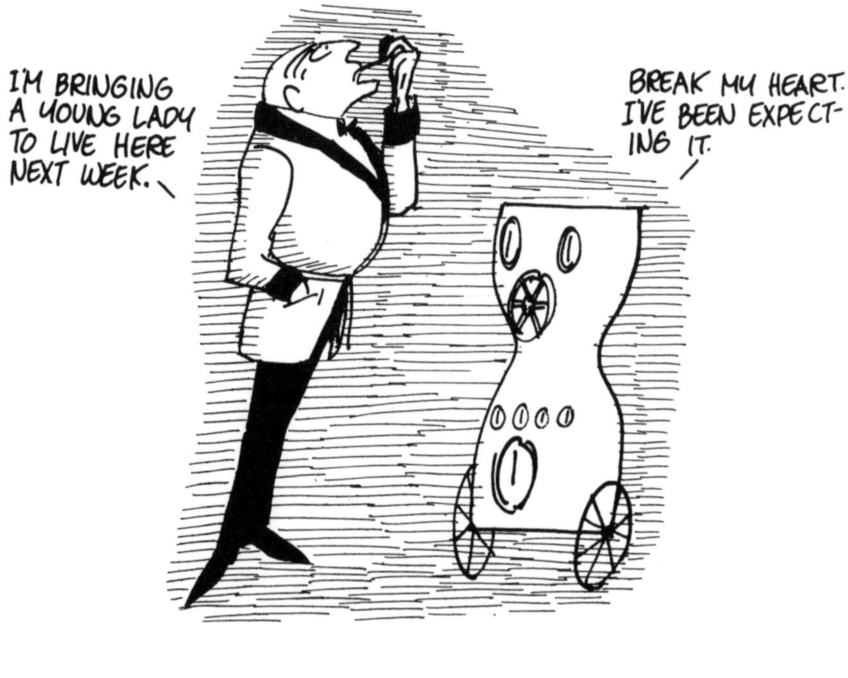
I'M BRINGING A YOUNG LADY TO LIVE HERE NEXT WEEK.
BREAK MY HEART. I'VE BEEN EXPECTING IT.

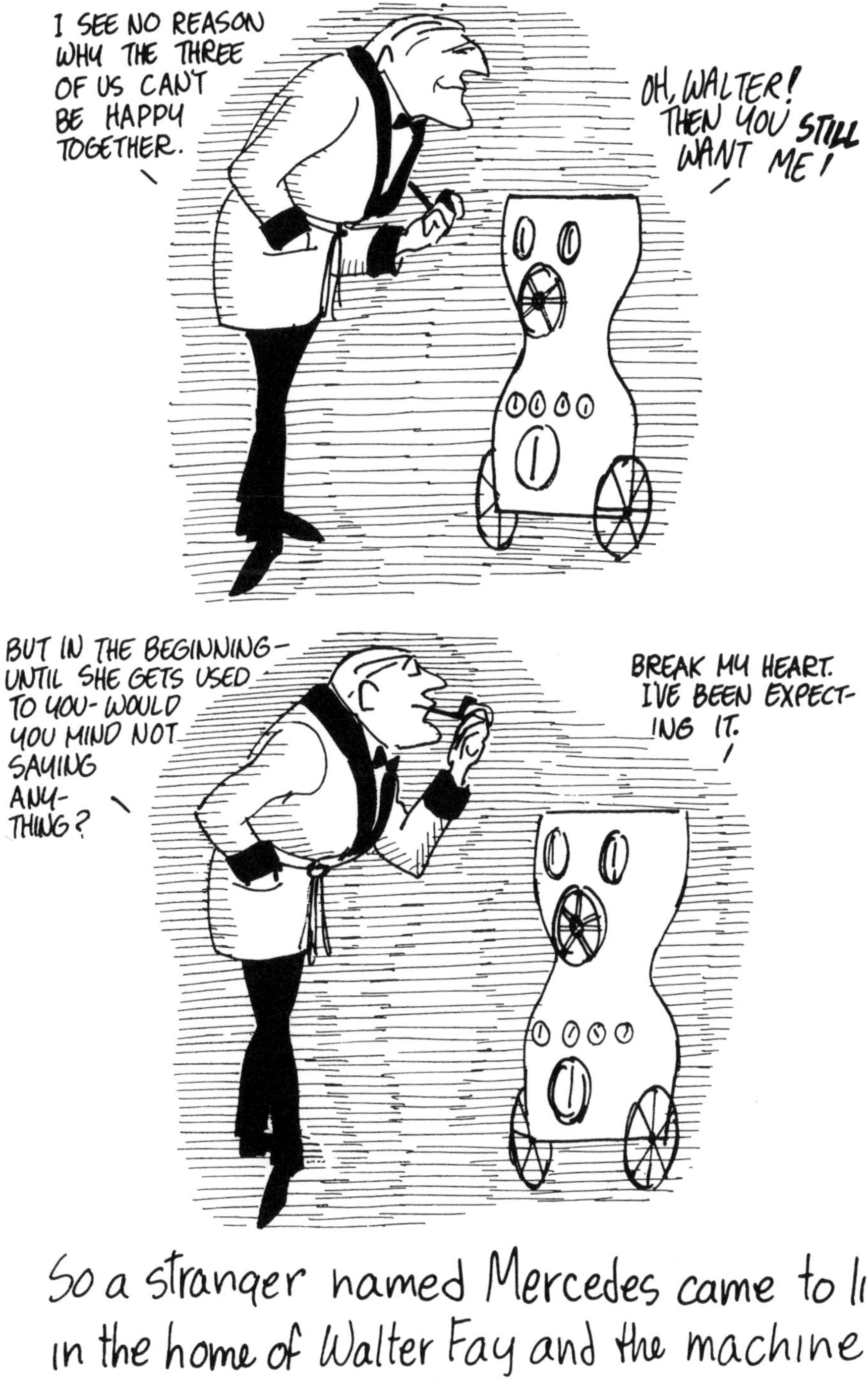
I SEE NO REASON WHY THE THREE OF US CAN'T BE HAPPY TOGETHER.
OH, WALTER! THEN YOU STILL WANT ME!
BUT IN THE BEGINNING- UNTIL SHE GETS USED TO YOU- WOULD YOU MIND NOT SAYING ANY-THING?
BREAK MY HEART. I'VE BEEN EXPECT-ING IT.

So a stranger named Mercedes came to live in the home of Walter Fay and the machine.

She was a mother to him-
WHEN YOU'RE IN TROUBLE WHO'S THE ONLY ONE YOU CAN TURN TO?
MY MERCEDES.
She was a father to him-
ARE YOU SURE YOU'VE MADE A WISE DECISION, MY WALTER?
MAYBE YOU'RE RIGHT.
She was his lover-
OH, WALTER- YOU HURT ME.
DID I REALLY?

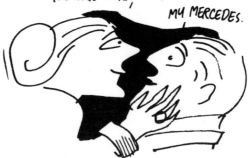

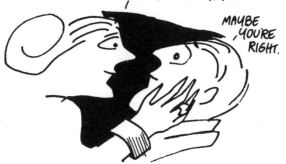

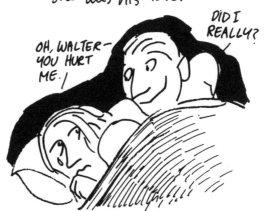

But at odd moments when Mercedes was out organizing a charity drive Walter Fay would wheel out his lonely machine.

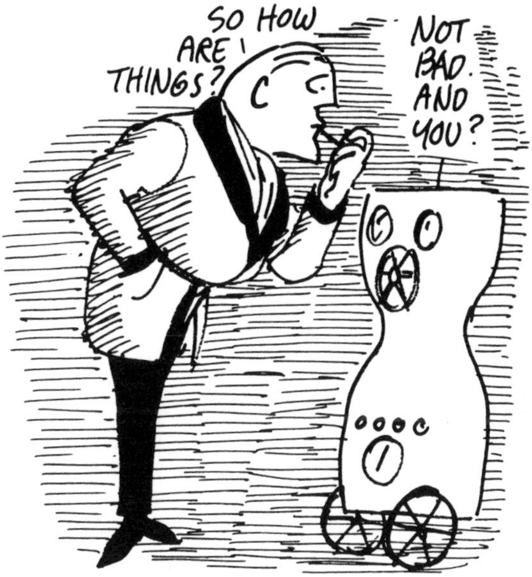
SO HOW ARE THINGS?
NOT BAD. AND YOU?

But there no longer seemed to be any contact

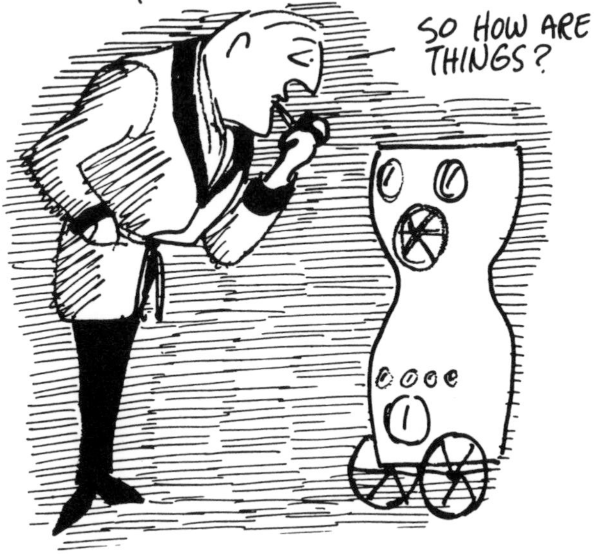
SO HOW ARE THINGS?

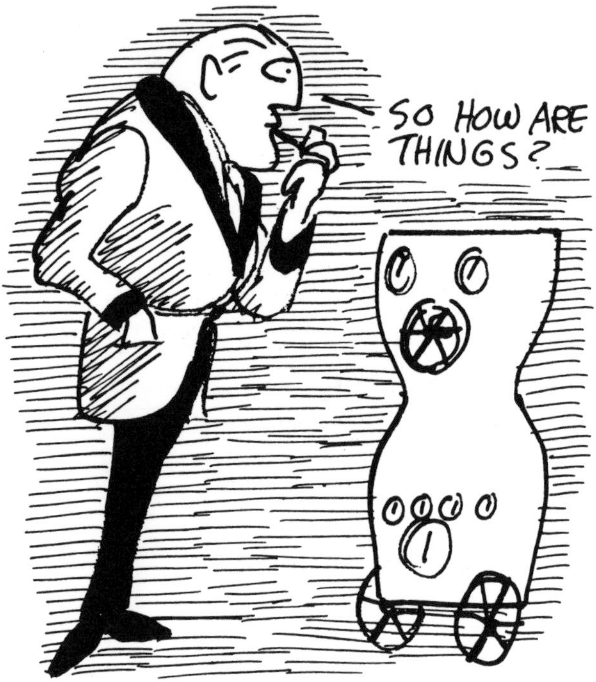
SO HOW ARE THINGS?

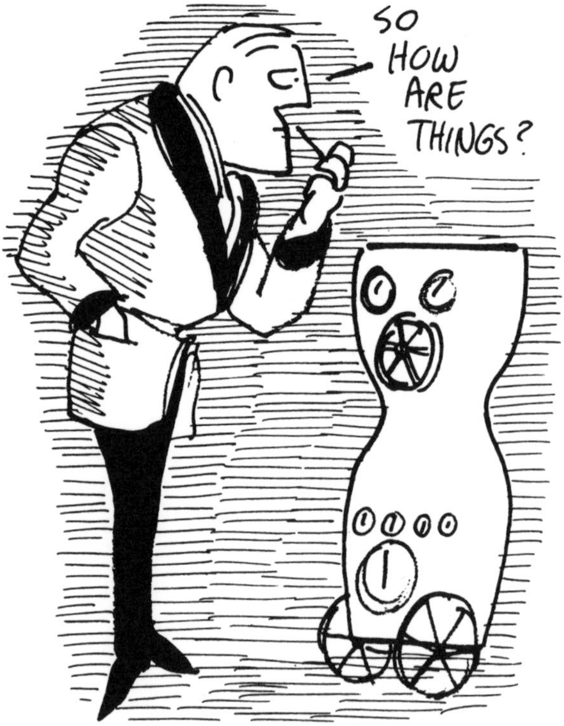
SO HOW ARE THINGS?

and receiving no answer, he wheeled it into the upstairs closet and never wheeled it out again.

And there it remained until one day Mercedes came upon it—

WALTER—
WHAT A
LOVELY
SURPRISE! —
A
DRESS-
MAKER'S
DUMMY!

And she made many dresses and gave many parties and Walter Fay never felt disappointed, ignored, rejected or betrayed — or any other feeling again.

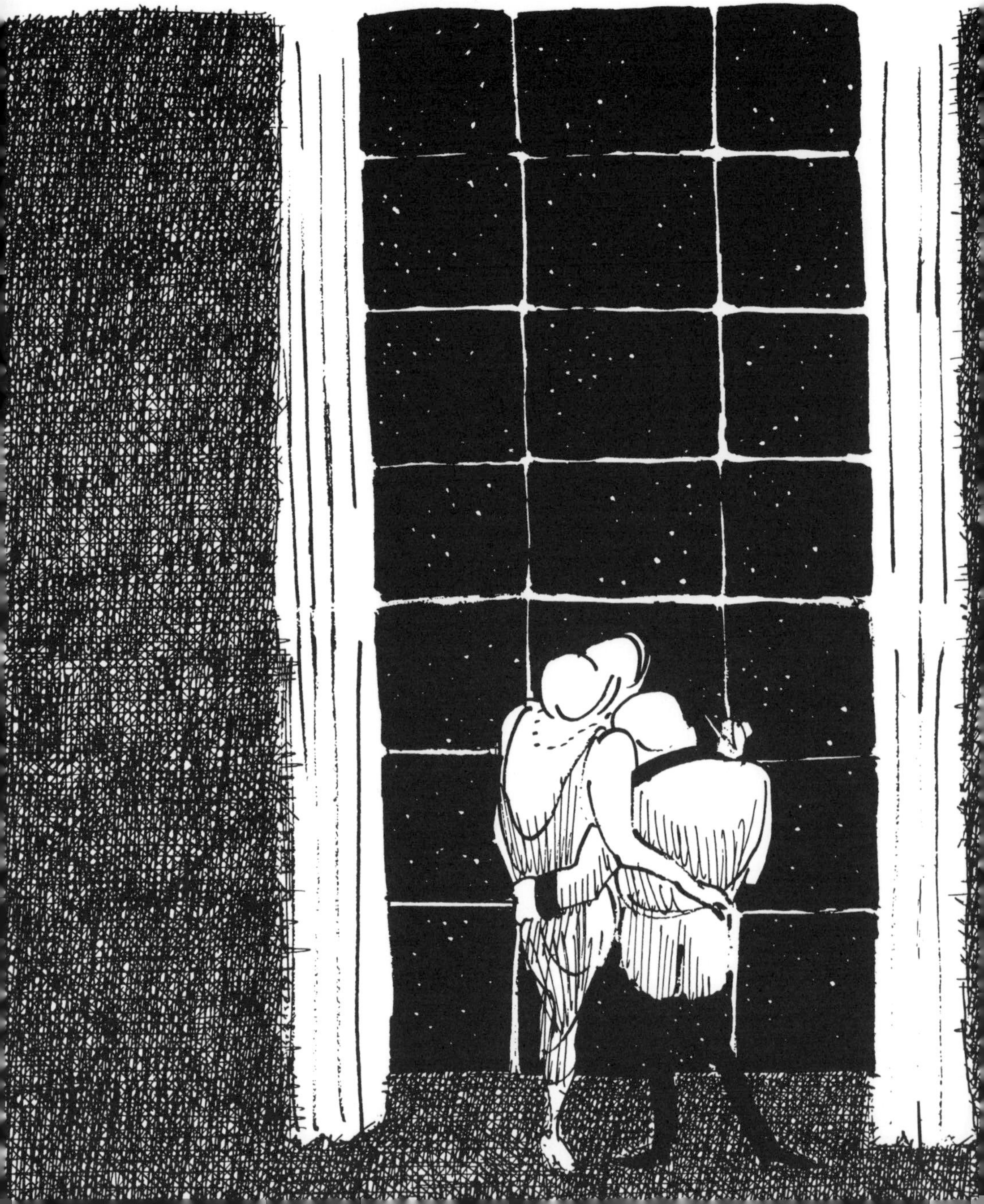

Not even for a second

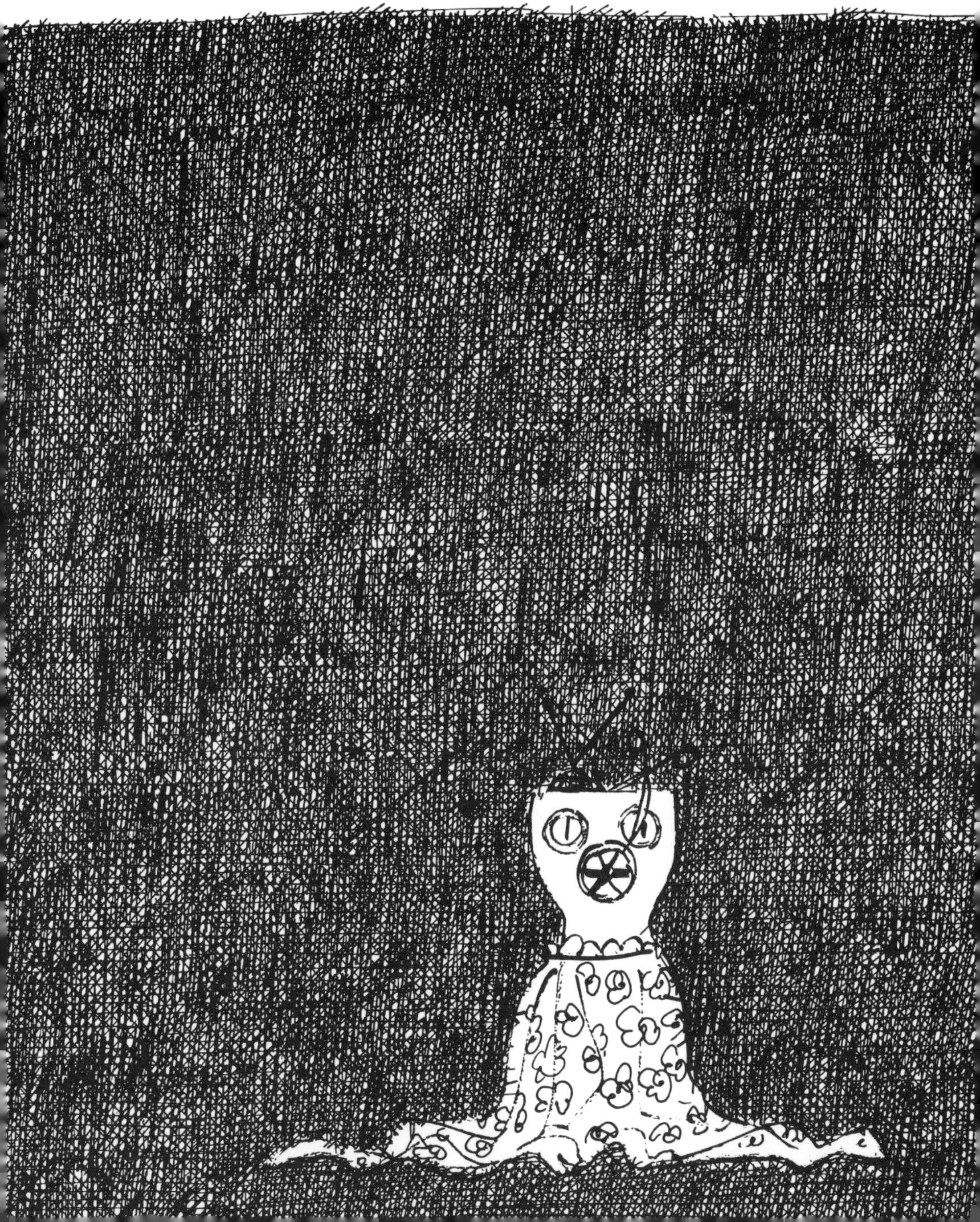

Harold Swera

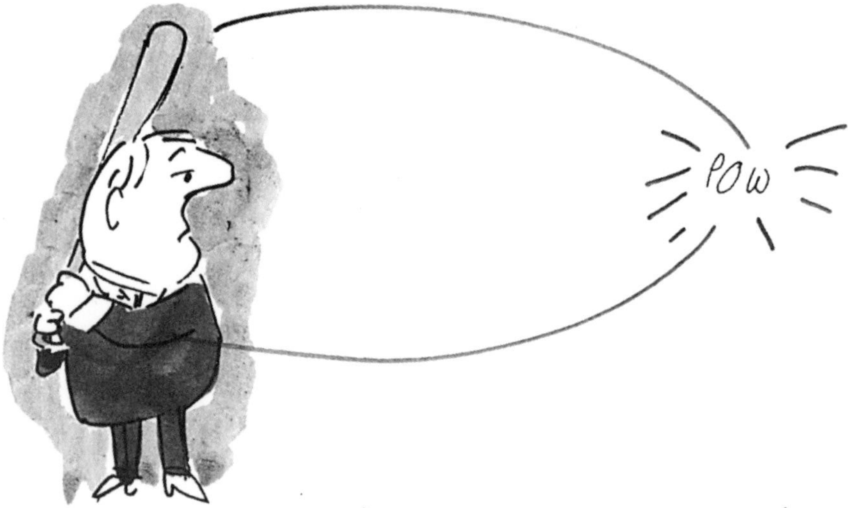
POW

could hit a baseball farther than any man alive -

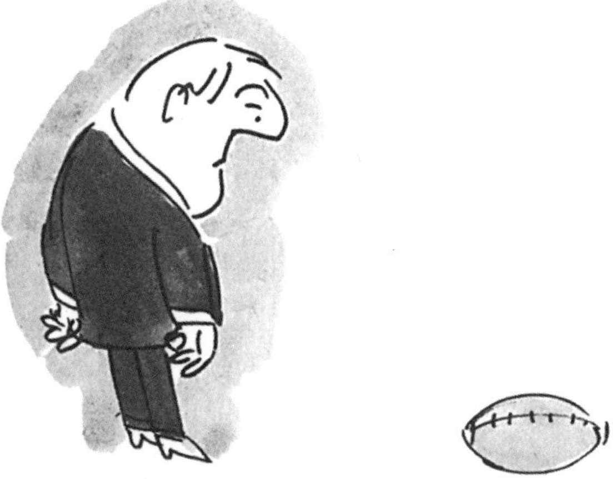

could -

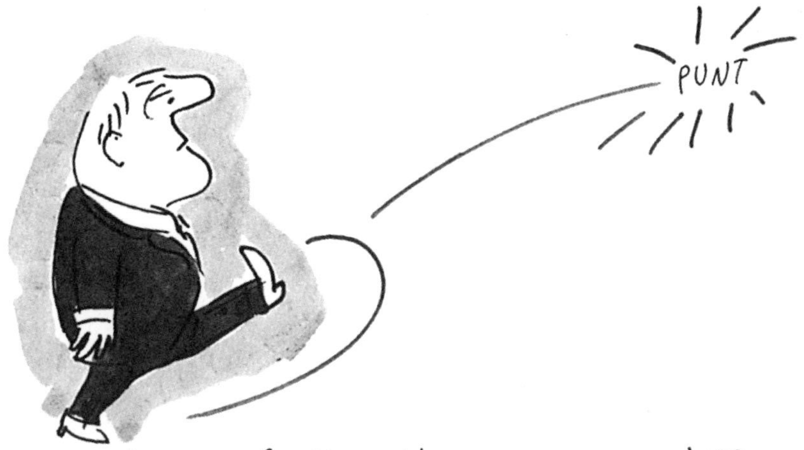
PUNT

Kick a football farther than any man alive -

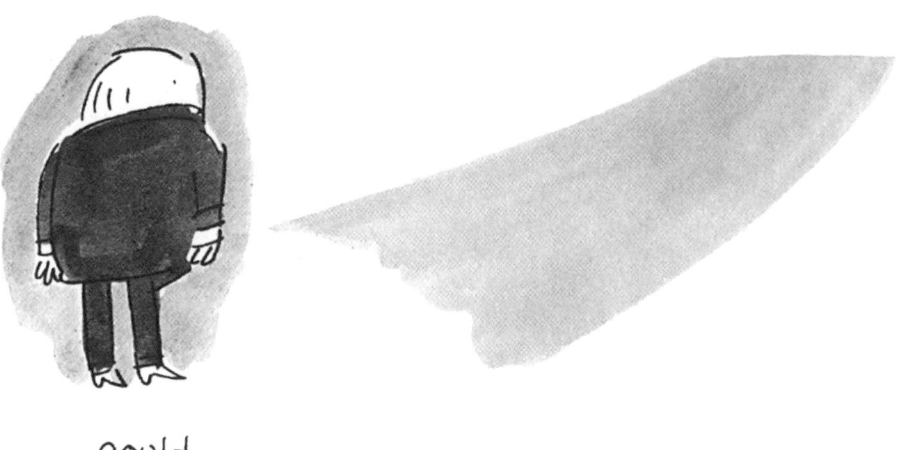

could -

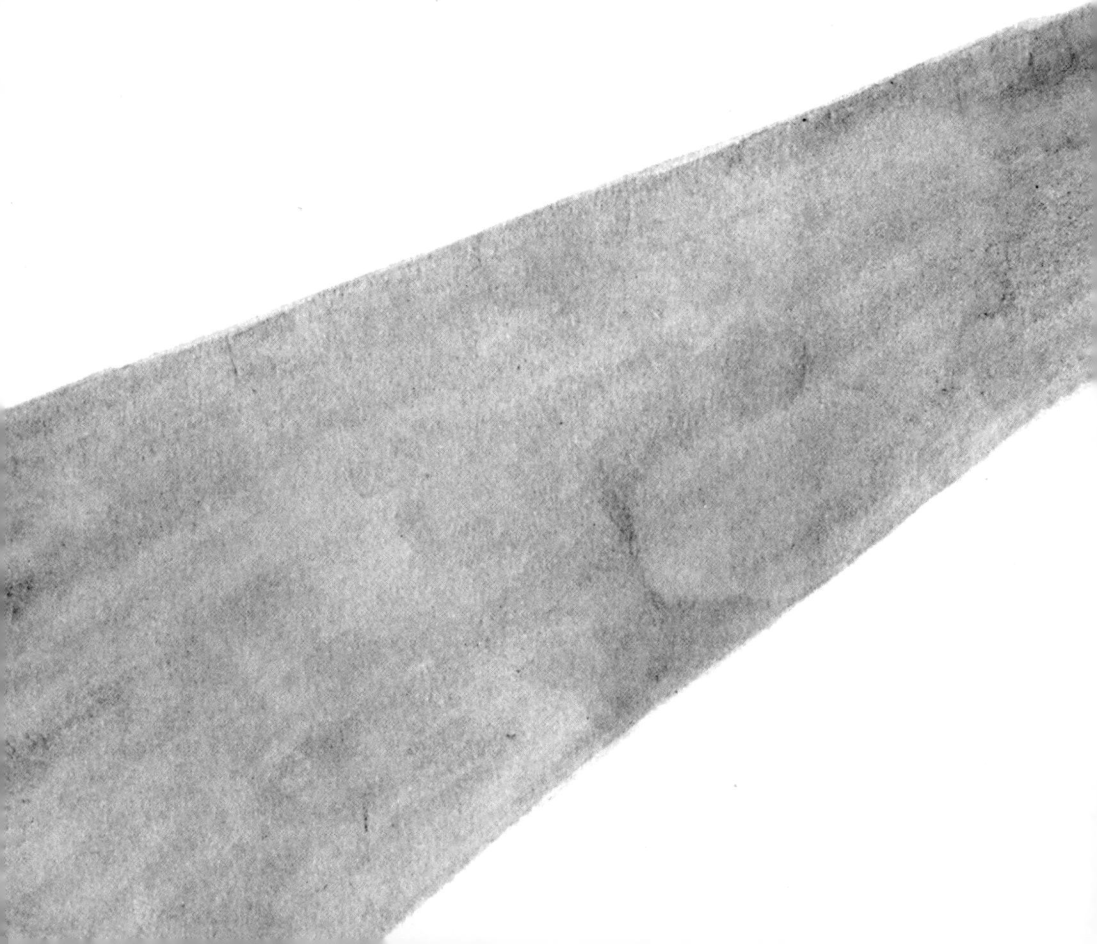

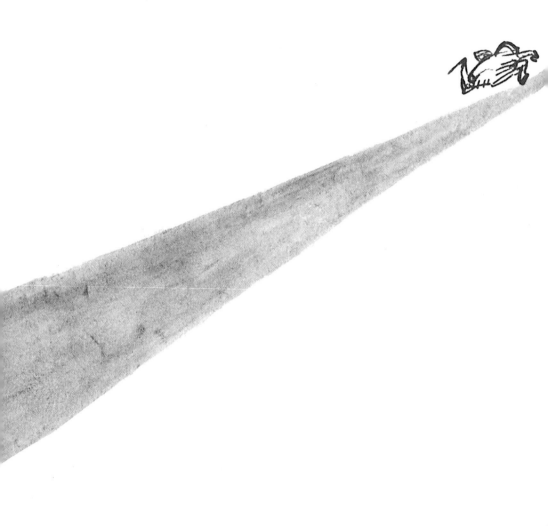

run the mile faster than any man alive.

Harold Swerg could do anything

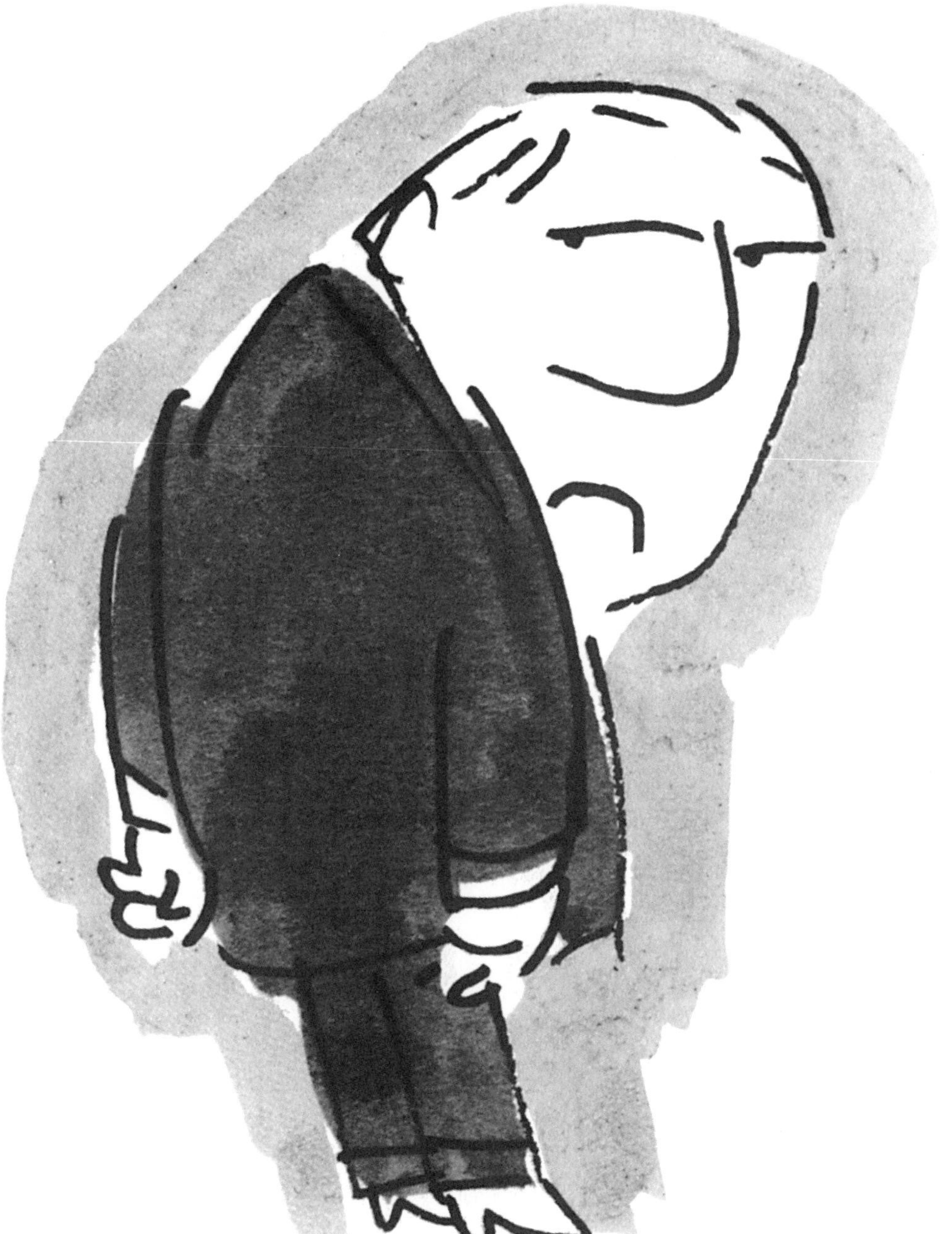

Only he wouldn't.

Baseball and football magnates came to Harold Swerg. They said:

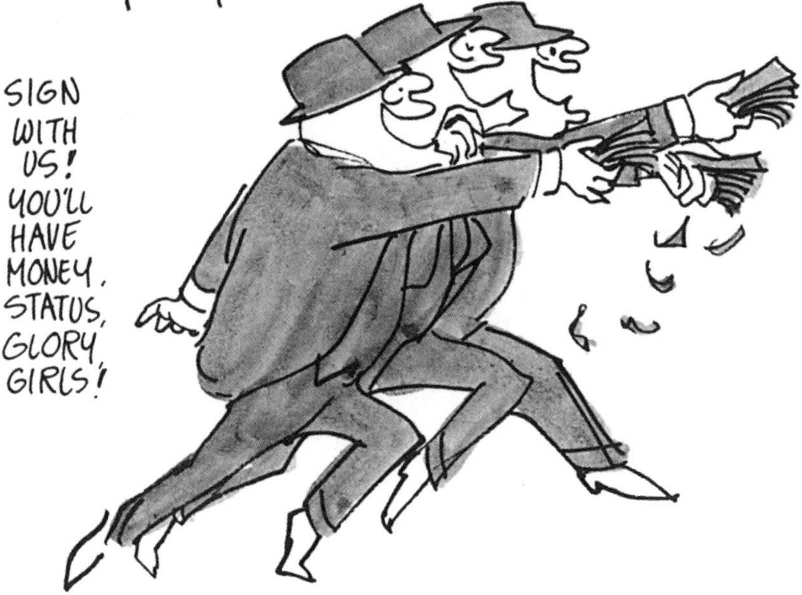
SIGN WITH US! YOU'LL HAVE MONEY, STATUS, GLORY, GIRLS!

Track and field magnates came to Harold Swerg. They said:

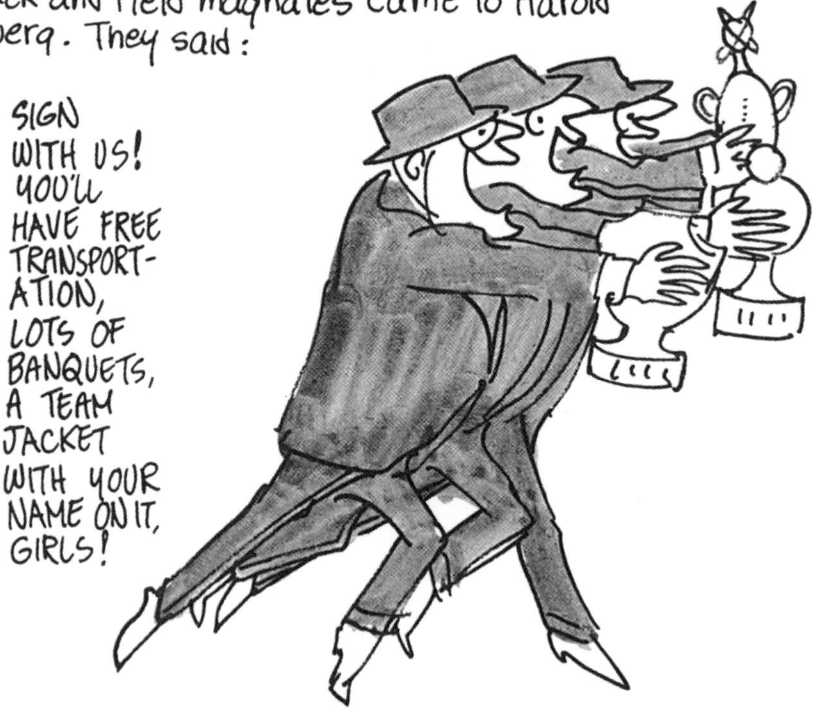
SIGN WITH US! YOU'LL HAVE FREE TRANSPORT-ATION, LOTS OF BANQUETS, A TEAM JACKET WITH YOUR NAME ON IT, GIRLS!

And to all of them Harold Swerq replied:

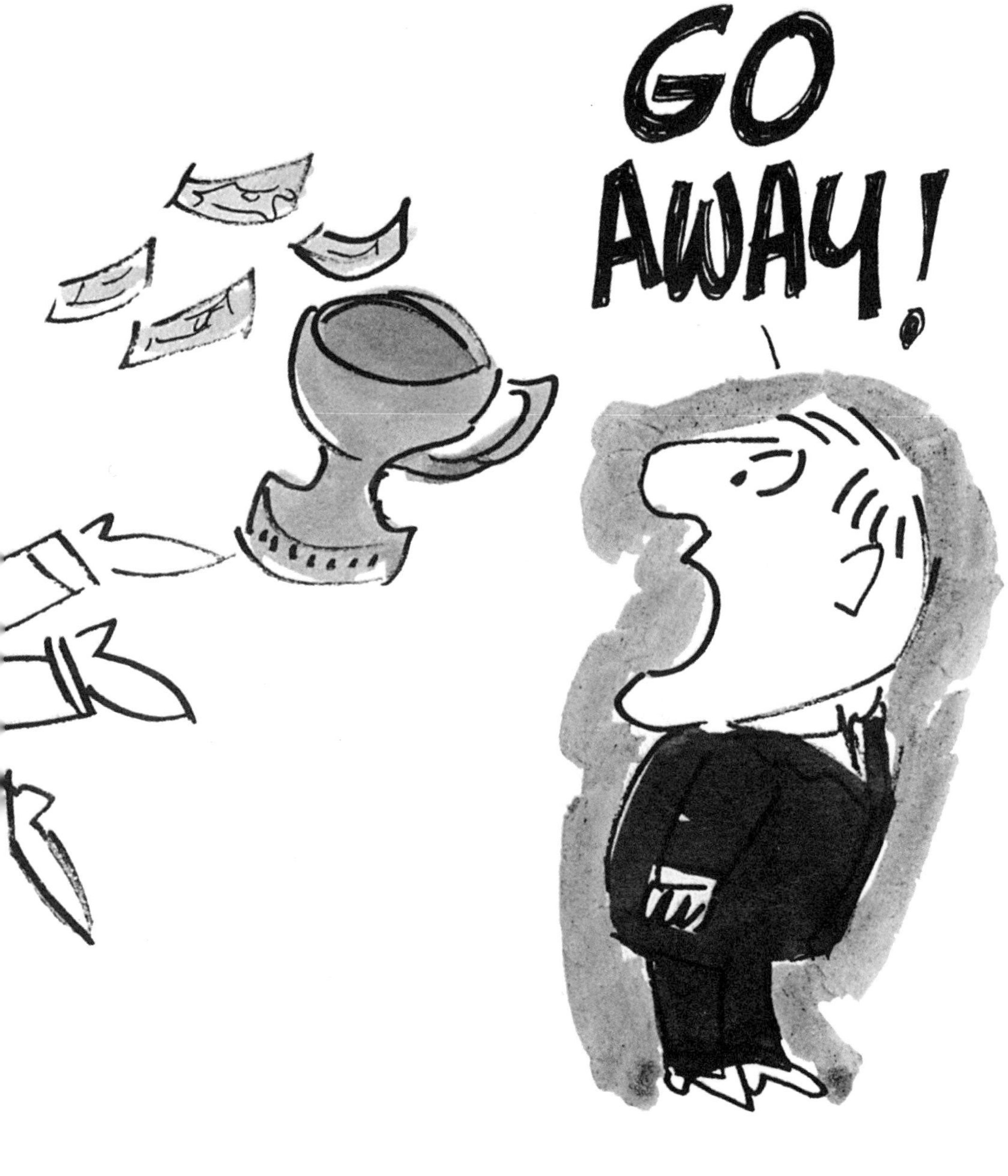
GO AWAY!

He just wanted to go on making his living as a filing clerk.

I DON'T **LIKE** THE SPORT BUSINESS. I **LIKE** THE FILING CLERK BUSINESS.

THE SPORT BUSINESS DOESN'T PRESENT A CHALLENGE. THE FILING CLERK BUSINESS PRESENTS A CHALLENGE.

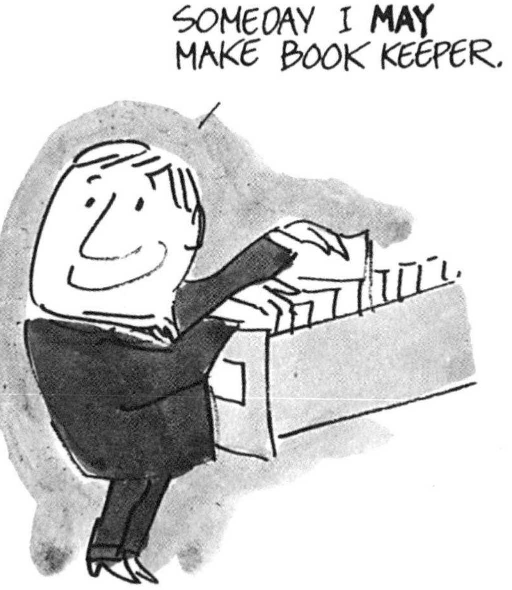
SOMEDAY I **MAY** MAKE BOOK KEEPER.

So the baseball magnates and the football magnates and the track and field magnates all got together and issued a press release.

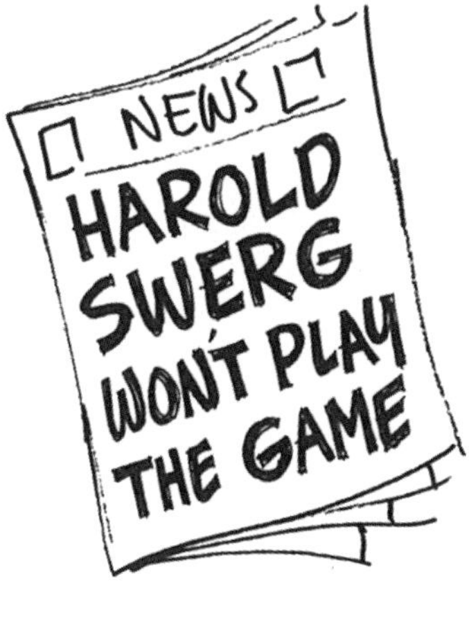
NEWS
HAROLD SWERG WON'T PLAY THE GAME

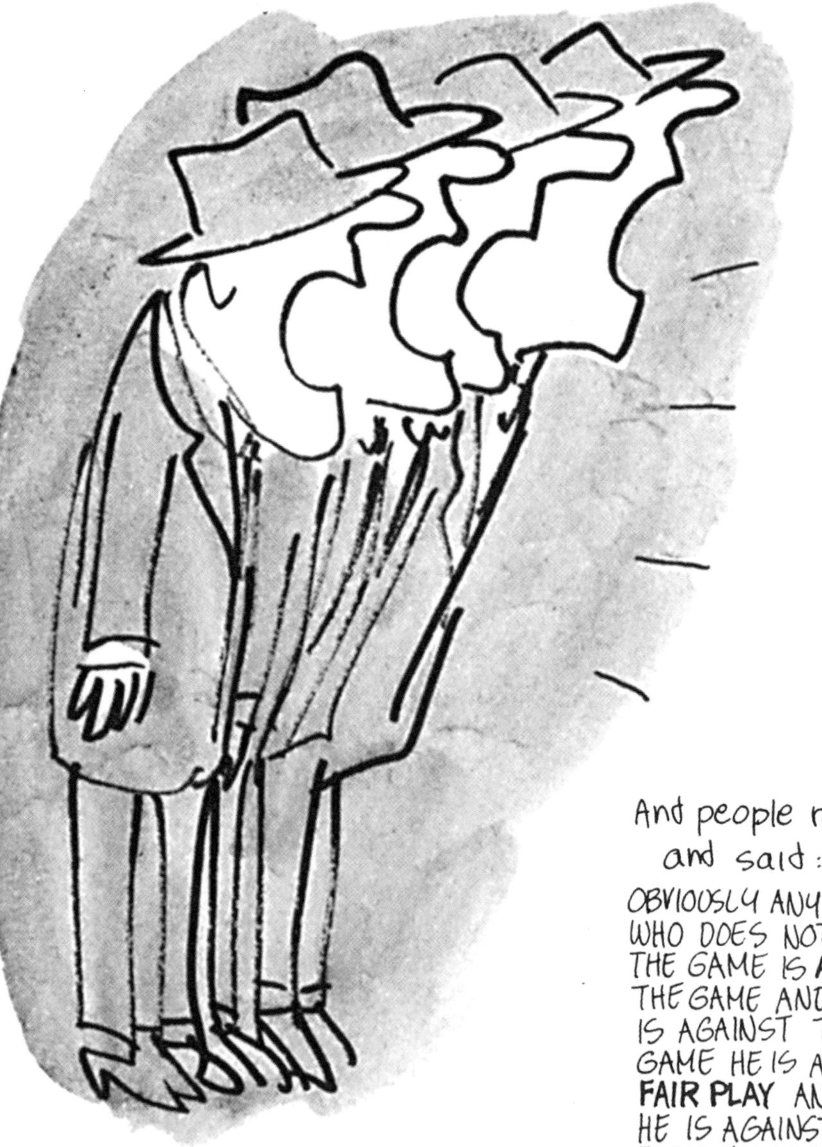

And people read it and said:

OBVIOUSLY ANY MAN WHO DOES NOT PLAY THE GAME IS **AGAINST** THE GAME AND IF HE IS AGAINST THE GAME HE IS AGAINST **FAIR PLAY** AND IF HE IS AGAINST FAIR PLAY HE IS AGAINST **OUR WAY OF LIFE!**

BOO!

To all of which Harold Swerg replied:
LEAVE ME ALONE.
And that was where things seemed to settle.

Then the new Olympics were announced. RUSSIA was to have its greatest team *ever*.

It had someone who could hit a baseball farther than anybody.

It had someone who could kick a football farther than anybody.

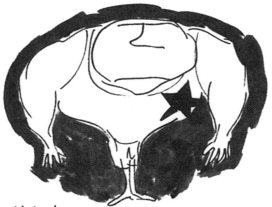

It had someone who could run a mile faster than anybody.

The State Department called a conference.

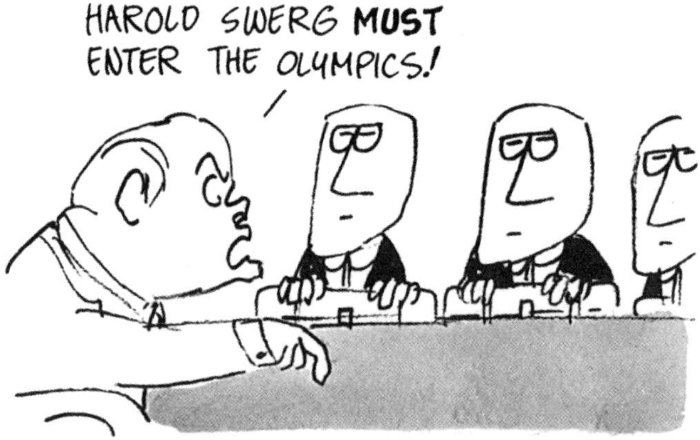
HAROLD SWERG **MUST** ENTER THE OLYMPICS!

So they sent a representative–

who returned with a message.

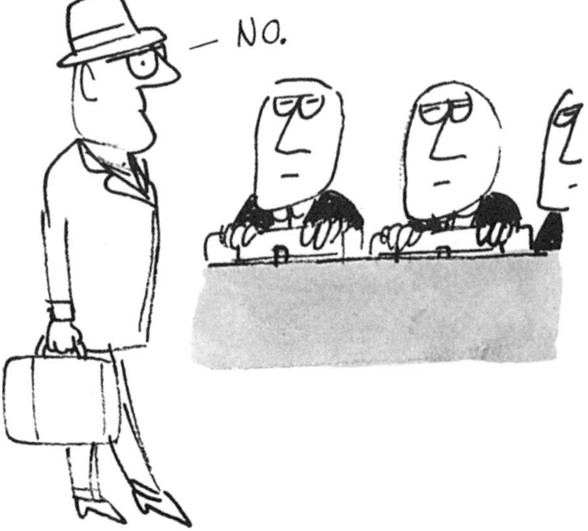
NO.

So they checked his loyalty file.

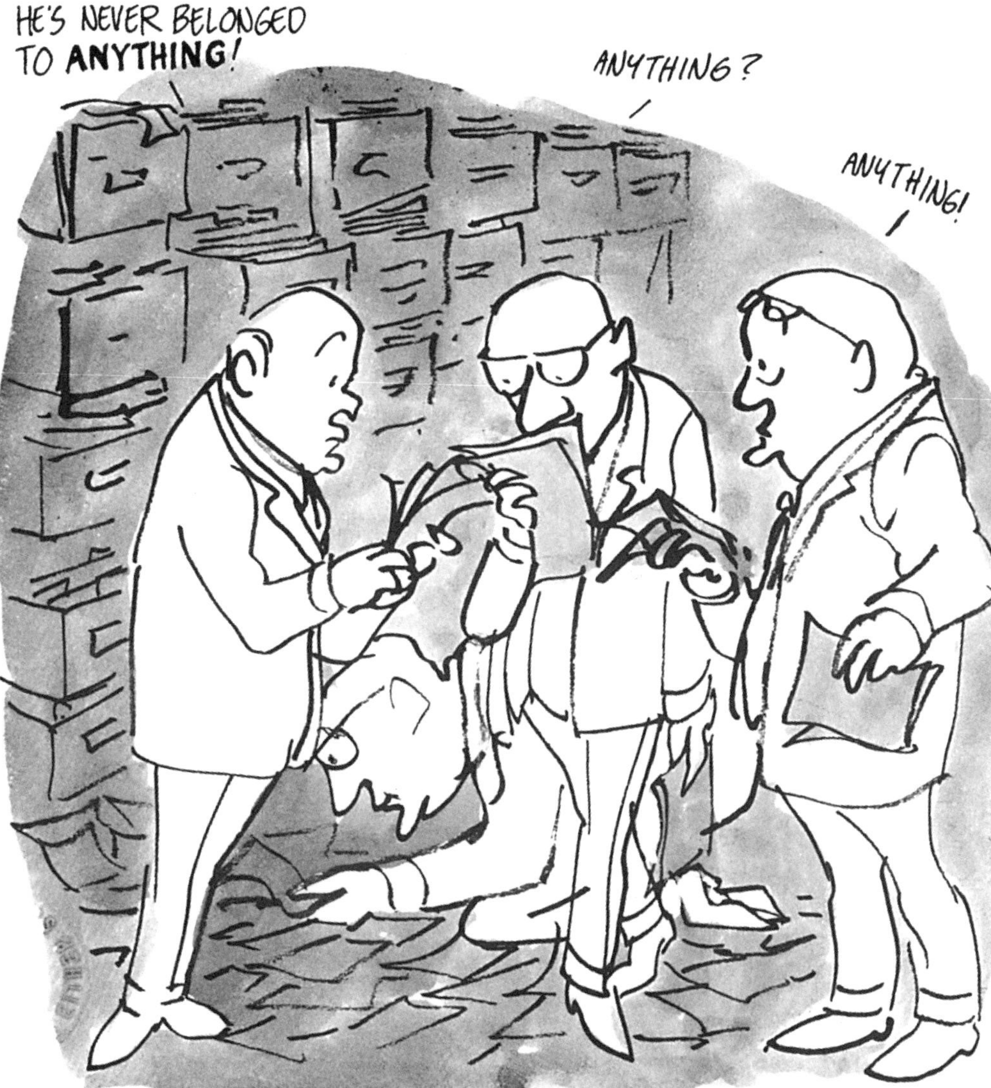
HE'S NEVER BELONGED TO **ANYTHING**!
ANYTHING?
ANYTHING!

And that seemed to be the answer. Harold Swerg was just not interested in belonging.

A higher State Department official
went to see him.

BUT YOU'VE **GOT**
TO **BELONG!**
EVERYONE
BELONGS TO
SOMETHING!

NOT ME. Said
Harold
Swerg.

They sent a bunch of congressmen.

IT'S THE RULE OF A DEMOCRACY THAT THE MAJORITY
DECIDES. A MAJORITY HAS DECIDED THEY WANT **YOU**
TO PLAY IN THE OLYMPICS. ARE YOU TRYING TO
CRUMBLE OUR FOUNDATIONS?

"I'M JUST TRYING TO BE
LEFT ALONE" said
Harold Swerg and
he sent them away.

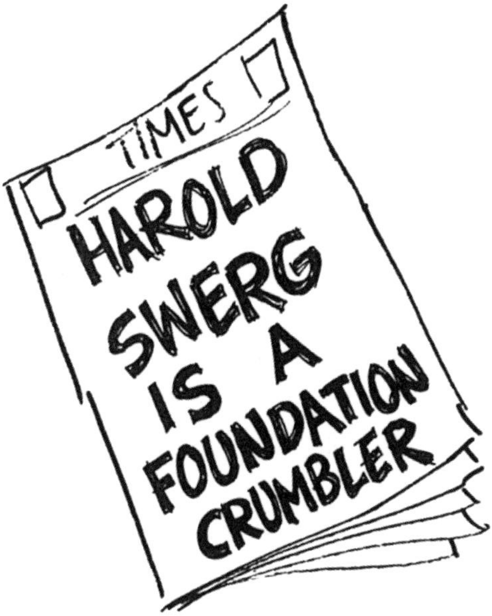
TIMES
HAROLD SWERG IS A FOUNDATION CRUMBLER

screamed the press. Congress threatened to draft him into the Olympics.

Finally there came a special appeal from the President.

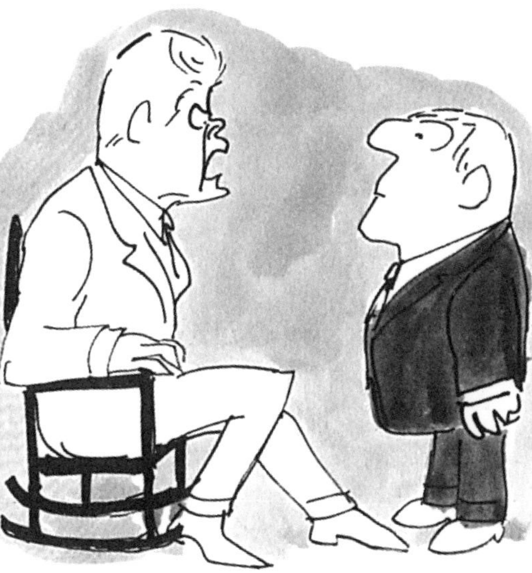
DO YOU WANT US TO LOSE?
SO THATS WHATS BOTHERING EVERYBODY.

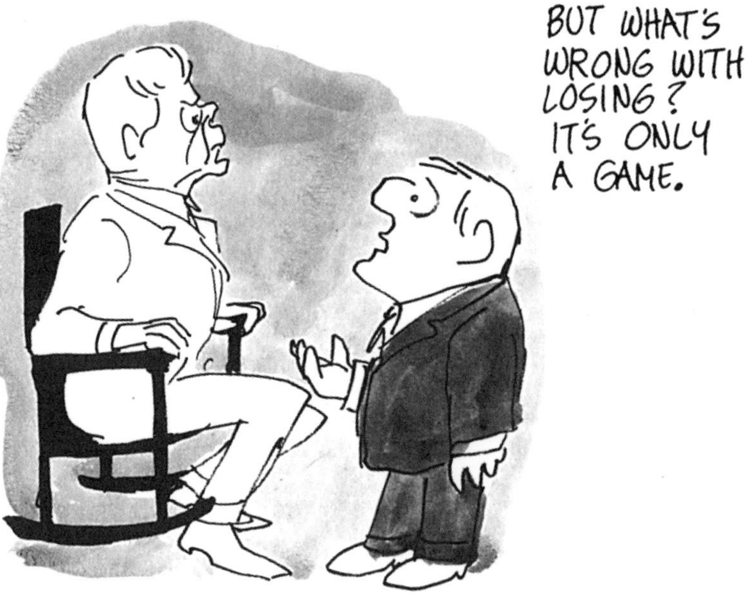
BUT WHAT'S WRONG WITH LOSING? IT'S ONLY A GAME.

Everyone was thrown into confusion.

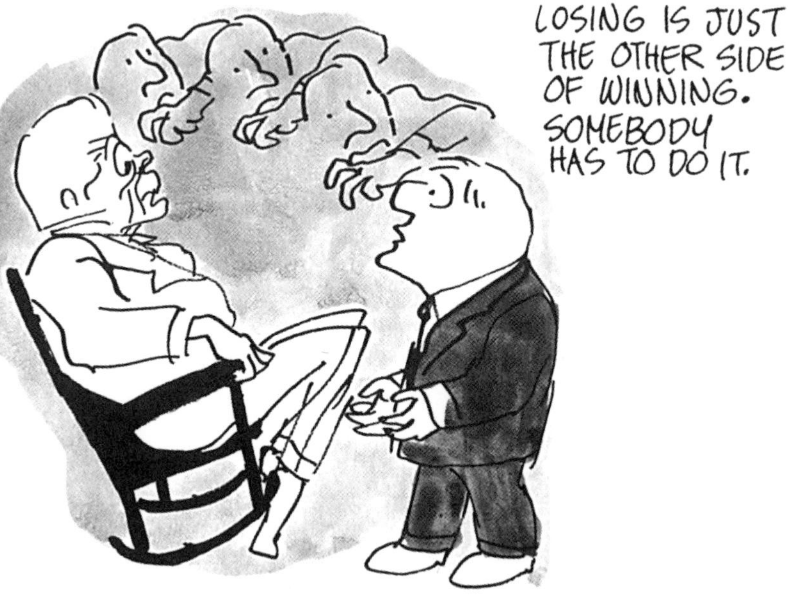
LOSING IS JUST THE OTHER SIDE OF WINNING. SOMEBODY HAS TO DO IT.

'DON'T LISTEN! DON'T LISTEN!' cried the President's advisors and they all closed their ears.

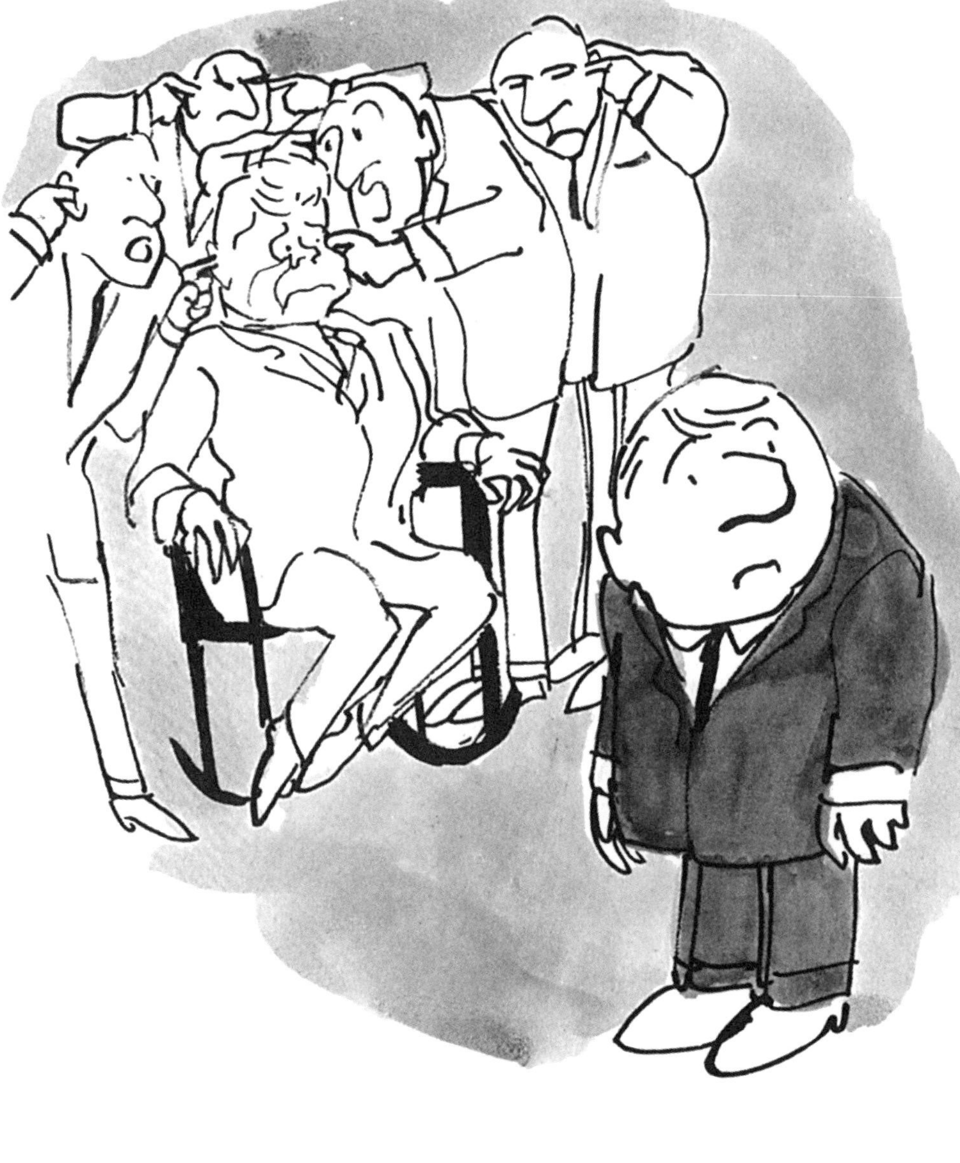

The public expressed its outrage. They booed. They hissed. They burned Olympic torches on his lawn.

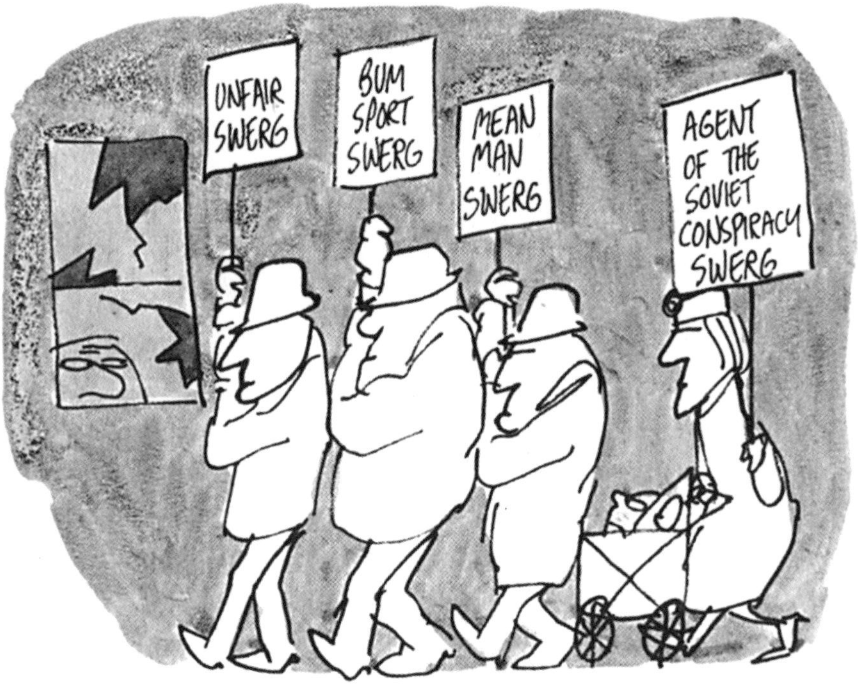
UNFAIR SWERG
BUM SPORT SWERG
MEAN MAN SWERG
AGENT OF THE SOVIET CONSPIRACY SWERG

The Soviet press offered its views on the subject.

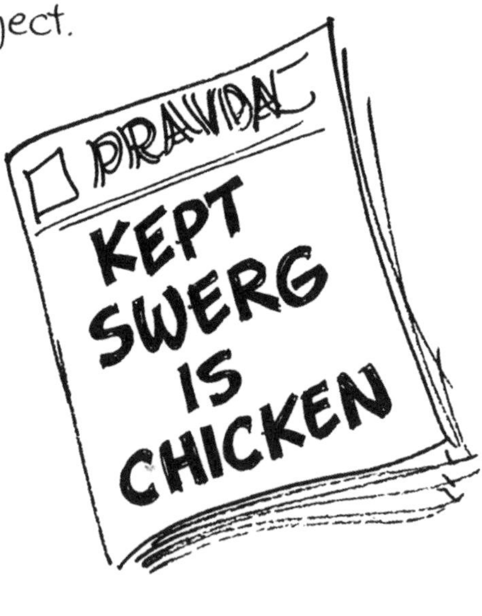
PRAVDA
KEPT SWERG IS CHICKEN

Then one day, just when things were at their hottest - Harold Swerg came out of his house and said:

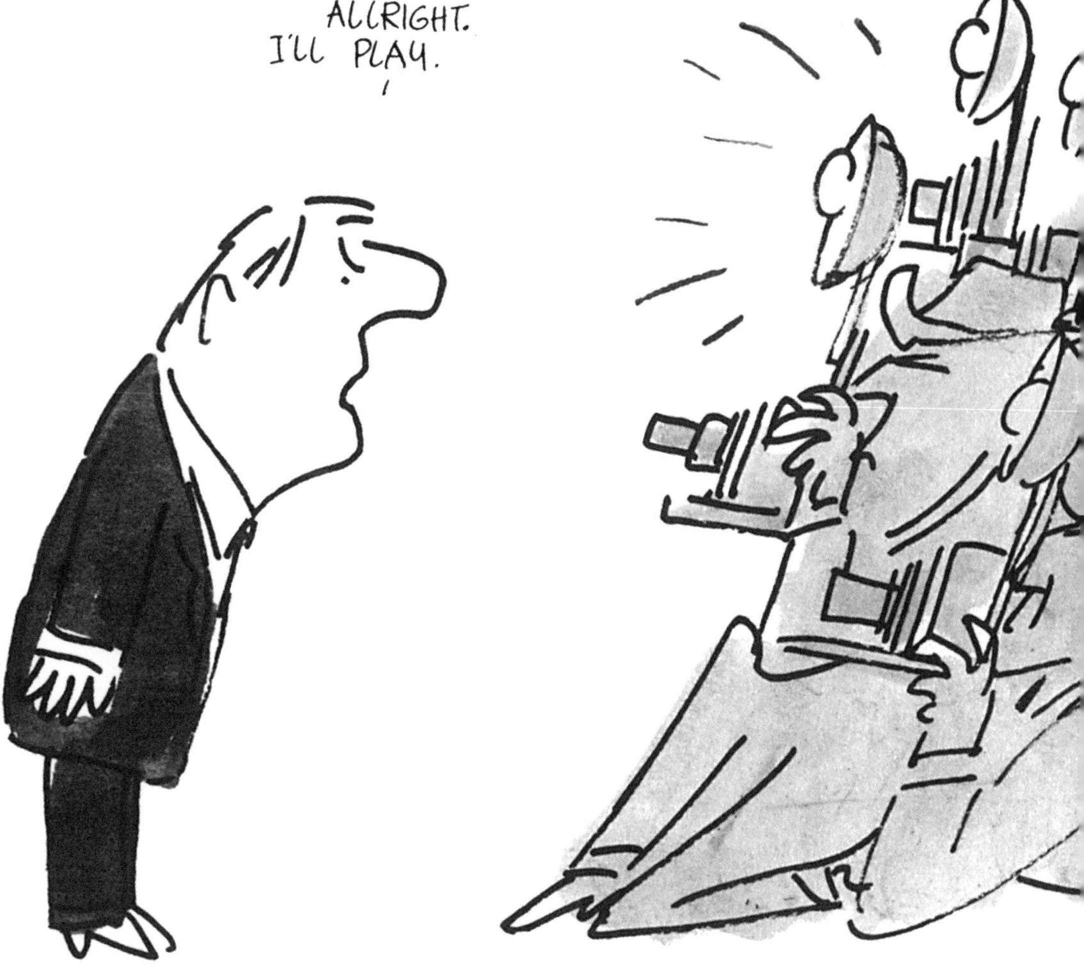
ALLRIGHT.
I'LL PLAY.

"**SWERG WILL PLAY!**" The country was electrified. "**SWERG WILL PLAY!**" Both political parties claimed credit. And so the games began!

The first event was who could hit a baseball the farthest. The Russian (Peoples Farthest Baseball Hero Smedyakov) went first.

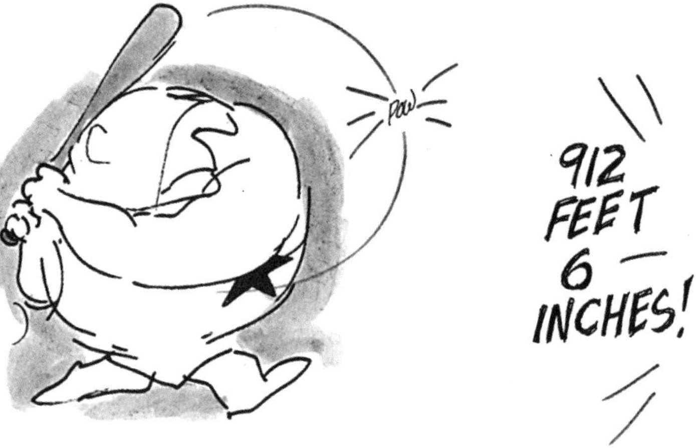
POW
912 FEET 6 INCHES!

Harold Swerg went second.

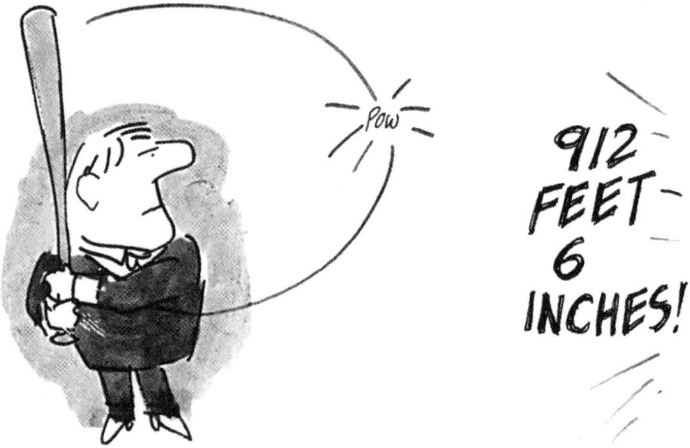
POW
912 FEET 6 INCHES!

The next event was who could kick a football the farthest. The Russian (People's Hero Kicker Brosnokopski) went first.

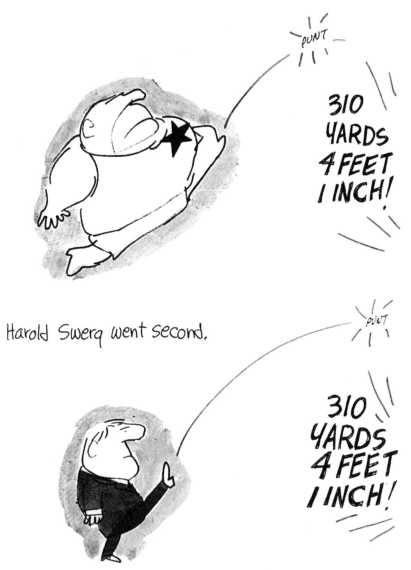

PUNT

310 YARDS 4 FEET 1 INCH!

Harold Swerg went second.

PUNT

310 YARDS 4 FEET 1 INCH!

Grumblings of discontent began to murmur through the crowd.

The last event was the mile. His opponent was Peoples Fastest Hero Runner Alive Kchawelshkov.

It was a tie.

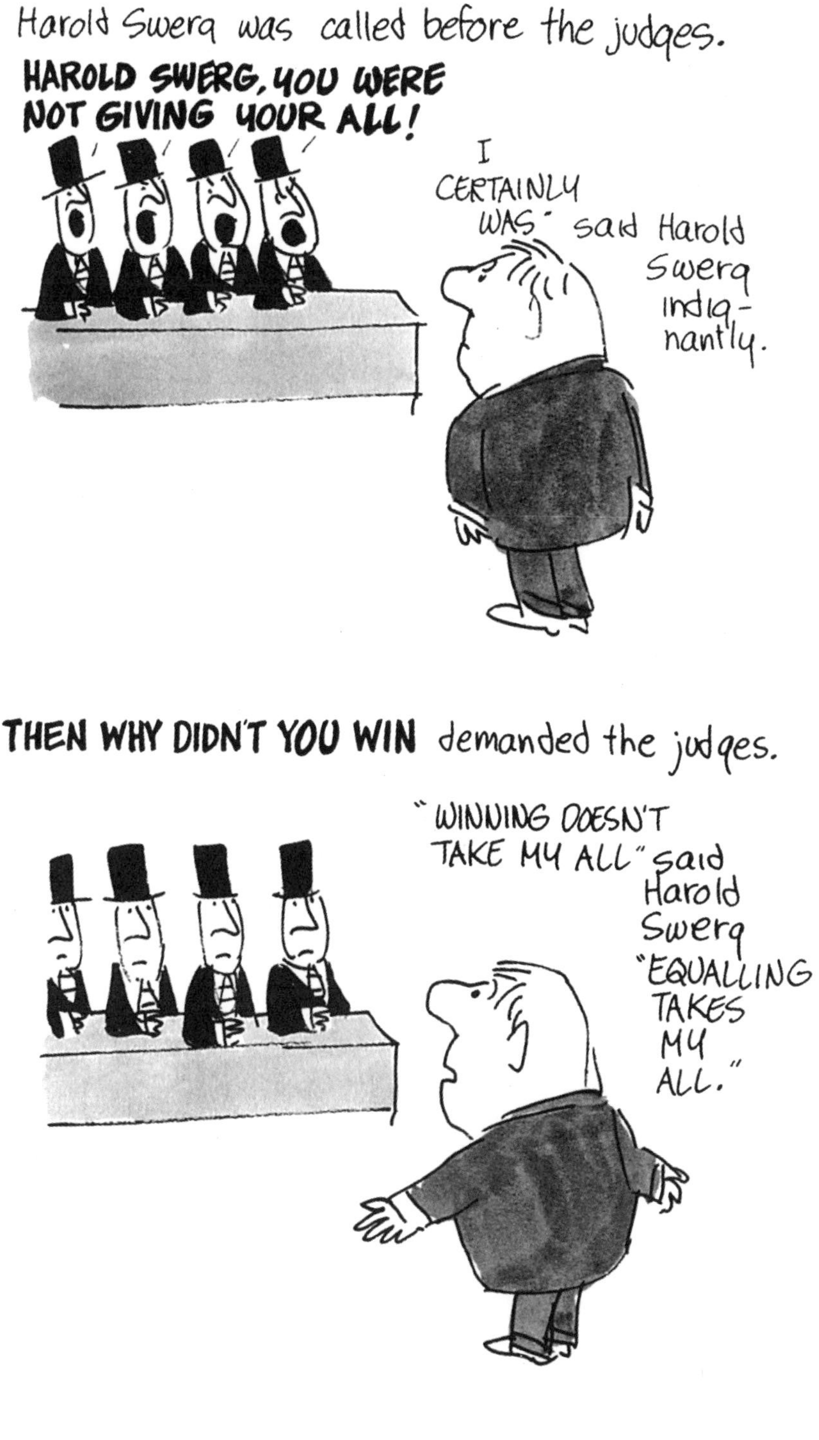
Harold Swerg was called before the judges.
HAROLD SWERG, YOU WERE NOT GIVING YOUR ALL!
I CERTAINLY WAS" said Harold Swerg indignantly.
" THEN WHY DIDN'T YOU WIN demanded the judges.
"WINNING DOESN'T TAKE MY ALL" said Harold Swerg "EQUALLING TAKES MY ALL."

"HUH?" said the judges

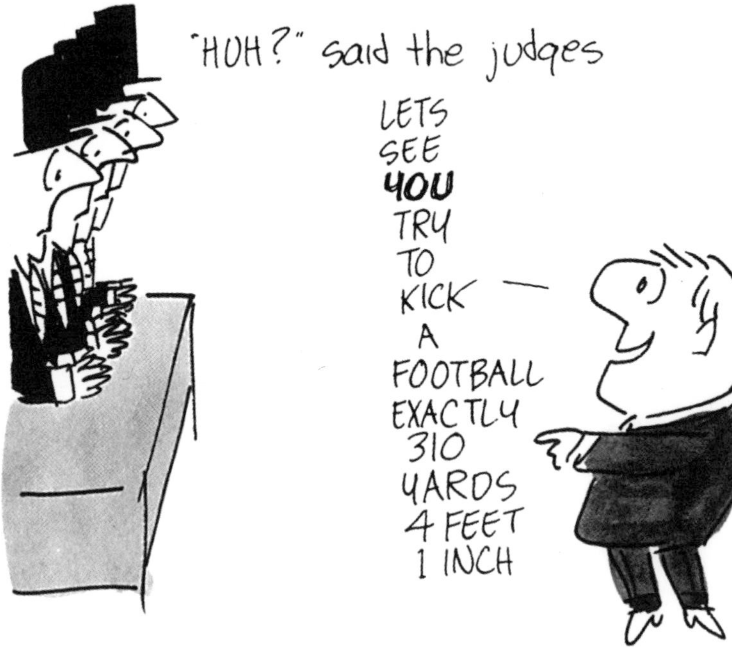
LETS SEE YOU TRY TO KICK A FOOTBALL EXACTLY 310 YARDS 4 FEET 1 INCH

But the judges just didn't understand.

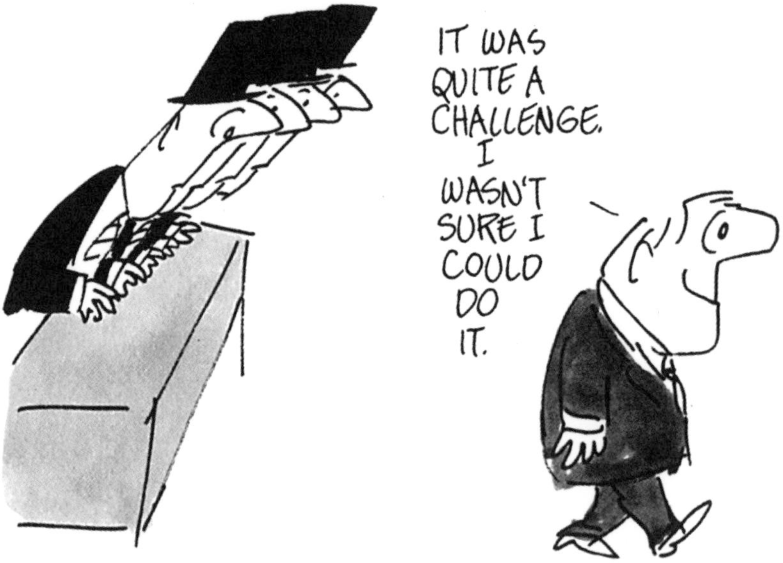
IT WAS QUITE A CHALLENGE. I WASN'T SURE I COULD DO IT.

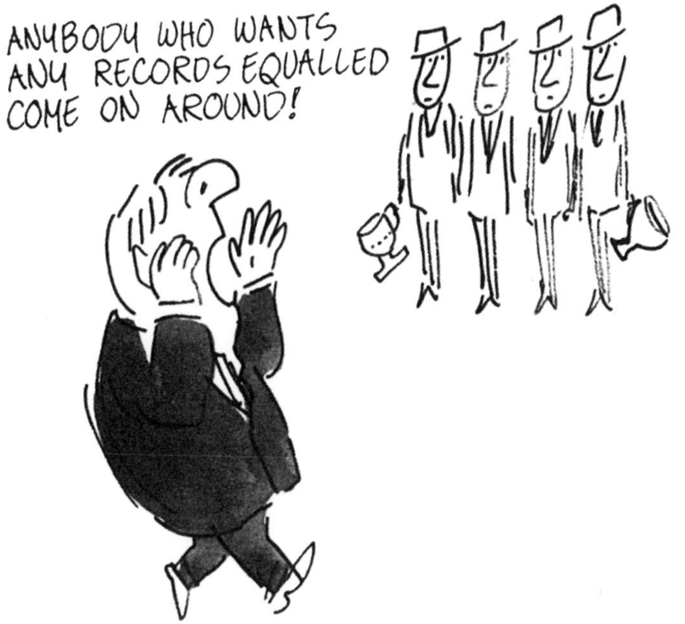
ANYBODY WHO WANTS ANY RECORDS EQUALLED COME ON AROUND!

But nobody did.

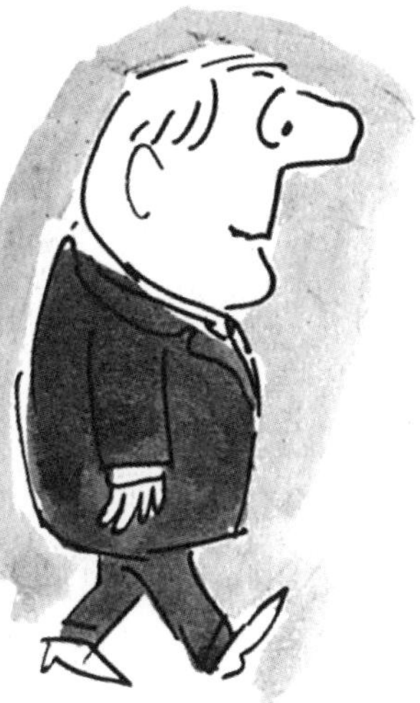

Because nobody is interested
in having records equalled.

So they left Harold Swerg alone—

which was just the way he wanted it.

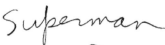

I USED TO BE **SUPERMAN**.

I USED TO GO RESCUING PEOPLE ALL THE HELL OVER THE PLACE. WHEREVER YOU LOOKED I WAS SAVING **SOMEBODY**.

THEN ONE DAY I PULLED THIS CHICK FROM THE RIVER. DO YOU THINK SHE **THANKED** ME? **NO!**

SHE JUST WANTED TO KNOW WHY I HAD THIS **COMPULSION** TO RESCUE.

SHE ACCUSED ME OF DOUBTING MY MASCULINITY AND HENCE MY EXHIBITIONIST TENDENCIES. SHE WANTED TO KNOW WHY I DIDN'T SPEND MORE TIME **READING**.

SHE TOOK ONE LOOK AT MY CAPE AND SAID I WAS A LATENT TRANSVESTITE, AND WHY WAS MY COSTUME SO SKIN TIGHT AND DID I RESCUE MORE **MEN** THAN **WOMEN** –

I TRIED TO TELL HER SHE SHOULDN'T JUDGE ME THE WAY SHE JUDGES **EARTH** PEOPLE. SHE JUST PATTED MY HEAD AND SMILED.

SO AFTER A LOT OF ARGUMENT BACK AND FORTH I FINALLY GOT HER TO ADMIT THAT ALTHOUGH I MIGHT NOT BE **SUPER**, I WAS A LOT BETTER THAN **AVERAGE!**

NOW I HAVE A REGULAR OFFICE JOB IN THE CITY AND A HOUSE IN THE SUBURBS. WE'RE BOTH **VERY** HAPPY.

JULES FEIFFER

Superman

A WOMAN *starts across the stage.* MUGGER *runs from behind her, stops in front of her and poses threateningly.*

MUGGER Don't scream. Give me your purse!

WOMAN I wasn't going to scream. I was going to try to discuss this with you.

MUGGER It won't work. Three times this week broads discussed me out of taking their pocketbooks. I got to live too, you know.

SUPERMAN (*Off stage*) Faster than the speed of light!

MUGGER Oh, my God!

SUPERMAN (*Off stage*) More powerful than an express train!

MUGGER It's – it's –

SUPERMAN (*Off stage*) Leaps over buildings in a single bound!

MUGGER (*Flees*) Superman!

SUPERMAN (*Enters running and leaping*) Ha! Ha! That scoundrel won't harm you again, madam. Else he'll have to reckon with *Superman*!

WOMAN (*Stares disbelieving*) What is this? A gag?

SUPERMAN Indeed no, madam. Superman does not gag. (*Proudly*) Superman doesn't have a sense of humor!

WOMAN You can't really be –

SUPERMAN Ha, ha! But I am!

WOMAN You mean – who I used to hear all the time on the radio?

SUPERMAN Superman, madam! Superman!

WOMAN (*Suspiciously*) Who sponsored you?

SUPERMAN (*Proudly*) Corn Kix, madam!

WOMAN (*Suspiciously*) Who were you on just before?

SUPERMAN Mandrake the Magician, madam. But you wouldn't remember him.

WOMAN Oh, wouldn't I? With Lothar?

SUPERMAN By George!

WOMAN (*Still suspicious*) And who was on *after* you?

SUPERMAN Jack Armstrong, all-American boy!

WOMAN (*Sings*) Raise the flag for Hudson High boys –

SUPERMAN (*Sings*) Won't you try Wheaties, the best breakfast food in the land. (*Stops himself*) That wasn't true, you know. Corn Kix was better.

WOMAN Do you remember "I Love A Mystery"?

SUPERMAN (*Excited*) With Jack, Doc, and Reggie?

WOMAN (*Hums the theme. SUPERMAN joins her. The WOMAN stops as SUPERMAN continues to hum. She stares hard at him*) There's something wrong.

SUPERMAN (*Politely*) Madam?

WOMAN Doesn't that costume make you look lumpy when you wear your street clothes? I mean, the cape and all?

SUPERMAN Well, it *is* a little warm. I usually take off summers.

WOMAN Why do you wear it?

SUPERMAN What?

WOMAN *You* know what I mean. The costume. The cape.

SUPERMAN It's the uniform of Superman, madam.

WOMAN It's rather effeminate don't you think?

SUPERMAN Hold on!

WOMAN It *is* terribly skin-tight. You're not a transvestite, are you? You don't have to answer if you don't want to.

SUPERMAN A *what*?

WOMAN (*Leering suspiciously*) *You* know. Do you rescue more men than women?

SUPERMAN I rescue only those in dire straits!

WOMAN Why?

SUPERMAN (*Shaken*) What? Why what? What?

WOMAN Why this compulsion to rescue. Are you a cop? Do you get paid for it? Is it your job?

SUPERMAN Well, nobody *hired* me, if that's what you mean.

WOMAN Then, you just do it for kicks. Run around in your skin-tight blue leotards and rescue people for the thrill of it.

SUPERMAN (*Weakly*) I fight crime.

WOMAN You can't fight crime in a business suit?

SUPERMAN (*Sadly*) You think I'm an exhibitionist.

WOMAN You *could* spend more time reading.

SUPERMAN I think it's wrong to judge Superman the way you judge *other* people.

WOMAN Everybody thinks he's special. But they don't run around in skin-tight. effeminate leotards –

SUPERMAN (*Hotly*) All right, so I do rescue more men than women – but more men get into trouble than women! *I'm* all right.

WOMAN I didn't say a word.

SUPERMAN Well, I know what you're thinking.

WOMAN How come you're not married?

SUPERMAN (*Wearily*) I fight crime – most of the time.

WOMAN (*Shrugs*) A man your age.

SUPERMAN You can't judge me the way you judge earth people. I admit that if I came from earth and wore effeminate skin-tight leotards and rescued more men than women it *would* seem suspicious – but I'm from Krypton!

WOMAN Look, I'm not arguing.

SUPERMAN Well, I don't want you to go away with the wrong idea.

WOMAN If it makes you more secure to be what you call Superman –

SUPERMAN I am. I tell you, I am. Do you want me to prove it? Do you want me to leap over a tall building in a single bound?

WOMAN Honey, you don't have to prove anything to me. Why *hurt* yourself? What are these doubts that torment you so terribly that you have to go around proving your masculinity to everybody?

SUPERMAN (*Bitterly*) O.K. Have it your way. I'm not Superman, all right? You feel better? I'm not! It's all a gag! All right?

WOMAN You'll see. You've come to a wise conclusion.

SUPERMAN But you will admit I'm better than average?

WOMAN (*Warmly*) I'm *sure* you are.

SUPERMAN (*Gratefully*) Can I take you to the theatre tomorrow night?

WOMAN I'm washing my hair.

SUPERMAN The next night?

WOMAN I'm sorry, I'm busy.

SUPERMAN Well, can I see you sometime?

WOMAN Well, the evenings are hard. Maybe for lunch. You won't wear that – that costume.

SUPERMAN No – a suit. I swear – a suit. I'll go out this minute and buy a suit.

WOMAN What's the matter? You're standing funny.

SUPERMAN I've got a stomach ache.

WOMAN Do you need help? Can you get home all right?

SUPERMAN It's only a little way. I think I can make it if I go slow. You're very considerate.

WOMAN Take it easy. And don't rush around so much. You'll find that you'll feel better.

SUPERMAN (*Begins to exit bent over*) You've been a great help. I'll be in touch.

WOMAN (*Calls to him*) Drink some hot soup! (*She turns, to exit. The* MUGGER *leaps out at her*)

MUGGER Don't scream. Give me your purse!

WOMAN (*Screams*) Superman! Come quick! Superman!

SUPERMAN (*Completely bent over, clutching hill stomach. turns weakly toward her*) Who?

George's Moon

Once

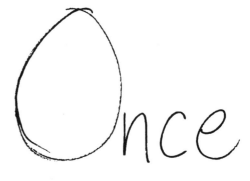

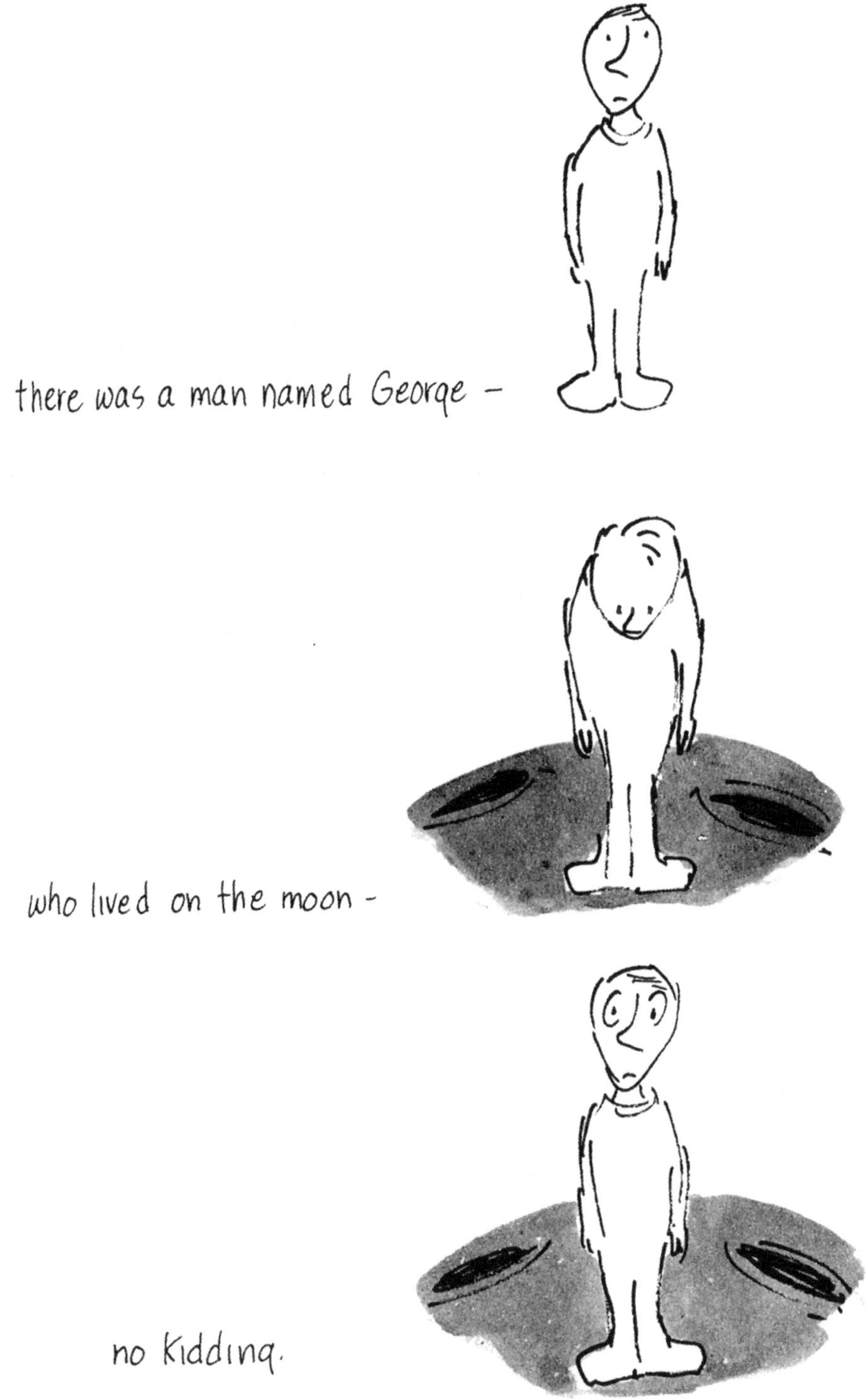
there was a man named George -
who lived on the moon -
no kidding.

George didn't have much to do on the moon.

He slept.

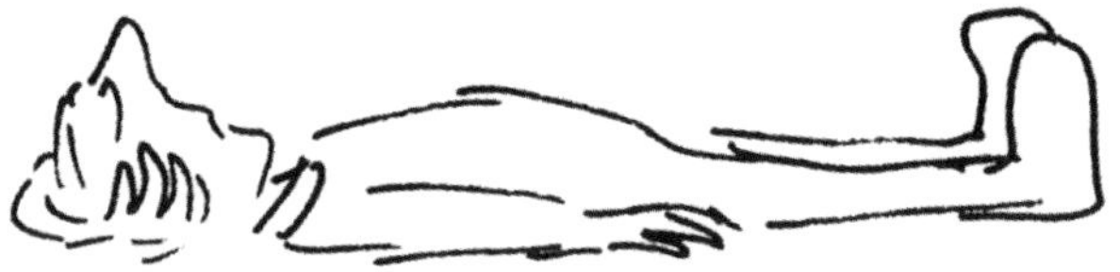

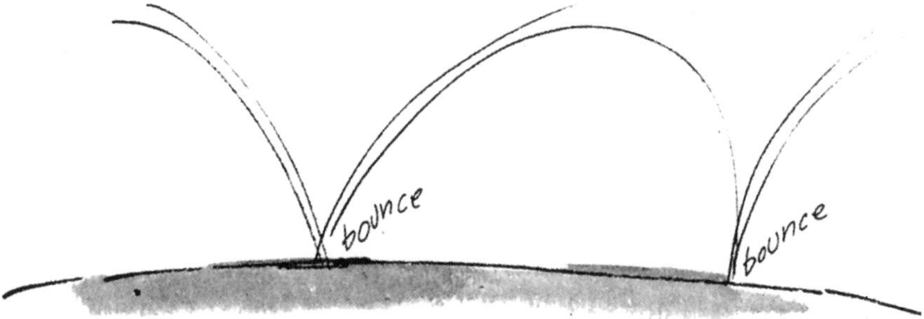
bounce
bounce

He took long walks.

He kept trying to figure out how he got there.

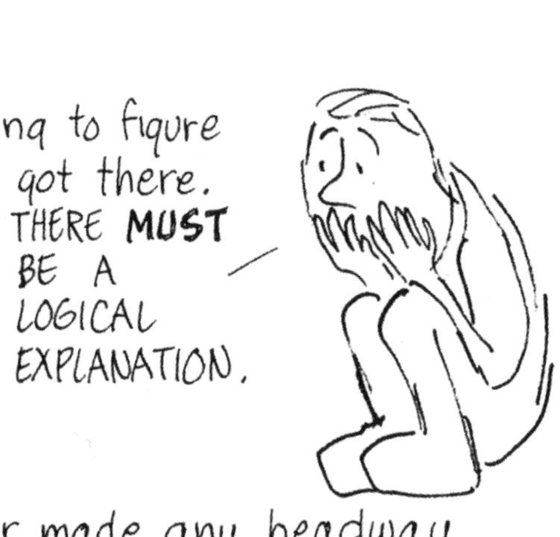
THERE **MUST** BE A LOGICAL EXPLANATION.

But he never made any headway.

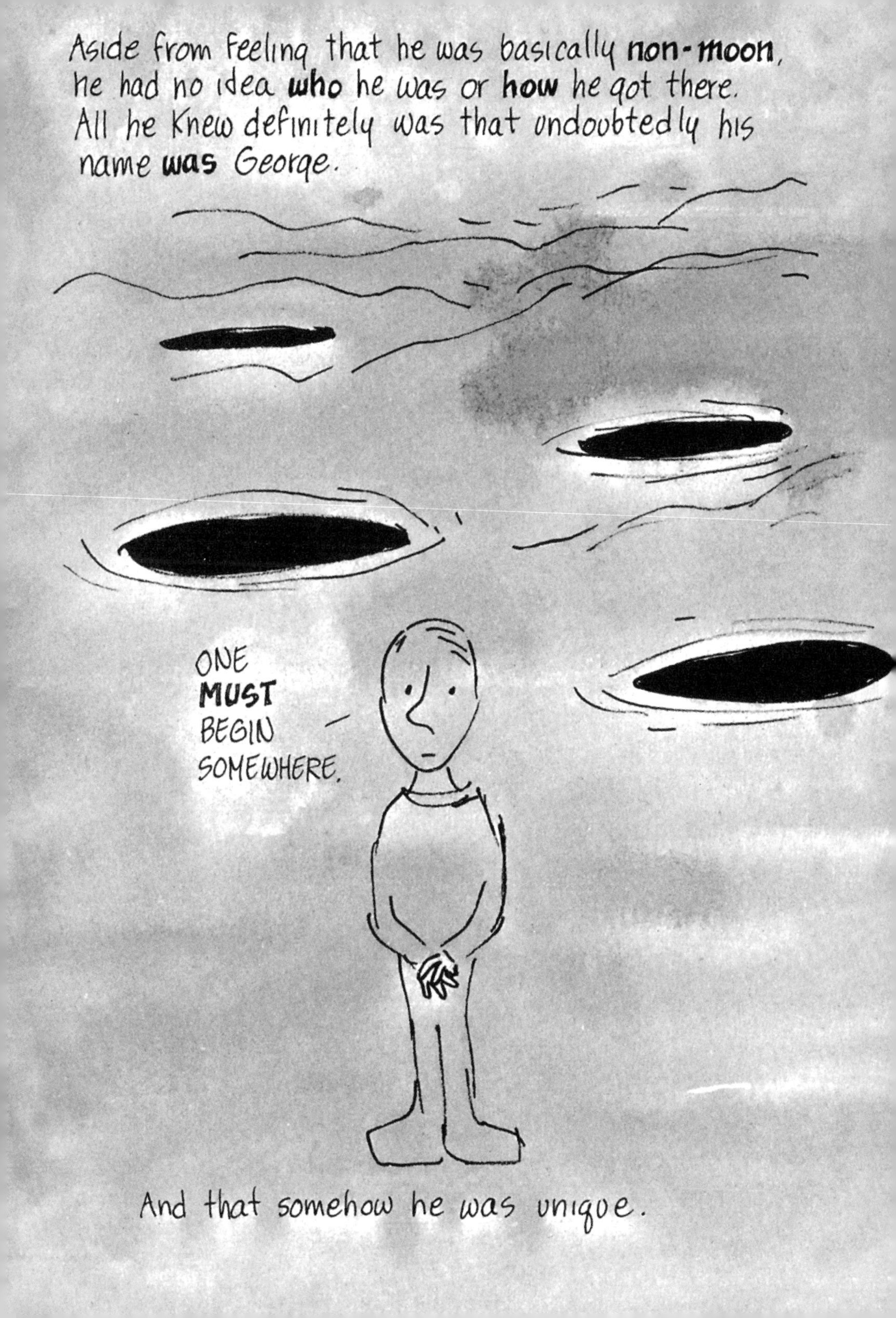
Aside from feeling that he was basically **non-moon**, he had no idea **who** he was or **how** he got there. All he Knew definitely was that undoubtedly his name **was** George.
ONE **MUST** BEGIN SOMEWHERE.
And that somehow he was unique.

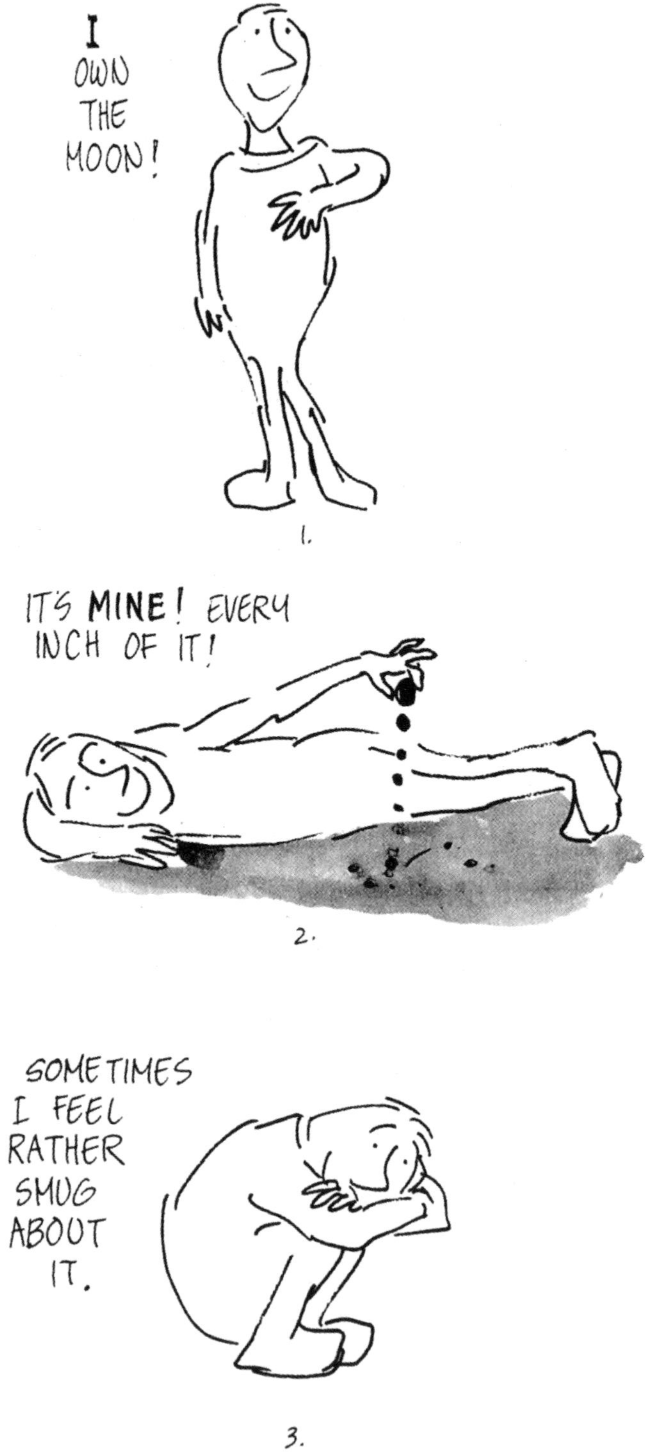
I OWN THE MOON!
1.
IT'S MINE! EVERY INCH OF IT!
2.
SOMETIMES I FEEL RATHER SMUG ABOUT IT.
3.

HI THERE,
MY MOON.

5.

SOMEDAY
I'LL CHANGE
YOUR NAME
TO **GEORGE**.

6

But this was a false exuberance. George felt no real connection with the land.

HOW
CAN I
WHEN I
BOUNCE
ALL
THE
TIME.

Mostly he was concerned with his **roots**. He thought about his roots quite a bit. But no matter how hard he thought he couldn't come up with a thing.

— SIGH.

So then he'd concentrate on his values. Because if he could sort out his values it would tell him something about his background and if he Knew something about his background it would then give him some indication of his roots.

s164.

But he couldn't come up with a single value.

All of which was pretty depressing.

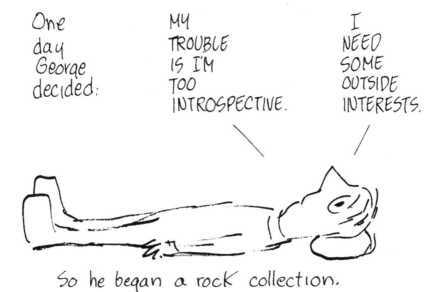

| One day George decided: | MY TROUBLE IS I'M TOO INTROSPECTIVE. | I NEED SOME OUTSIDE INTERESTS. |

So he began a rock collection.

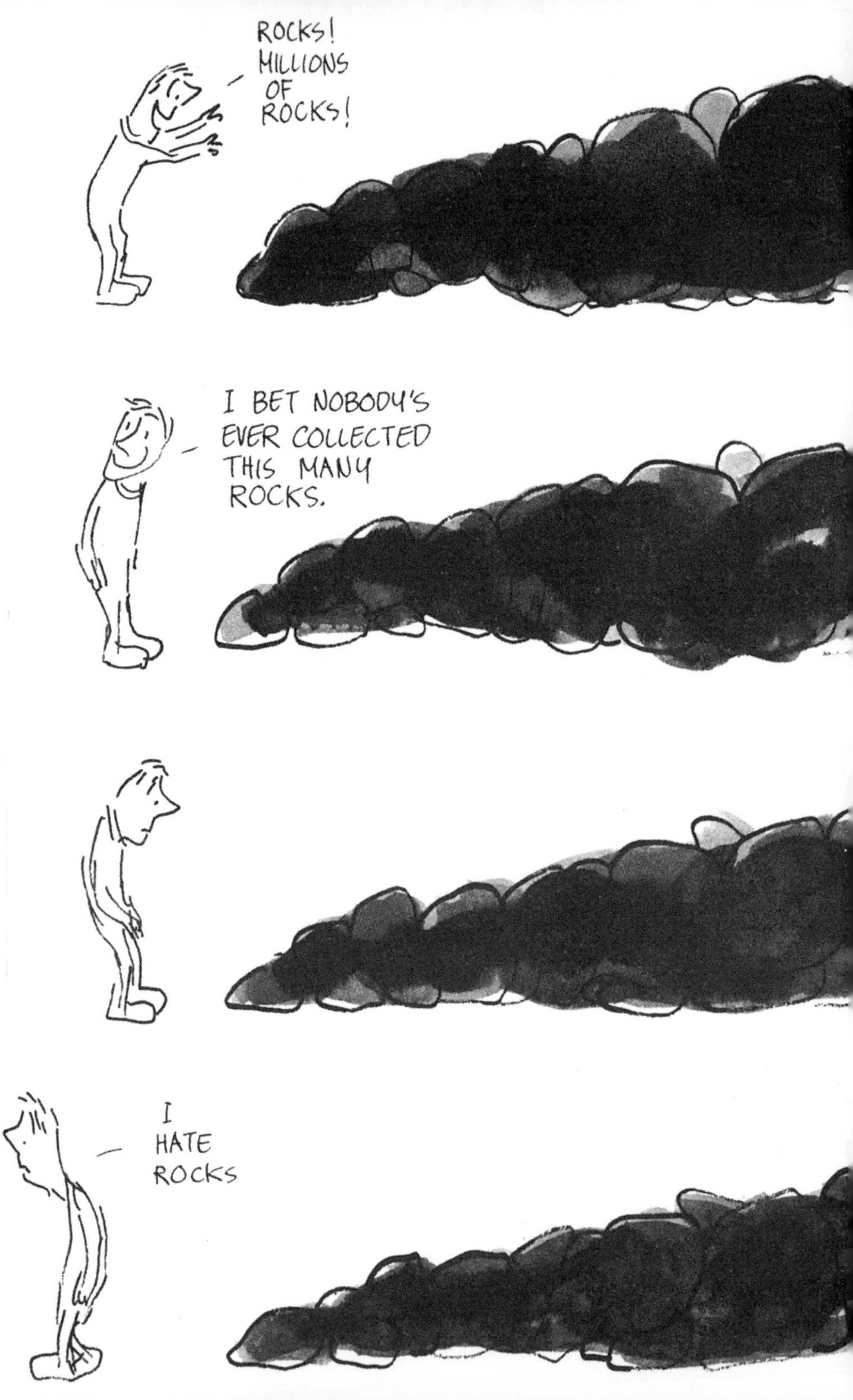
ROCKS! MILLIONS OF ROCKS!
I BET NOBODY'S EVER COLLECTED THIS MANY ROCKS.
I HATE ROCKS

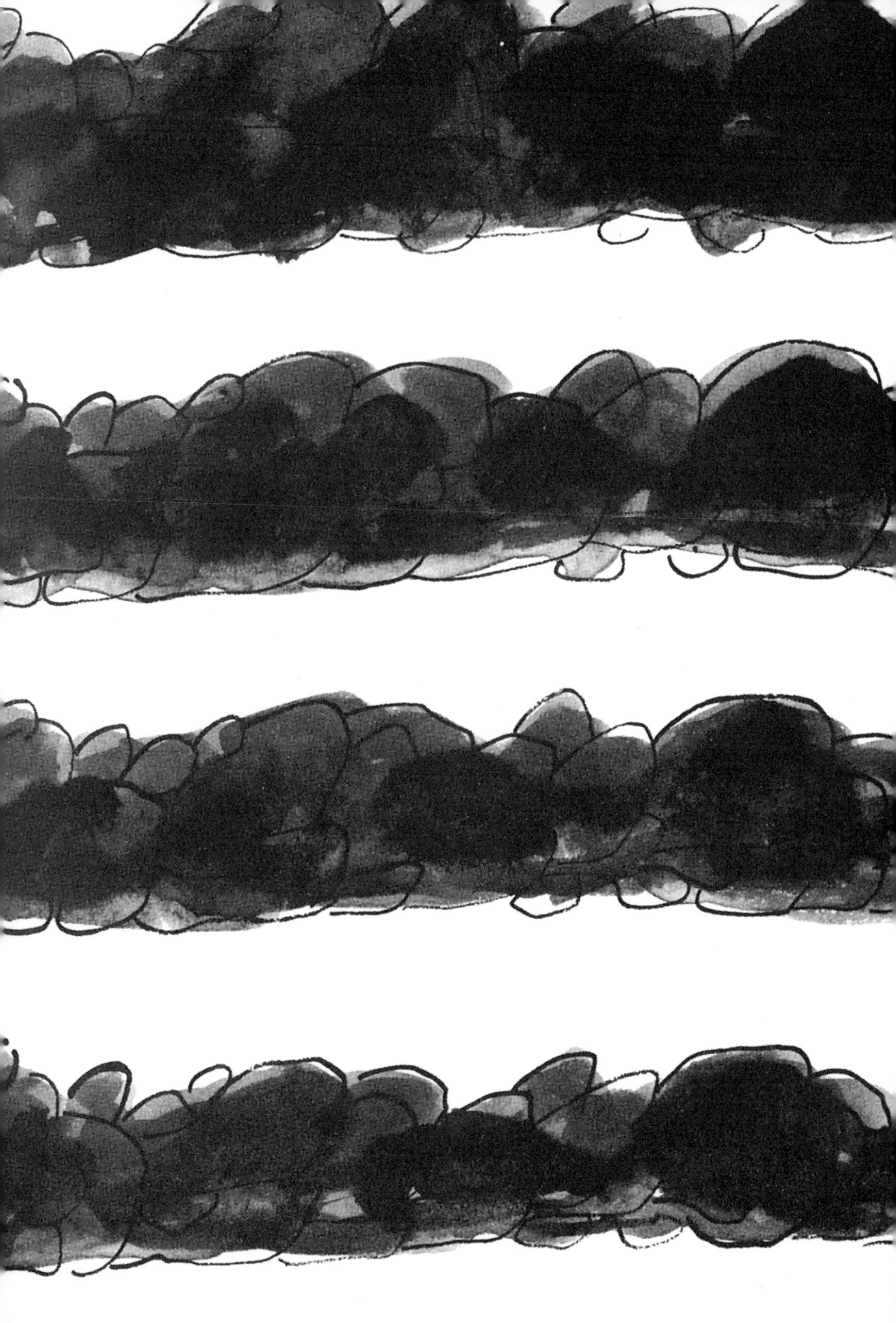

Rocks had no meaning for George. He began to count craters.

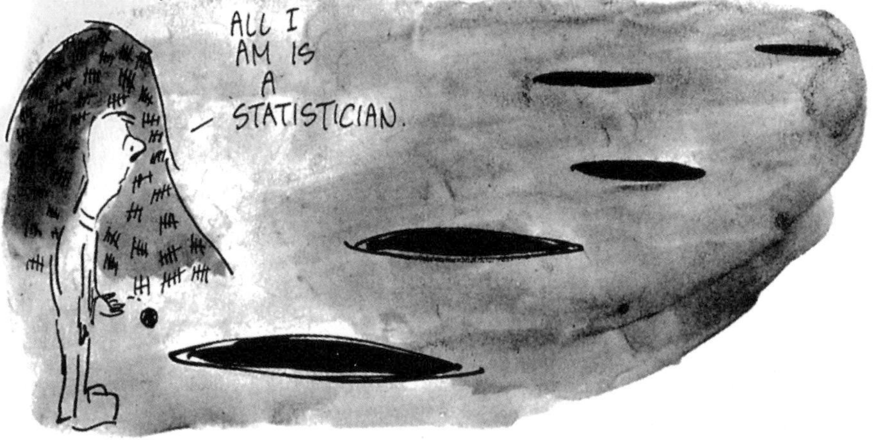
ALL I AM IS A STATISTICIAN.

George felt he was thinking too much. He needed to regain the feeling of his body. So he learned to drop kick his rock collection into his craters.

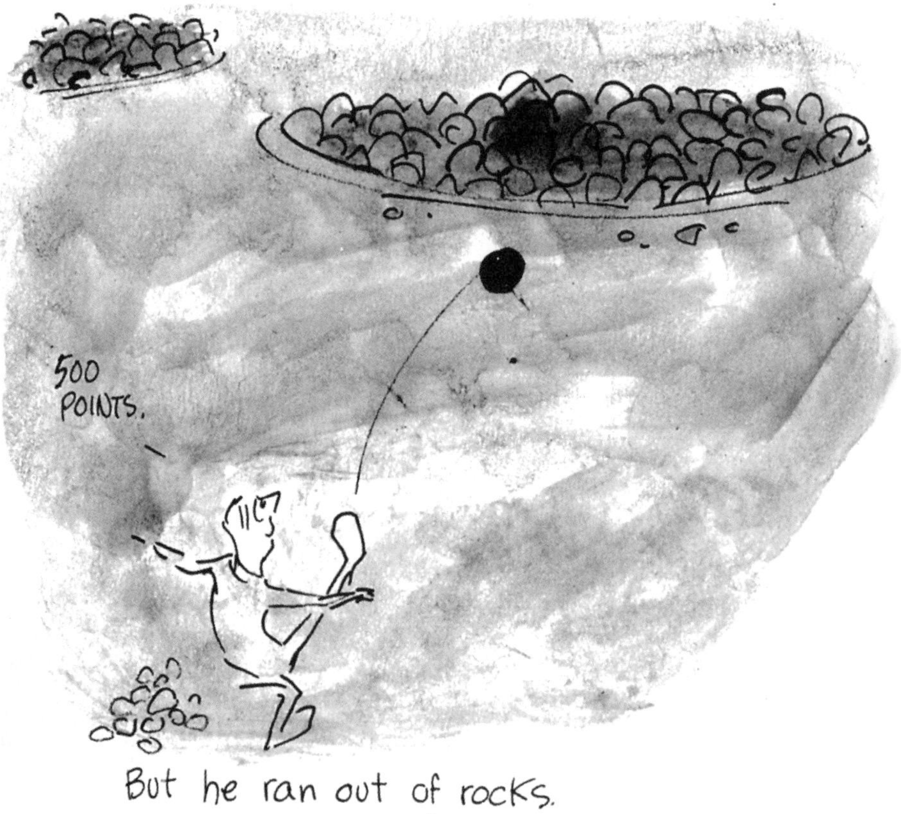
500 POINTS.

But he ran out of rocks.

He was just filling up time and he knew it. What good was it to collect rocks, to count craters, to fill the craters you've counted with the rocks you've collected, to empty the craters and collect the rocks all over again?

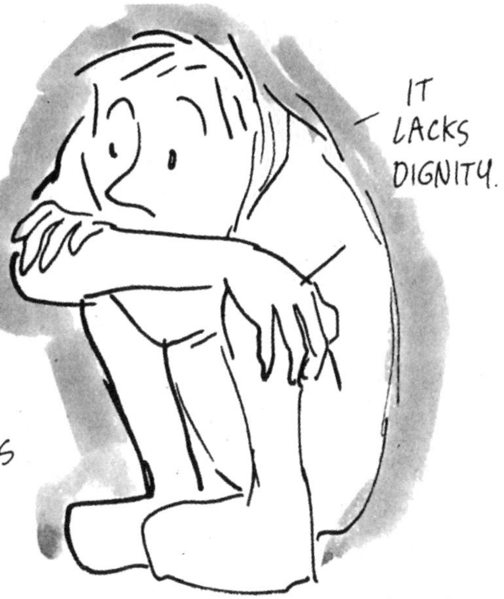
IT LACKS DIGNITY.

Was this a way for a man to spend a life?

George recognized he had no sense of himself. Also that he had no sense of others. How could he have any dignity without a context? He didn't know who he was or what or anything.

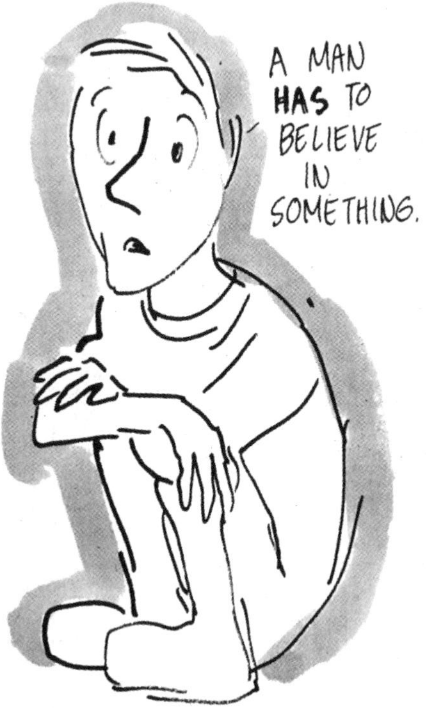
A MAN **HAS** TO BELIEVE IN SOMETHING.

So since **he** was the only thing around, George decided to believe in himself.

HAIL GEORGE.

He made up poems to himself.

GEORGE
George
GEORGE
george
GEORGE
George
GEORGE.

He made up stories to himself.

SO GEORGE CURED THE PLAGUE, ENDED THE FAMINE, TURNED BACK THE FLOOD.

And then he awoke one morning and found that he had forgotten his name.

THAT'S WHAT I GET. SERVES ME RIGHT.

So he stopped believing in himself.

He looked around for something
else to believe in. He tried to
believe in rocks.

HAIL.

But they seemed so ordinary.

He tried to believe in craters.

HAIL.

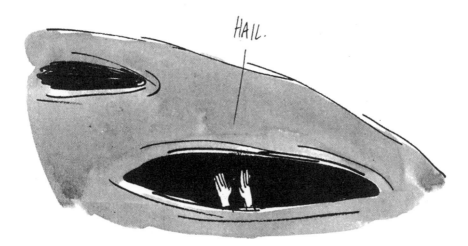

But since he had kicked rocks into them
he hadn't much respect for craters.

He made up other things to believe in. But they were all inadequate. He needed something spectacular. Something way beyond his experience. Then one day he looked up and noticed space.

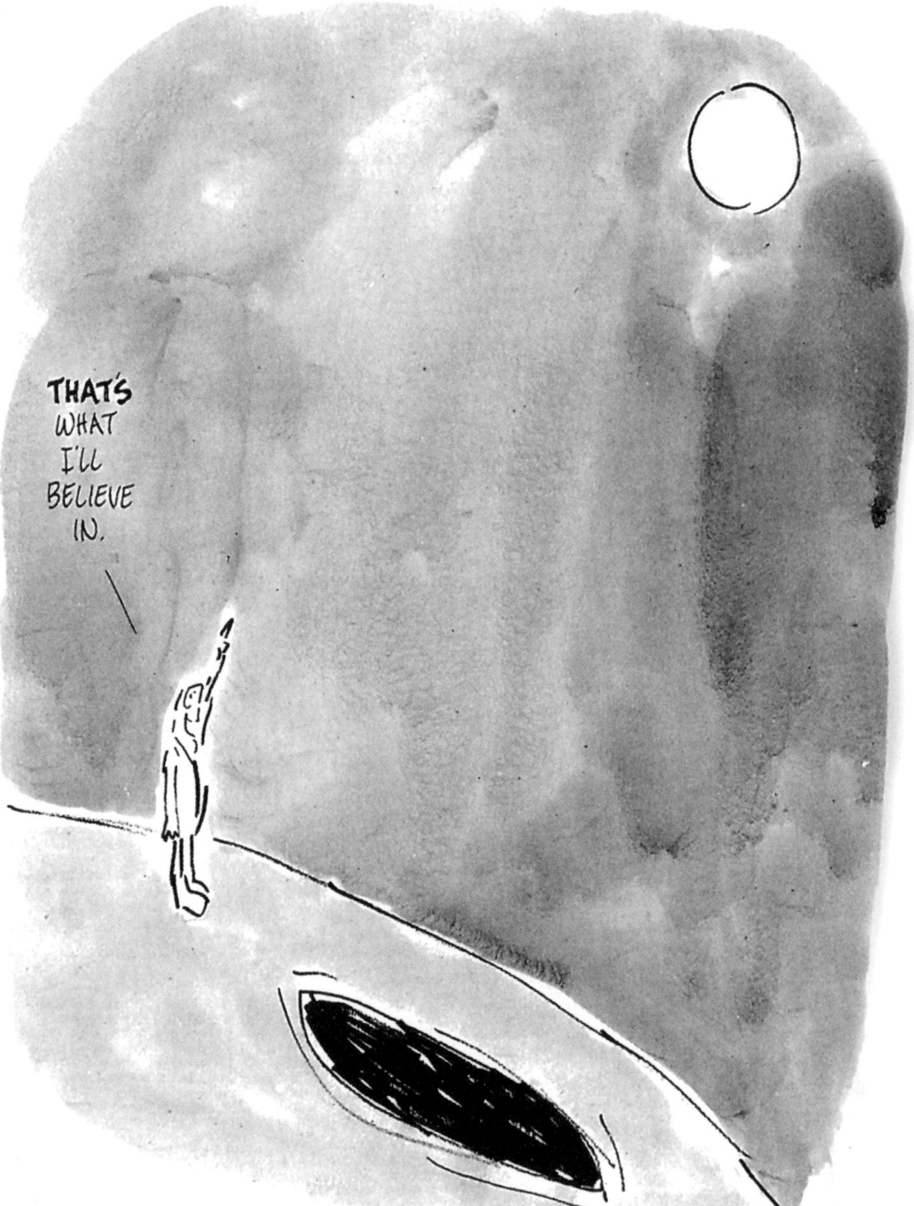
THAT'S WHAT I'LL BELIEVE IN.

There were all sorts of advantages to believing in space.
For one thing it was out there - **way** out there —

AND IT
FILLS UP
EVERYTHING.
THAT'S PRETTY
IMPRESSIVE.

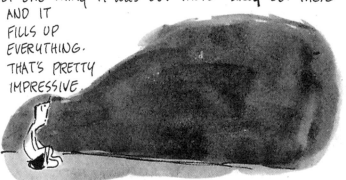

And it was obviously unknown.

IT COULD
NEVER BE
DISILLUSIONING.

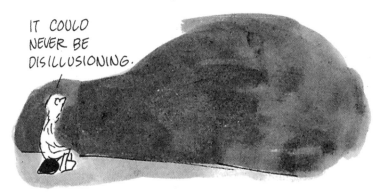

And it was dark with white blotches - very attractive
really - much more imposing than all those rocks
and craters he **used** to worship.

IT'S AMAZING
HOW I'VE
MATURED IN
MY BELIEFS.

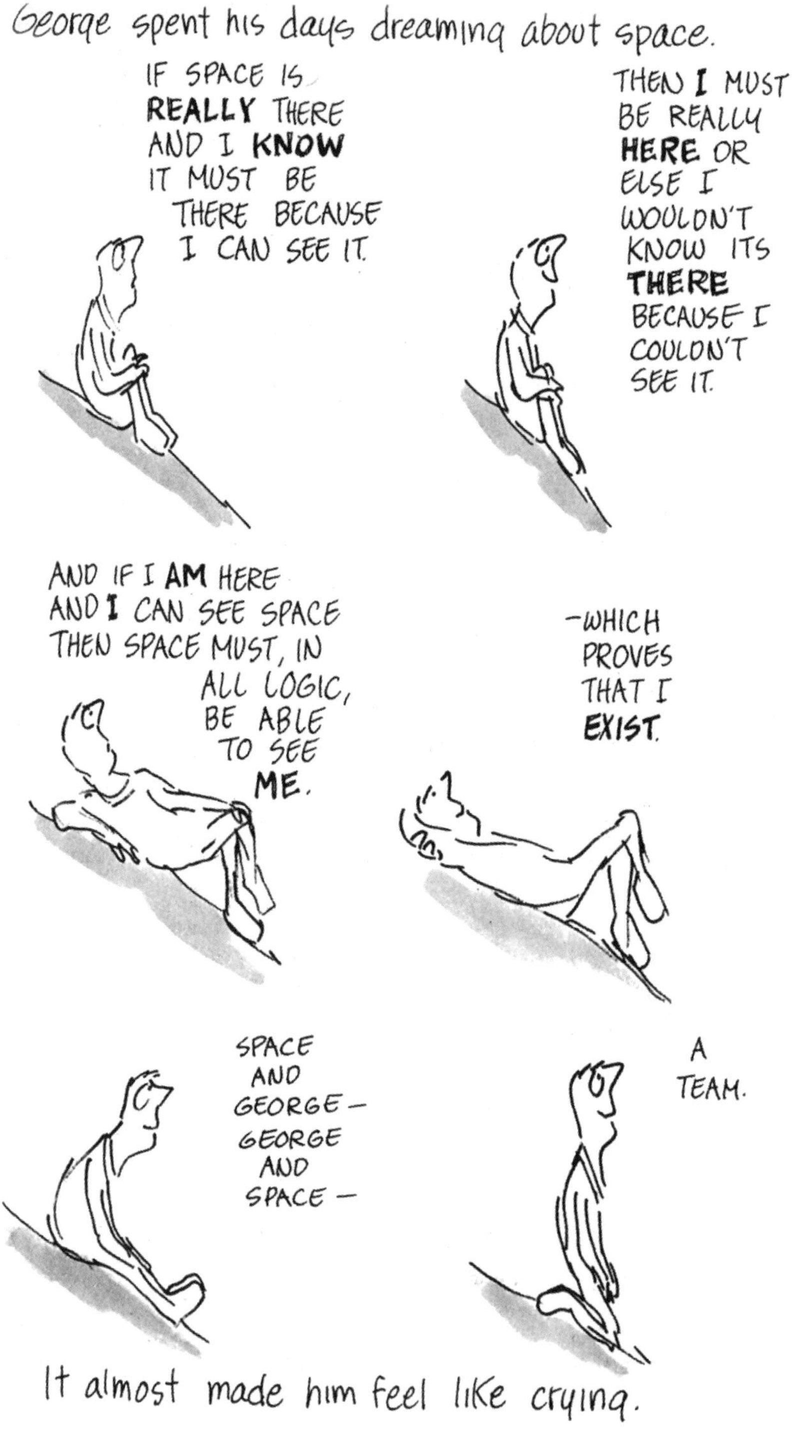
George spent his days dreaming about space.
IF SPACE IS REALLY THERE AND I KNOW IT MUST BE THERE BECAUSE I CAN SEE IT.
THEN I MUST BE REALLY HERE OR ELSE I WOULDN'T KNOW ITS THERE BECAUSE I COULDN'T SEE IT.
AND IF I AM HERE AND I CAN SEE SPACE THEN SPACE MUST, IN ALL LOGIC, BE ABLE TO SEE ME.
-WHICH PROVES THAT I EXIST.
SPACE AND GEORGE— GEORGE AND SPACE—
A TEAM.
It almost made him feel like crying.

Then one day they started shooting rockets off at him.

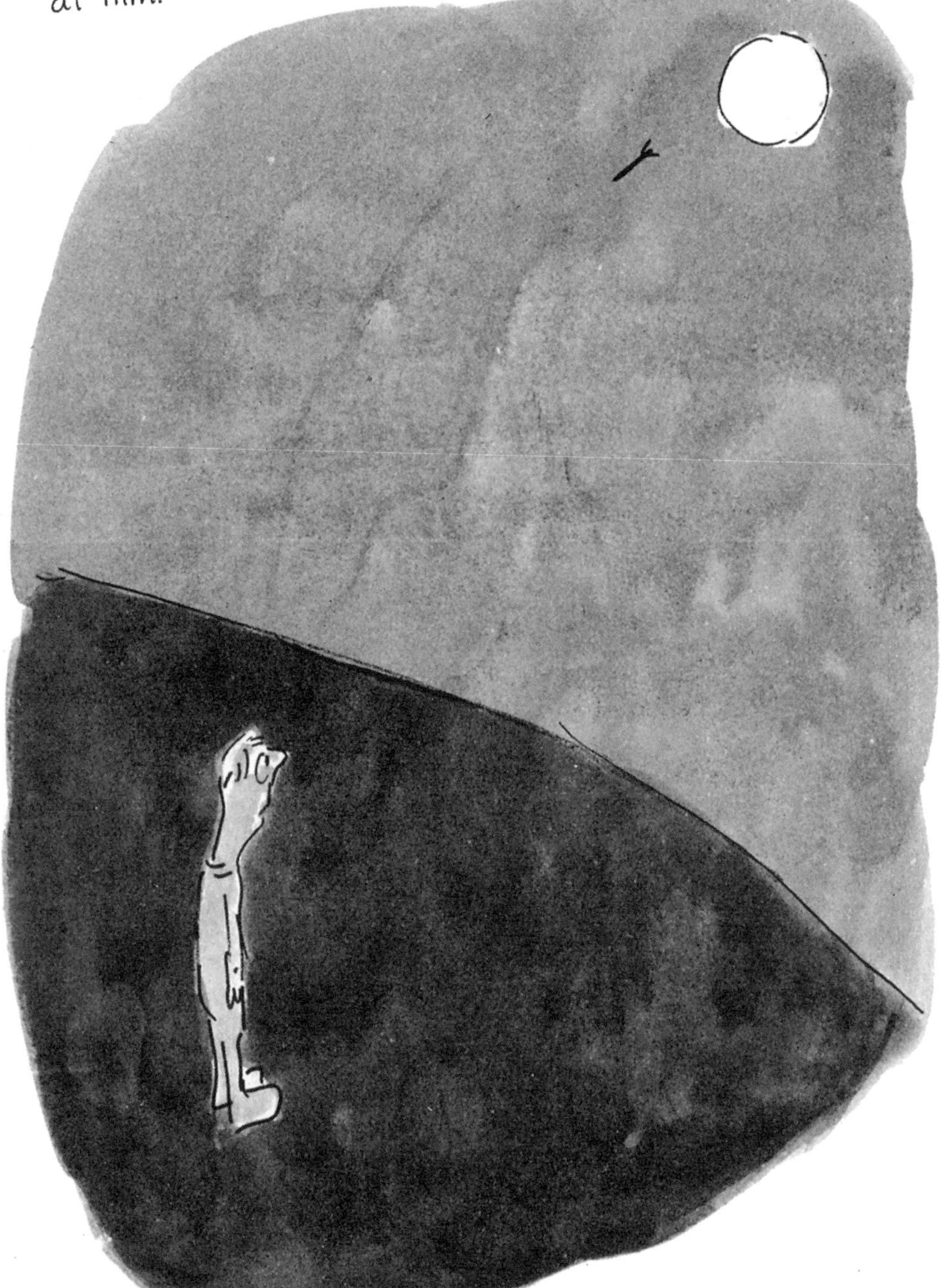

George was overjoyed.

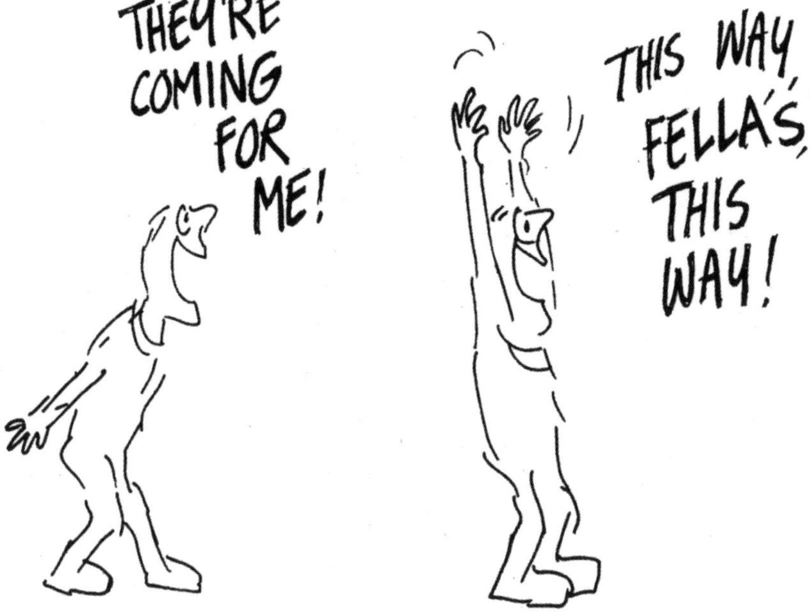
THEY'RE COMING FOR ME!
THIS WAY, FELLA'S, THIS WAY!

George tied a red undershirt to a big rock.

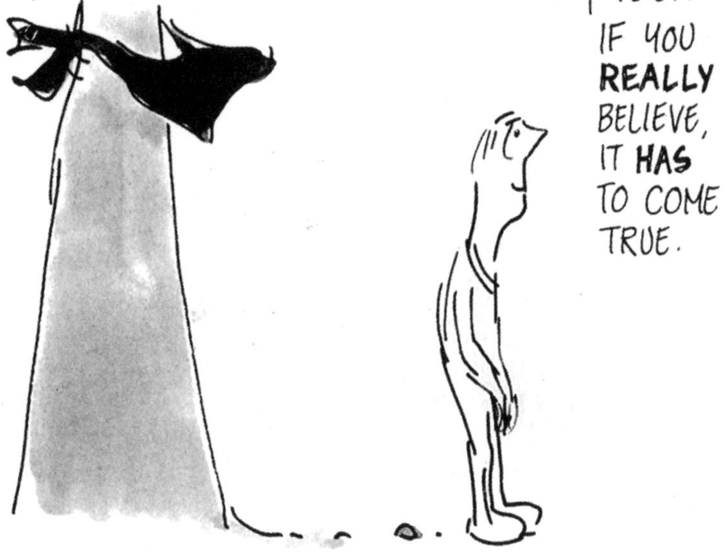
IF YOU **REALLY** BELIEVE, IT **HAS** TO COME TRUE.

But the rocket didn't even come close.

George wasn't too sad. Space was no longer mysterious and intangible. Space had people in it and they were trying to rescue him. He sat all day on the dark side and dreamed about them:

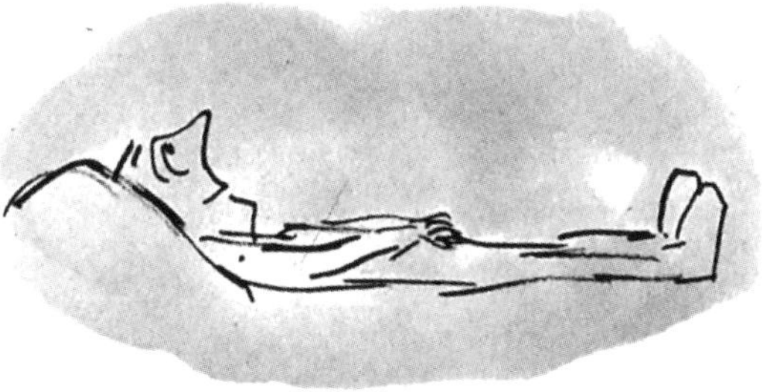
FIRST OF ALL THEY MUST BE VERY KIND TO GO TO ALL THIS TROUBLE. THEY MUST BE VERY HUMAN-ITARIAN AND HAVE LOTS OF FAVORITE CHARITIES.

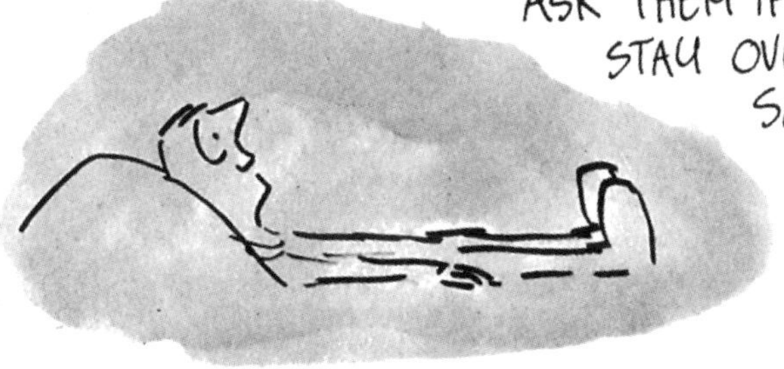
THEY WILL COME HERE AND WE'LL HAVE A BIG PARTY AND I'LL BE VERY POLITE AND ASK THEM IF THEY'D LIKE TO STAY OVER BUT THEY'LL SAY - "WELL, WE **DO** HAVE TO GET BACK."

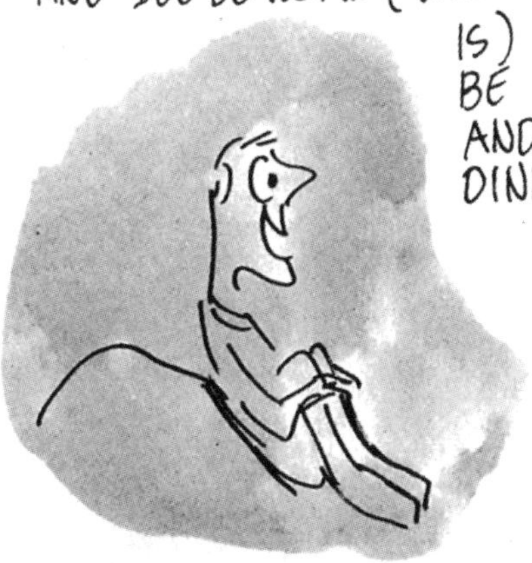
AND THEN WE'LL TAKE OFF AND I'LL BE **HOME** (WHEREVER THAT IS) AND THERE'LL BE BIG PARADES AND TESTIMONIAL DINNERS.

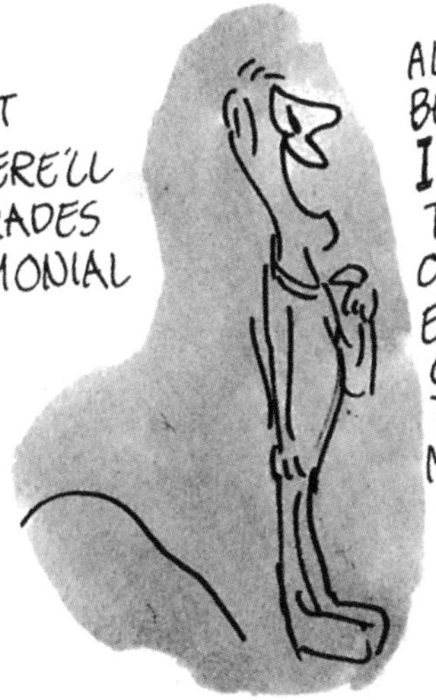
ALL BECAUSE **I'M** THE ONLY EXPERT ON THE MOON!

But then George realized he **wasn't** an expert on the
moon. In fact he really didn't know much about it at all.

He didn't know whether those holes actually **were**
craters or not. Maybe they were coal mines.

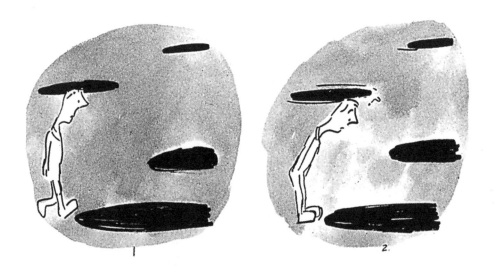

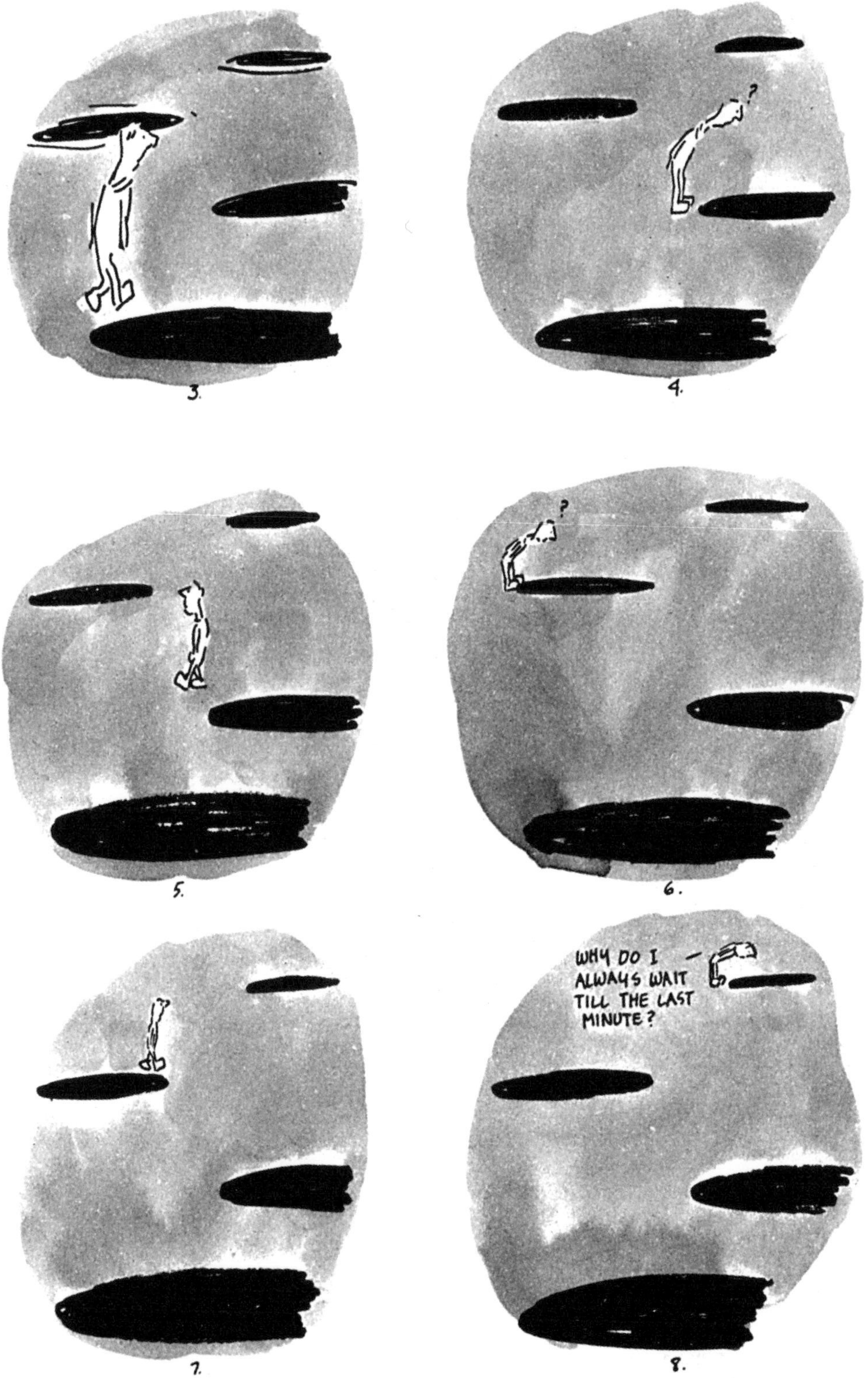
3.
4.
5.
6.
7.
WHY DO I ALWAYS WAIT TILL THE LAST MINUTE?
8.

He didn't know why it was that he could bounce or how come he could breathe without a helmet or why he was never hungry though there wasn't any food to eat.

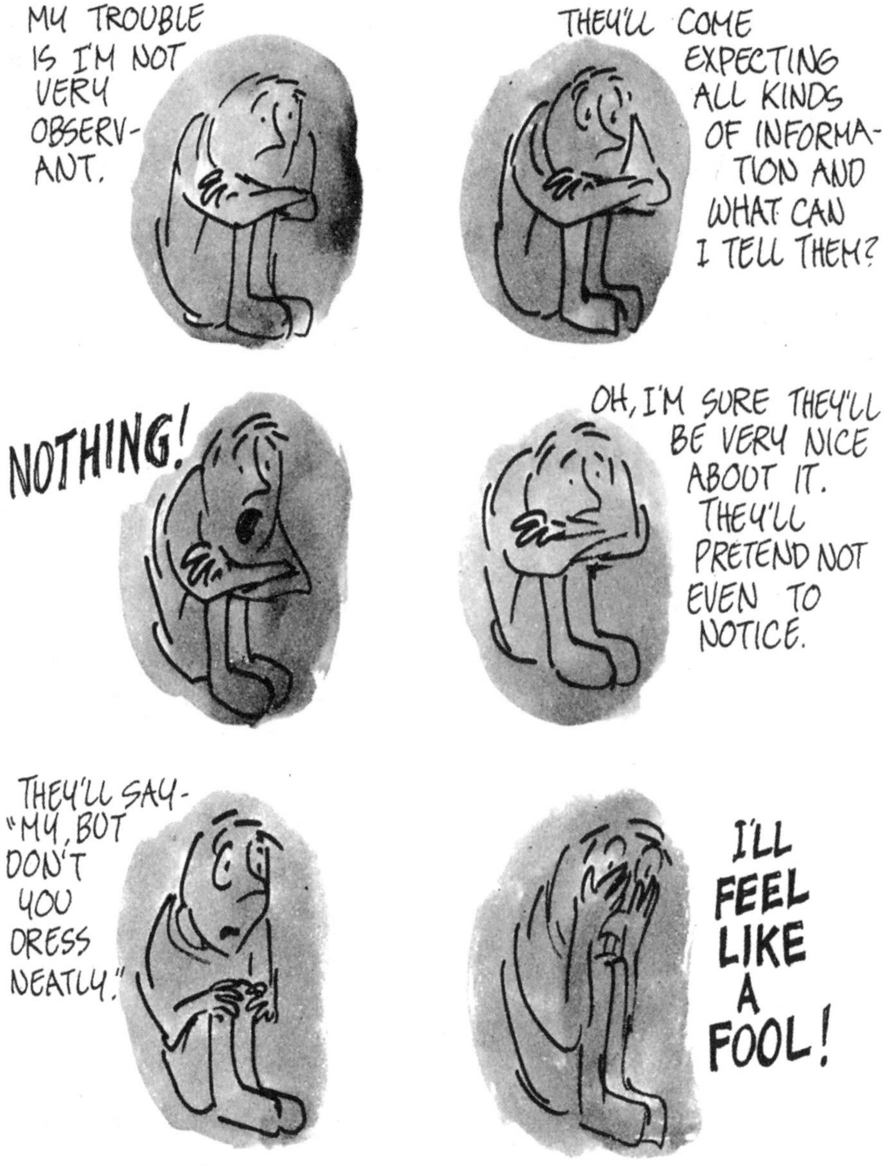
MY TROUBLE IS I'M NOT VERY OBSERV-ANT.
THEY'LL COME EXPECTING ALL KINDS OF INFORMA-TION AND WHAT CAN I TELL THEM?
NOTHING!
OH, I'M SURE THEY'LL BE VERY NICE ABOUT IT. THEY'LL PRETEND NOT EVEN TO NOTICE.
THEY'LL SAY- "MY, BUT DON'T YOU DRESS NEATLY."
I'LL FEEL LIKE A FOOL!

And then one day they shot off another rocket.

George hung up his undershirt again but on a less conspicuous rock. He began to feel anxious about the whole thing.

WHAT DO THEY WANT FROM ME? I'M NOT ANALYTICAL. THEY'LL JUST HAVE TO UNDERSTAND.

A FAT LOT **THEY'LL** CARE! THEY'LL BE **SCIENTISTS!** COLD- DISPASSIONATE— NO TIME FOR **MY** PROBLEMS.

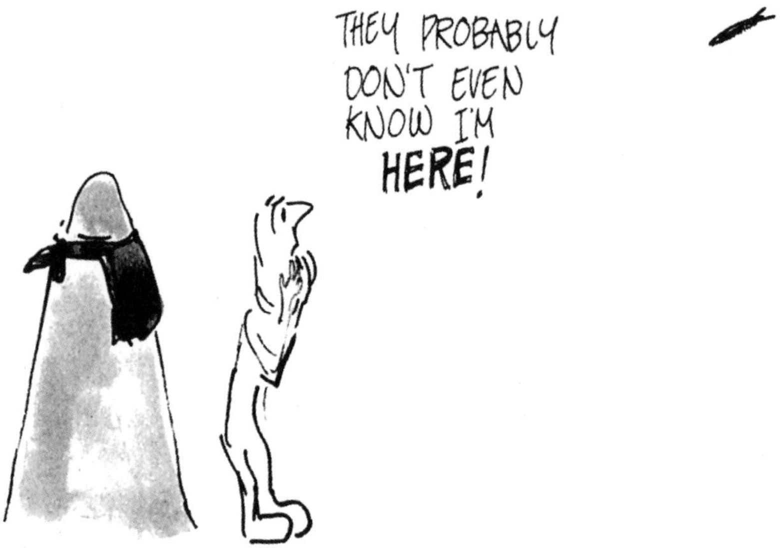
THEY PROBABLY DON'T EVEN KNOW I'M **HERE**!

But once more the rocket did not come close.

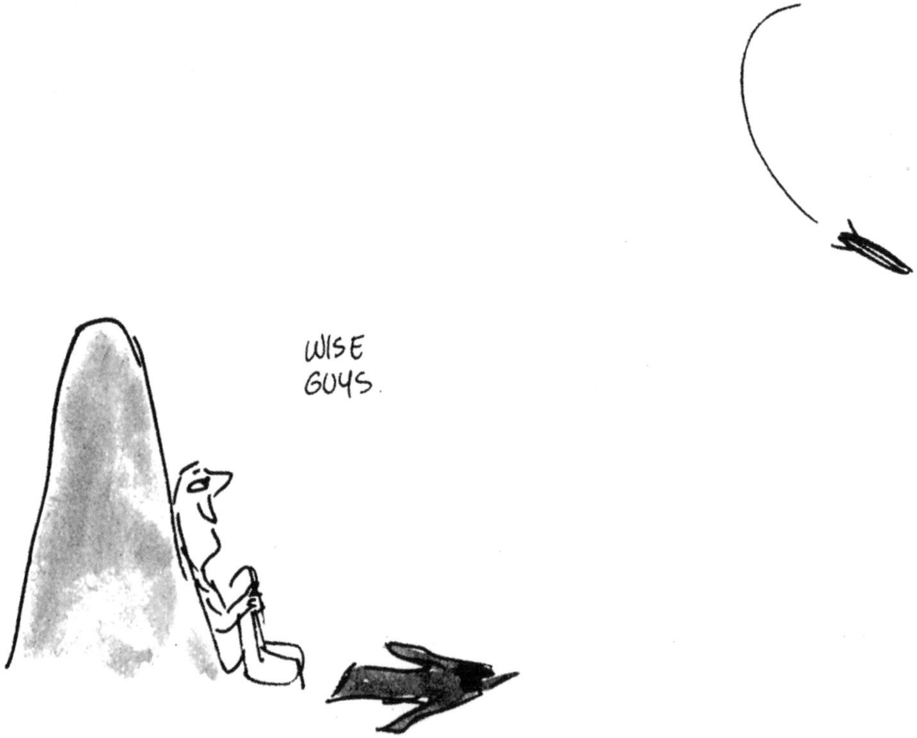
WISE GUYS.

But George knew that ultimately they **would** come.
He spent all his days sitting on the dark side
and dreaming about what it would be like.

THEY'LL COME OUT OF
THOSE DAMN ROCKETS
AND I BET FIRST
THING THEY'LL DO IS
STICK UP A **FLAG**

THEIR
FLAG
ON MY
MOON!

THEN THEY'LL
GIVE ME THEIR
BAGS TO CARRY.

THEY'LL MAKE FUN OF ME-
"YOU MEAN **YOU** DIDN'T
KNOW ABOUT **GRAVITY**?
YOU HEAR THAT GANG?
BEEN ON THE MOON
ALL THIS
TIME AND
HE DIDN'T
KNOW
ABOUT
GRAVITY!"

AND THEY'LL
TELL LOTS
OF INSIDE
JOKES.

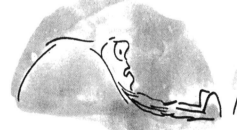

"WELL WE'D **LOVE** TO TAKE
YOU BACK " THEY'LL SAY-
"BUT YOU SEE HOW
CROWDED WE ARE WITH
ALL THESE ROCK
SAMPLES. WOULD YOU
MIND GIVING US A
SHOVE ? "

George thought about the way it used to be. The fun he had drop kicking rocks into craters. What a ball it was to sit around the moon and think about his roots.

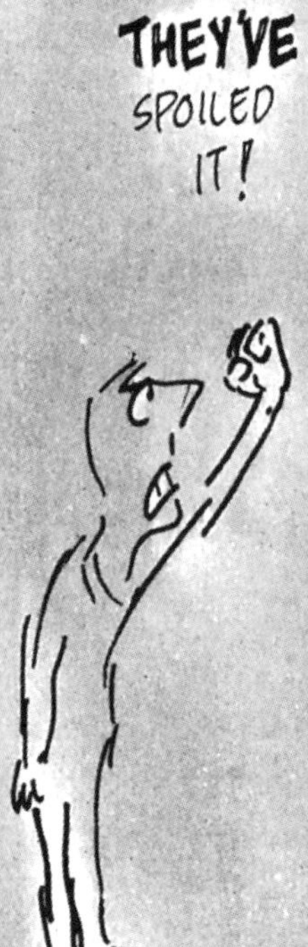
THEY'VE SPOILED IT!

And then one day they shot off another rocket.

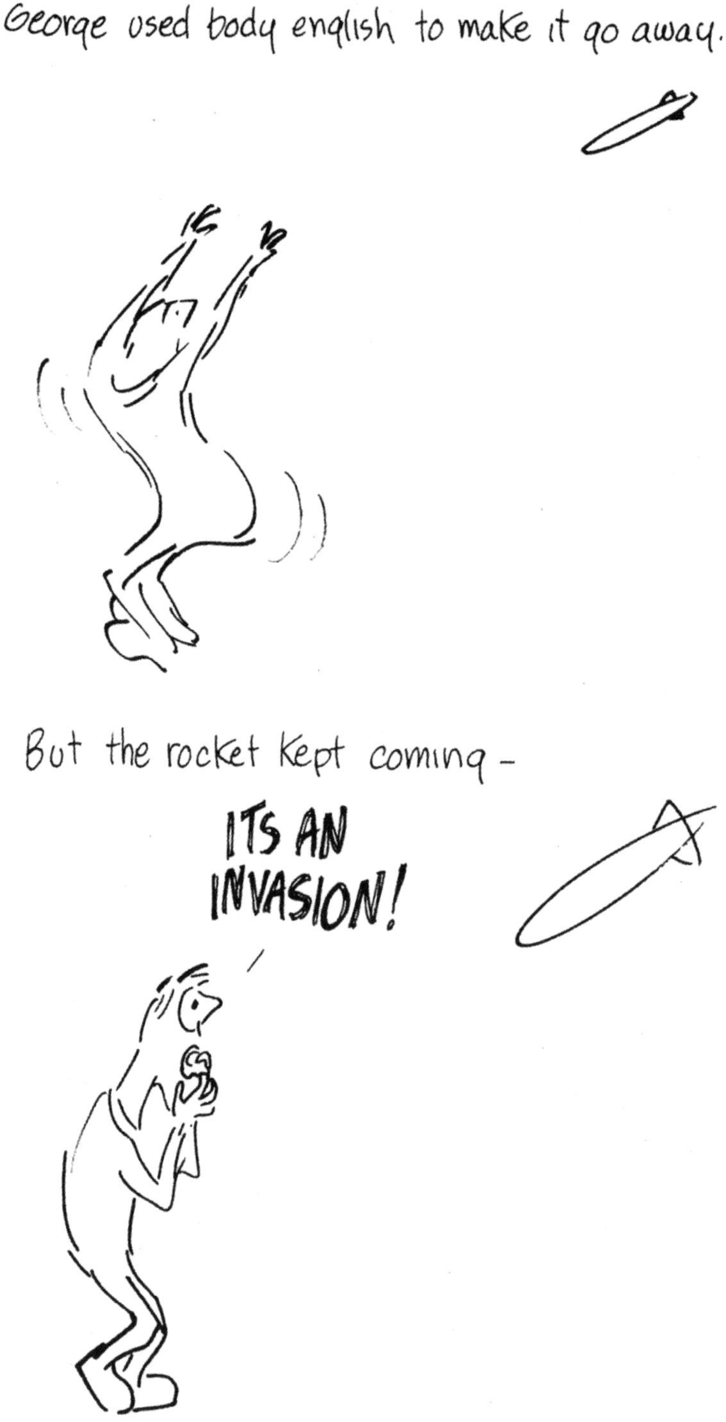
George used body english to make it go away.
But the rocket kept coming -
ITS AN INVASION!

Then, suddenly the fear and indecision which had held him for weeks was no more. George knew what he had to do.

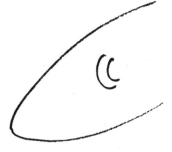

THIS
IS
WAR!

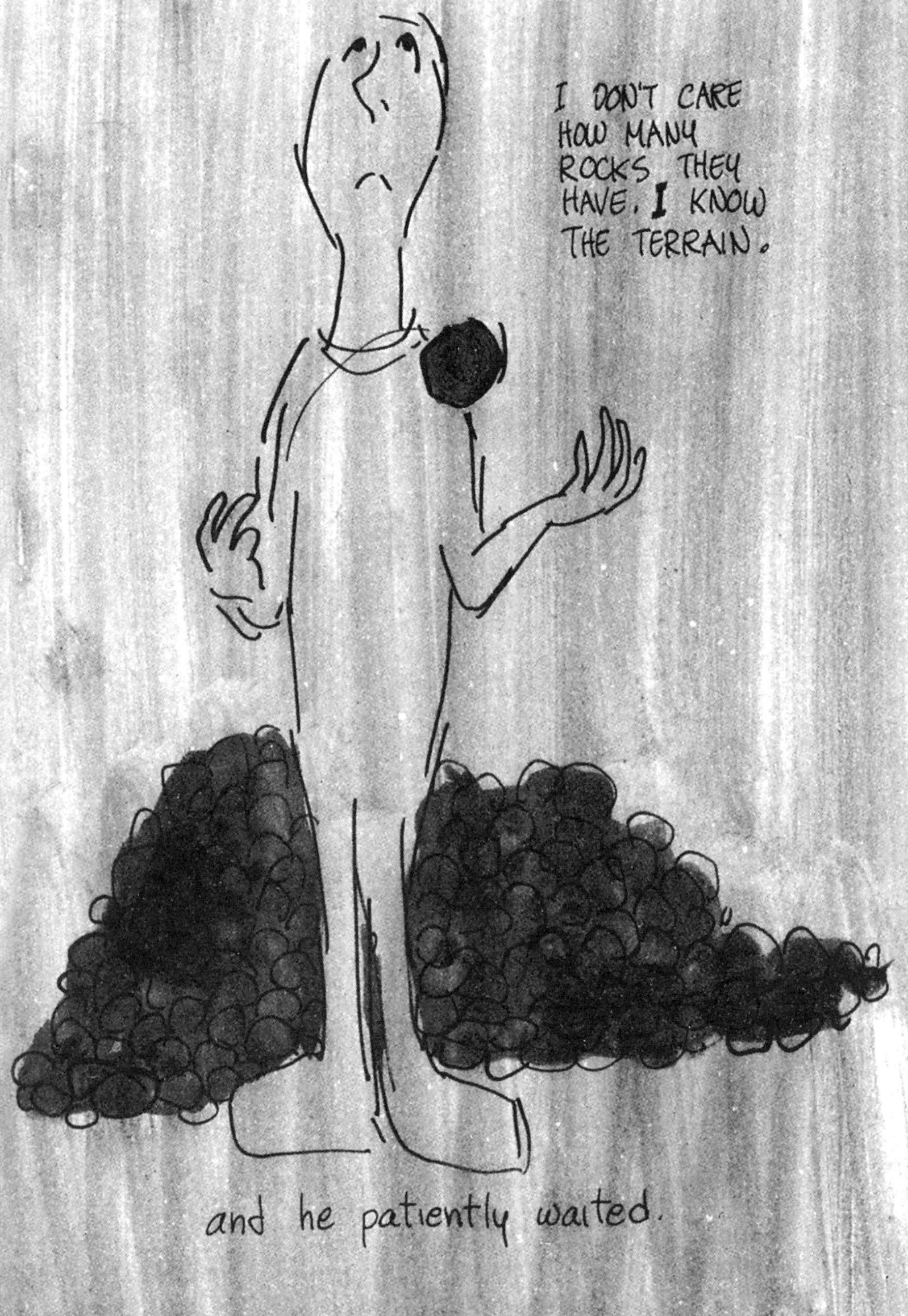
I DON'T CARE HOW MANY ROCKS THEY HAVE. I KNOW THE TERRAIN.
and he patiently waited.

Crawling Arnold

The curtain rises on a projection: an enormous color slide of a smiling baby. The stage is dark and voices come out of the darkness. Everybody "oohs" and "ahhhs" at the projection.

BARRY That's little Will at six months.

GRACE Eight months, dear. Even little Will wasn't that big at six months.

BARRY Seven months then. What a big bad bandit of a boy, eh, Miss Sympathy?

MISS SYMPATHY An alert child.

BARRY (*Clicks slide changer*) Next slide please. (*The projection changes*) There he is at only one year! Did you ever see such a rough and tough customer, Miss Sympathy?

GRACE Fourteen months, dear.

BARRY Thirteen months.

MISS SYMPATHY He does seem like an alert child.

BARRY Alert? You should see him crawl around down in the shelter. Arnold just goes down when the siren sounds and sits there. But little Will! He has to touch everything. Won't keep out of anything – the oxygen tank, the gas masks, the plastic bombs

MISS SYMPATHY The shelter? (*The lights come up slowly to reveal the expensively bedecked patio of the* ENTERPRISE *home.* BARRY *and* GRACE ENTERPRISE, *a vigorous, athletic couple in their seventies are sitting with* MISS SYMPATHY, *a young and pretty social worker, in deck chairs partly facing the slide screen. The projector is behind them being operated by* MILLIE, *the Negro maid. She, expressionlessly, begins to wheel it off*)

BARRY Our *fallout* shelter! Wait till you see it! (*To* MILLIE) You can serve our helmets now, Millie.

(MILLIE *coolly exits.* BARRY *and* GRACE *look hostilely after her.*)

GRACE It's the only shelter in the country that has a television set and a whatayoucall them dear?

BARRY Stereo rig.

GRACE Stereo rig.

(*She begins to fuss with the baby, making small gurgling noises at it*)

MISS SYMPATHY A television set? But what good would a –

BARRY It's not a real television set. It's the frame of one and then I have a sixteen millimeter movie projector and a library of films – *Tim McCoy, Our Gang* – a variety of fare. The idea, you understand, is that under enemy attack the family can survive down there for *weeks*, while being able to simulate normal conditions of living. For example, I've had cards made up with the names of our favorite shows and at the time they would ordinarily go on, we run a picture – a slide picture on the screen showing the title of the show –

GRACE *Lassie – Ben Casey –*

BARRY And during the half-hours those shows normally run, we sit and reminisce about our favorite episodes.

MISS SYMPATHY You've *done* this?

BARRY Several times. Before Little Will was born, Mrs. Enterprise and I – *and Arnold* – used to spend many happy weeks – many happy weeks in our shelter.

GRACE One gets to *know* Ben Casey so much more deeply after one has talked about him in a fallout shelter for two weeks. (MILLIE *enters with four air-raid helmets on a serving tray. There is evident tension between herself and the* ENTERPRISES. BARRY *and* GRACE *each sullenly take a helmet*) You may serve cocktails now, Millie. (GRACE *places a helmet in baby carriage.* MISS SYMPATHY *quietly demurs*)

BARRY You're making a mistake, Miss Sympathy. Today's drill begins pretty soon. (MILLIE *exits, with* MISS SYMPATHY *looking after her, curiously*) You should see our library down there! Four years' worth of back copies of the *Readers Digest*. I didn't know how long we'd be down there so I wanted to get articles of *lasting* interest. (*He takes the baby carriage from* GRACE *and begins to fuss with the baby, making small gurgling noises*)

GRACE (*Proudly*) It's the only shelter in the country to be written up in *Good Housekeeping*.

MISS SYMPATHY Little Will is how old?

GRACE (*Proudly*) He'll be –

BARRY (*Jealously*) He'll be two in September. (*He buries his face in the blankets of the carriage, muffling the sound of his voice*) Isn't this the biggest, baddest, toughest little fellow who ever lived? I'll tell the world this is the biggest, baddest, toughest little fellow who ever lived!

MISS SYMPATHY (*Peering into the carriage*) My, he's a *large* baby.

BARRY Arnold was half his size at that age. Arnold couldn't crawl until he was almost *two*. Little Will's been crawling for four months now. *Four* months.

MISS SYMPATHY And Arnold?

BARRY (*Nervously*) Wasn't Millie supposed to bring us some drinks?

GRACE Well, that's why we asked you to come, Miss Sympathy.

BARRY (*Embarrassed*) Yes. Arnold is crawling again too. For four months.

GRACE (*Sadly*) Regressed.

MISS SYMPATHY (*Taking out a pad and making notes*) That sometimes happens when the first child feels over-competitive with the second child. *Sibling rivalry.*

GRACE Crawl. As soon as he enters the house he falls on all fours and crawls, crawls, crawls. I say to him, "Arnold, you know you can walk beautifully. At business you walk beautifully – "

MISS SYMPATHY At business?

BARRY (*Embarrassed*) Arnold is thirty-five.

(*He fusses with the carriage*)

MISS SYMPATHY (*Making a long note*) *Advanced* sibling rivalry.

GRACE (*Distressed*) That's what we wanted to talk to you about. I know there's nothing seriously wrong with Arnold. He's always been a good boy. Done everything we told him. Never talked back. Always well-mannered. Never been a show-off.

MISS SYMPATHY (*Taking notes*) He's never had any previously crawling history?

GRACE I'm afraid he took the news of Little Will's birth rather hard. I imagine when one has been raised as an only child and has lived happily all one's years in one's parents' home, it's hard to welcome a little stranger.

BARRY (*Buries his head in the blankets, muffling his voice*) Who's Daddy's brave big bandit of a man? Little Will's Daddy's brave big bandit of a man.

GRACE Please, dear. Don't talk with your mouth full. (MILLIE *enters with three drinks on a platter. A coolness immediately settles in the room.* BARRY *and* GRACE *lapse into a sullen silence.* GRACE *coldly receives her drink*) Thank you, Millie.

(BARRY *grumbles something under his breath as he receives his.* MISS SYMPATHY *is obviously perturbed*)

MISS SYMPATHY (*Whispers to* MILLIE *as she is served her drink*) I strongly sympathize with the aspirations of your people. (MILLIE *exits*)

BARRY (*Rocking the carriage*) A nationwide alert! All the American people mobilized as one, sitting it out in shelters all over the country. That's what I'd like Little Will to grow up to see. I guess it's just an old man's dream.

GRACE Here's Arnold! Please, Miss Sympathy, don't tell him you're here because we asked –

ARNOLD (*Enters crawling. He is an attractive young man in his thirties. He wears a hat and a business suit and carries an attaché case*) Father – Mother – (*He notices* MISS SYMPATHY, *sizes her up for a long moment then coolly turns to his mother*) Company?

GRACE Arnold, dear, this is Miss Sympathy. Miss Sympathy, this is our son, Arnold Enterprise.

MISS SYMPATHY I'm pleased to meet you.

ARNOLD (*Turning away*) That's O.K. (*To his mother*) Dinner ready?

BARRY You're being damned rude, Arnold!

ARNOLD I apologize. I have things on my mind. Are you having drinks?

GRACE Oh, I'm sorry dear. With you on the floor that way I forget that you drink.

ARNOLD Occasionally to excess. (*Crawls around*) Did anyone see my coloring book?

GRACE Millie!

(ARNOLD *crawls around. There is an awkward pause.* MILLIE, *finally, enters with a drink.* MISS SYMPATHY *leans forward examining everyone's reaction*)

ARNOLD (*Accepting the drink*) It's got an olive in it!

GRACE Please, dear.

ARNOLD (*To* MILLIE) You know I drink martinis with a lemon peel!

GRACE (*Placating*) Millie – would you mind –

(MILLIE *coolly takes back the glass and starts off*)

MISS SYMPATHY (*Whispers to* MILLIE *as she exits*) I have great regard for the aspirations of your people!

GRACE (*To* ARNOLD) Did you have to –

ARNOLD (*To himself*) When I began drinking martinis ten years ago I ordered them with an olive. I didn't know any better, I guess. They always came back with a lemon peel. (*To* MISS SYMPATHY) There was something so garbagey about a lemon peel lying at the bottom of my martini.

BARRY (*Angry*) Arnold! I'm sorry, Miss Sympathy.

MISS SYMPATHY (*Waving* BARRY *off*) No. No. I understand. (*To* ARNOLD) Please go on.

ARNOLD (*Shrugs*) There's nothing to go on. I got used to it. I got to like it. I got to want lemon peels in my martinis. It still looked garbagey, but I found that *exciting!* I've always been surrounded by lots of money, cut off from life. That lemon peel floating there in its oil slick that way was to me my only contact with The People. It reminded me of East *River* movies – the Dead End Kids. Remember the Dead End Kids?

MISS SYMPATHY No, I'm afraid not –

ARNOLD (*Suspiciously*) What do you do?

(BARRY *and* GRACE *look distressed.* MISS SYMPATHY *warns them off with her eyes*)

MISS SYMPATHY I'm a social worker.

ARNOLD (*Astonished*) And you don't remember the Dead End Kids?

MISS SYMPATHY A *psychiatric* social worker.

ARNOLD Oh, *you'd* remember Ingrid Bergman movies. Where's my coloring book, Mother?

GRACE Where did you leave it yesterday, dear?

ARNOLD (*Restlessly*) I've got to find my coloring book. I feel in the mood for coloring.

GRACE I'll help you look, Arnold, if you'll just tell me where you think you left it.

(ARNOLD, *perturbed, crawls around the room looking for his coloring book.* GRACE *follows him anxiously.* BARRY, *flushed with embarrassment, rocks the baby carriage almost violently)*

BARRY That's a good boy, Little Will, that's a nice, big good boy Little Will.

ARNOLD I found it!

(He crawls off in a corner with the coloring book. GRACE *follows him. As he begins coloring, she looks over his shoulder)*

BARRY *(Miserably, to* MISS SYMPATHY*)* I've tried to know that boy.

MISS SYMPATHY Communications between the generations is never easy, Mr. Enterprise.

BARRY We wrote away to Dear Abby about him. She was snotty.

MISS SYMPATHY I'm not sure you acted wisely. She's not licensed, you know.

BARRY I tried in every way to get close to him, like a father should.

MISS SYMPATHY Perhaps if you had been a bit more patient –

BARRY I've tried, believe me, I've tried. I introduced him into my way of life – my friends – I even got him accepted into my athletic club, and they don't usually take Jews.

MISS SYMPATHY Arnold's Jewish?

BARRY *That* week. It's not worth discussing. The next week he converted to Buddhism. They don't take Buddhists at my club either. But I got him in. It didn't do any good. All he ever did was go down to the gym and ride one of those vibrating horses for hours. He'd just sit there and ride till closing time. And he'd have a far-away look in his eyes. It became the scandal of the club.

GRACE *(To* ARNOLD*)* The sky is blue, dear. Not red; *blue.*

ARNOLD Picasso colors it red.

GRACE Picasso is an artist, dear. Artists can color the sky red because they *know* it's blue. Those of us who aren't artists must color things the way they really are or people might think we're stupid.

BARRY *(Flushed, strides over to* ARNOLD*)* For Christ's sake, stop embarrassing us in front of the woman! Color the goddamn sky blue!

(He glares over ARNOLD's *shoulder.* GRACE *flutters nervously over to* MISS SYMPATHY*)*

GRACE Another drink perhaps, Miss Sympathy?

MISS SYMPATHY I'm fine, thank you. You mustn't allow yourself to get too depressed, Mrs. Enterprise.

GRACE *(Hopefully)* I manage to keep myself busy. Organizational work. I'm the block captain of the "Let's Be a Friend to Our Children Society." It's made up of mothers who've had somber histories with their children and are trying to profit others with their experience.

MISS SYMPATHY That sounds very ambitious.

GRACE And I'm chairman of the gratification committee of the Husband's Fulfillment League. We prepare and distribute many useful pamphlets based on lessons learned from many somber experiences with fulfillment. And, of course, there's still tennis.

MISS SYMPATHY It all sounds very ambitious.

GRACE But primarily my life has been my husband's. When he's happy I try to be happy. When he's unhappy I try to be unhappy. When he wants me I try to want him. The key to a successful marriage is giving. *I've* given. Everything.

(MILLIE *enters and serves* ARNOLD *his drink*)

ARNOLD That's it. A lemon peel! (*He drops coloring book and examines the martini*) I can't tolerate a martini without a lemon peel. (*To* MILLIE) Have you been back to the U.N., Millie?

MILLIE (*Coolly*) Not since last time.

ARNOLD (*To* MISS SYMPATHY) Millie was on television at the U.N. We all watched her.

MISS SYMPATHY (*Interested*) Oh, what were you doing there?

(GRACE *and* BARRY *writhe uncomfortably*)

MILLIE Rioting.

(*She exits*)

BARRY (*Furious*) I swear we've got to replace that girl.

GRACE It doesn't do any good. Any of the girls you get these days, they're all the same. One time or another they've *all* rioted at the U.N.

MISS SYMPATHY I, naturally, don't agree with her means but if we examine her motivation we should be able to understand why she may have felt that such a form of protest was in order. A misguided protest, I admit, but –

BARRY She wants her own shelter!

MISS SYMPATHY What?

BARRY When I started work on the shelter I was going to build two of them. One for us and one for Millie and any friends she'd want to invite. Same dimensions, same material, exactly like ours in every way.

GRACE Millie resented the idea.

BARRY That girl has been with us ten years, hardly a peep out of her in all that time. Before her, the girl we used to take in was Millie's mother. When Millie's mother was ill, her *grandmother* would come in to clean.

GRACE Millie's grandmother was a *good* girl.

BARRY We never had any trouble before. But when I tell Millie I'm building her a shelter, same dimensions, same material, exactly like ours in every way – she nearly quits!

MISS SYMPATHY I sympathize with her aspirations. She wanted to share *your* shelter of course.

BARRY (*Outraged*) Yes!

MISS SYMPATHY You see, while on the surface it would seem that the two shelters are alike in every way, the simple fact that Millie is excluded from one of them can have a devastating psychological effort on her. I have always been opposed to separate but equal fallout shelters.

BARRY But now she *wants* one!

MISS SYMPATHY Oh?

BARRY She comes back from the U.N. and we're having a practice air-raid drill – and you understand we're all Americans here, *we* accept the law of the land – so we invite Millie into our shelter. And she refuses! Suddenly she wants her *own* shelter!

MISS SYMPATHY But why? For what reason?

GRACE (*Distraught*) She says she's a neutralist!

ARNOLD She's a hypocrite. A real neutralist wouldn't take shelter at all.

BARRY Do you hear that kid? He's worse than she is!

MISS SYMPATHY Are you a neutralist, Arnold?

ARNOLD No, the neutralists are too extreme. I'm neutral.

GRACE (*Maneuvering to leave* MISS SYMPATHY *alone with* ARNOLD) Barry dear, don't you think we should make a final check of the shelter? The drill should start any time now.

BARRY Good thinking. I wonder what the delay is? The block captain mentioned last week that they were having a little trouble with the siren.
(*They exit wheeling the baby carriage*)

MISS SYMPATHY (*There is an awkward silence. She decides to get right to it*) Don't you know how to walk?

ARNOLD That's a funny question. Why do you ask?

MISS SYMPATHY Well, you're not walking.

ARNOLD I'm not smoking either. Why don't you ask me if I know how to smoke?

MISS SYMPATHY (*Containing herself*) That's very good. (ARNOLD *shrugs*) Do you mind if I crawl with you?

ARNOLD (*Hotly*) Yes, I do!

MISS SYMPATHY But *you* do it!

ARNOLD I do it because I believe in it. You do it because you think you're being therapeutic. You're not. You're only being patronizing. I realize that in your field it's sometimes difficult to tell the difference.

MISS SYMPATHY (*With difficulty*) That's very good.

ARNOLD If you really feel the urge to crawl with me – *really* feel it, I mean – then you'll be most welcome. Not any more welcome or unwelcome than you are now by the way. I am by no means a missionary. Did you see my coloring book?

MISS SYMPATHY When anyone says anything you don't like you retreat into that coloring book.

ARNOLD I admit it's rude. I shouldn't do it unless I have a coloring book for you too. (*He studies her*) Do you wear glasses?

MISS SYMPATHY Contact lenses.

ARNOLD (*Suddenly shy*) You'd be prettier with glasses. Or rather *I* think you'd be prettier with glasses. I like the way a girl looks with glasses. It makes her face look – less undressed.

MISS SYMPATHY You think contact lenses make me look naked?

ARNOLD I think the more people have on the better they get along with each other. If everybody in the world wore big hats, thick glasses and dark overcoats they'd all pass each other by thinking, "What an interesting person must be inside all that." And they'd be curious, but they wouldn't ask questions. Who'd dare ask questions like "What are you really like" to a person in a big hat, thick glasses and a dark overcoat? The desire to invade privacy rises in direct proportion to the amount of clothing a person takes off. It's what we call "communication." Take off the big hat and they say, "Good morning, sir!" Take off the thick glasses and they say, "My, don't you have *haunted* eyes!" Take off the overcoat and they say, "Tell me *everything!*" So there you have intimacy, followed by understanding, followed by disillusion, followed by – (*Shrugs*) if only everybody wore more clothing we wouldn't have wars.

MISS SYMPATHY You're saying you'd like to wear an overcoat with me. Is that it?

ARNOLD I'd feel better if one of us at least wore a big hat. Do you ever have fantasies?

MISS SYMPATHY Aren't you getting intimate?

ARNOLD *You* decided to wear the contact lenses.

MISS SYMPATHY Everybody has fantasies.

ARNOLD What are yours about?

MISS SYMPATHY Being a better social worker.

ARNOLD Dear God.

MISS SYMPATHY (*Sadly*) I used to have fantasies about Adlai Stevenson. But that's all over now.

ARNOLD I have fantasies all the time. When I'm awake, when I'm asleep, I *live* with them. I embellish them. Polish them day after day. You cultivate a good fantasy long enough and soon it can seep out into the real world. Do you know how old my parents are?

MISS SYMPATHY I hadn't thought of it. Middle fifties?

ARNOLD They're both over seventy.

MISS SYMPATHY And they had a *baby?*

ARNOLD (*Shrugs, reaches for the coloring book, changes his mind*) My father doesn't look very much older than me does he?

MISS SYMPATHY (*Evasive*) I don't know if I noticed.

ARNOLD You're kind. But that's how it's been always. They're both alert, involved, aggressive people. So while I'm out trying, unsuccessfully, to make it with a girl and I come home, mixed up and angry and feeling like not much of anything, what are they waiting up proudly to tell me? *They're* having a baby. I'll try to say this in as uninvolved and unneurotic a way as I know how – it's hard to face a daily series of piddling, eroding defeats and, in addition, have the fact thrown in your face that your *father* at *age seventy* can still do better than you can. (*There is a long pause.* ARNOLD *fishes a ball out from under a chair and tosses it to* MISS SYMPATHY. *She one-hands it*) You catch pretty good. (*She cocks her arm back.* ARNOLD *throws out one hand defensively)* No, don't throw it. I'm not ready to compete yet.

MISS SYMPATHY These fantasies – were any of them about crawling?

ARNOLD In my fantasies, it was everyone else who crawled. For instance, in one of them I had this uncle. Uncle Walter –

(A weak siren begins to wail erratically)

BARRY *(Enters, running with the baby carriage)* That's it! The alert! Down to the shelter everyone!

GRACE *(Enters with a fire extinguisher and shopping bag)* Oh, it's so exciting! It's so exciting!

(BARRY switches on a transistor radio)

RADIO VOICE Stay tuned to this frequency. All other frequencies have left the air. This is Conelrad!

BARRY *(Listening intently)* I met that fellow down at civil-defense headquarters once. You'd be surprised. He's just like you and me.

(GRACE is in a sudden, heated conversation with ARNOLD)

GRACE But you *have* to go down! You went down with us last year!

RADIO VOICE It is the law that everyone on the street take shelter –

ARNOLD We're *not* on the street. We're on the patio.

BARRY *(Exasperated)* You think the Russians give a damn we're not on the street?

GRACE It's the spirit of the law one should follow, dear.

BARRY Arnold, I've had enough of this nonsense! Downstairs! That's a parental order!

ARNOLD *(Hotly)* I colored the sky blue, didn't I? Why don't *you* ever meet *me* halfway?

BARRY *(Exits wheeling the baby carriage)* I can't do anything with him.

GRACE We can't leave our oldest out on the patio!

BARRY *(Re-enters with the baby carriage)* He's the one who's breaking the law. Let's go!
    (He exits with the carriage)

GRACE You'd better follow me, Miss Sympathy. It's dark in the basement.

MISS SYMPATHY *(Weakly, to ARNOLD)* It *is* the law.

ARNOLD I told you I'm not asking for converts.

GRACE For the last time, won't you come, Arnold? It's not going to be any fun without you.

ARNOLD I'm doing something *else*, Mother.

BARRY *(Re-enters with the baby carriage)* The hell with him. The law doesn't mean a thing to *our* son. Come on!

(He exits with the baby carriage. GRACE exits)

MISS SYMPATHY *(To ARNOLD)* I, as do you, question the sense of such a drill, but objecting to this law by defying it robs *all* laws of their meaning. Now, I can see working for its reform while continuing to *obey* it, but to be both against it and defy it at the same time seems to me to weaken your position.

ARNOLD They're all downstairs. You'd better go.

MISS SYMPATHY (*Starting away*) You do understand?

ARNOLD (*Dryly*) I think I hear planes.

(*She exits running. Sound of offstage pounding.*)

BARRY (*Offstage*) Goddamit, Millie! What are you doing in there? Unlock the door! (*Sound of pounding*)

GRACE (*Offstage*) That's not nice, Millie! Let us into our fallout shelter! (*Sound of pounding*)

BARRY (*Offstage*) Millie! There is such a thing as the laws of trespass! You're in *my* shelter!

(*Sound of pounding.* MISS SYMPATHY *enters*)

ARNOLD (*Grinning*) Millie locked herself in the shelter?

MISS SYMPATHY She says, "Let the white imperialists wipe each other out." (ARNOLD *laughs*) I can appreciate her sensitivity and support her aspirations but I reject the extremes to which she's gone. (*Brightly*) But I do understand her motivations. (*Sound of pounding*)

BARRY (*Offstage*) Millie, you're not playing fair!

ARNOLD You really shouldn't be up here, you know.

MISS SYMPATHY I thought we were having an all clear by default.

ARNOLD I doubt it.

BARRY (*Offstage*) All right, Millie. We'll stay down here anyway! We'll use the basement as our shelter! Down on your stomach, Grace. Where's Miss Sympathy? Miss Sympathy!

MISS SYMPATHY (*Yelling*) Upstairs! I thought it was over!

BARRY (*Offstage*) The law's the law, Miss Sympathy. We can't come up till we hear the all clear. Otherwise we'd be making Khrushchev happy!

ARNOLD It *is* the law.

MISS SYMPATHY What if I lay on my stomach up here? It's so dusty down there.

ARNOLD I guess that would be *semi*-compliance.

MISS SYMPATHY Does it seem within the spirit of the law to you?

ARNOLD Well, I know lying on your stomach *is* the accepted crisis position. I don't imagine you'd be penalized because of location. (*She lies on her stomach.* ARNOLD *views her with wry amusement*) Don't you know how to stand?

MISS SYMPATHY (*Dryly*) That's quite witty. You were telling me about your fantasy.

ARNOLD Which one?

MISS SYMPATHY Your uncle. (*Checks notes*) Walter.

ARNOLD Well, in a fantasy it's you who are in control, isn't it? So you can make things any way you want them. So I wanted an uncle. I guess I was eight or nine at the time. So I made him up. Uncle Walter. Uncle Walter was a mess. His eyes were very bad and he wore big, thick bifocals – about this size – half the size of his face and he had a beard. Hair all over. I mean it started with his nose hairs and blended with his ear hairs and went all the way down to his chest hairs. Except I never saw his chest. He was frail and he always wore a scarf. And a big heavy black overcoat. Even inside the house. It used to shed. *He* used to shed. My mother and father were always embarrassed when he came to visit. And I was too – but for *them*, not for him. I kept hoping Uncle Walter would understand that I was as normal as he was and that it wasn't my fault my parents were a little strange. He would never let me near him. He *hated* children. So I hated children. Anything Uncle Walter did I wanted to do. I tried to get bad eyes. I'd let them blur out of focus until they'd tear. I began seeing my parents as Uncle Walter saw them. I don't mean I began to understand them the way Uncle Walter did. I mean I *became* Uncle Walter looking at my parents. I became Uncle Walter looking at *me!* Then – I don't know how it happened – my father talked Uncle Walter into joining his athletic club. I thought it was a big joke – that in a week Uncle Walter would have them all wearing overcoats, bifocals and beards – (*Mimes sign*) "The Unhealthy Athletic Club." But all that happened was that Uncle Walter got healthy. He got rid of his overcoat. He shaved his beard. He took pills for his vitamin deficiency and his eyes became twenty-twenty. He began to smile at me and say, "Howsa boy!" He talked business with the family. It was *my* fantasy and he had sold me out! He died a month later. Never trust a grownup.

MISS SYMPATHY Will you tell me why you're crawling?

(*Arnold crawls over to* MISS SYMPATHY)

ARNOLD I find that in crawling like a child I begin to act like a child again.

MISS SYMPATHY Is that why you started?

ARNOLD Possibly. I did a very childlike thing on the way home. I never would have thought of doing such a thing before I crawled. As an adult my values encompassed a rigid good, a rigid evil and a mushy everything in between. As a child I've rediscovered one value I had completely forgotten existed.

MISS SYMPATHY What's that?

ARNOLD Being naughty.

MISS SYMPATHY You did something naughty on the way home. Is that what you're telling me?

ARNOLD I don't think I want to talk about it right now. I want to enjoy it by myself for a little while longer.

MISS SYMPATHY (*Exasperated*) God, you're as hard to reach as a child!

(*Quickly*) I understand why, of course.

ARNOLD Why?

MISS SYMPATHY First you tell me what you did today that was naughty.

ARNOLD First you tell me why I'm as hard to reach as a child.

MISS SYMPATHY (*As if to a child*) First you tell me what you did that was naughty.

ARNOLD (*Kidding*) You first.

MISS SYMPATHY (*As if to a child*) Oh no, you!

ARNOLD (*Kidding*) I asked you first.

MISS SYMPATHY (*As if to a child*) Then will you tell me?

ARNOLD (*Trying to withdraw*) Yes.

MISS SYMPATHY (*Very arch*) Promise?

ARNOLD (*Serious*) Yes.

MISS SYMPATHY (*Very arch*) Cross your heart and hope to die?

ARNOLD (*Stares at her, unbelieving*) I can understand why you have trouble reaching children.

BARRY (*Offstage*) Hey, up there. Have you heard the all clear sound yet?

MISS SYMPATHY (*Yelling angrily*) No, it hasn't, Mr. Enterprise!

BARRY (*Offstage*) Funny. It should have sounded by now.

GRACE (*Offstage*) I'm getting a chill lying on my stomach this way.

BARRY (*Offstage*) It's the proper position, Grace.

GRACE (*Offstage*) Can't we go up soon, Barry?

BARRY (*Offstage*) When the all clear sounds we'll go up. That's the law. Is that Millie yelling something?

GRACE (*Offstage*) Yell louder, Millie. We can't hear you – (*Pause*) She wants to know if the all clear sounded yet.

BARRY (*Offstage*) Tell her to go to hell.

ARNOLD (*After a long study of* MISS SYMPATHY) Do you really want me to get up?

MISS SYMPATHY (*Petulantly*) It's not what I want. It's what's best for yourself.

ARNOLD You mean if I got up I'd be doing it for myself.

MISS SYMPATHY (*Petulantly*) Not for me. Not for your mother. Not for your father. Strictly for yourself.

ARNOLD That's too bad. I don't care much about getting up for myself. I would have liked to have done it for you though.

MISS SYMPATHY (*With sudden warmth*) I *would* be very pleased.

ARNOLD If I got up right now?

MISS SYMPATHY (*Warmly*) Yes.

ARNOLD (*Begins to rise*) Okay.

MISS SYMPATHY (*Tackles him*) No!

ARNOLD But you said –

MISS SYMPATHY Not *now*. Later! (*Whispers*) It's against the law!

ARNOLD (*Shrugs. Returns to his crawling position*) Did you see my coloring book?

MISS SYMPATHY (*Furious*) You're not being *honest!* You blame me for accepting the rules of society. Well, without those rules we'd have anarchy. Every mature person has to operate within the warp and woof of society. You want to operate outside that warp and woof, to return to a *child's* world – to start all over again!

ARNOLD (*Appreciatively*) Yeah!

(*From his pocket he plucks a lollipop*)

MISS SYMPATHY (*Impatiently*) Well, you *can't* start all over again. It will all come out the *same way!*

ARNOLD (*Sucking the lollipop*) Then I'll start all over again.

MISS SYMPATHY But it will all come out the same way *again!*

ARNOLD Then I'll start all over again, again, again. It's *my* game.

(*He takes a long, loud suck on the lollipop*)

BARRY (*Offstage*) Wasn't that the all clear?

MISS SYMPATHY I'm afraid not, Mr. Enterprise.

GRACE (*Offstage*) I'm catching cold.

BARRY (*Offstage*) Let me put my jacket under you.

GRACE (*Offstage*) I'm *tired* of this.

BARRY (*Offstage*) But it's only a few minutes. We've spent over two weeks in our shelter.

GRACE (*Offstage*) But we had television.

BARRY (*Offstage*) The law is there for the citizens to obey. If *we* are irresponsible how can we attack *others* for being irresponsible?

MISS SYMPATHY (*Coldly, to* ARNOLD) You have a very irresponsible attitude.

ARNOLD Naughty is the word I prefer.

MISS SYMPATHY You were going to tell me something.

ARNOLD I forgot.

MISS SYMPATHY What you did on the way home from work – (*With sarcasm*) Something naughty.

ARNOLD Do you find me attractive, Miss Sympathy?

MISS SYMPATHY (*A long pause. She begins to sniffle*) Yes, I do.

ARNOLD (*Surprised*) You can say it just like that?

MISS SYMPATHY (*Barely restraining tears*) Because I do. I know I do. You're the kind of person I find attractive *always*. From previous examples I know you fall into my spectrum of attractiveness. Actually, it's because I find you so attractive that I'm having trouble with you. If I didn't find you attractive I could explain your problem without the slightest difficulty.

ARNOLD Everything's so complicated.

MISS SYMPATHY We live in a complex world.

ARNOLD *Children* are complex. Adults are just complicated.

MISS SYMPATHY Why did you ask if I found you attractive?

ARNOLD Because we've been alone for a while and we'll be alone for a while longer. I thought it was the right thing to say.

MISS SYMPATHY We have a time limit. The all clear will probably sound any minute.

ARNOLD Four months ago you wouldn't have found me attractive.

MISS SYMPATHY Why do you say that?

ARNOLD Because four months ago I didn't crawl. Crawling has made me a more attractive person.

MISS SYMPATHY It has? How?

ARNOLD Well, for one thing I'm conspicuous now. I never used to be. There's a certain magnetism conspicuous men have for women. (*More cautiously*) I *think* conspicuous men have for women.

MISS SYMPATHY No, don't stop. In some ways you're right.

ARNOLD I'm more assertive now. Everybody used to have *their* road. My mother, my father, my friends, Millie – with me the question was whose road would I take? Whose side was I on? Now I have *my* road, *my* side.

MISS SYMPATHY You're terribly sweet. Do you mind if I crawl over to *you?*

ARNOLD I'd like it. (*She does. For a while they stare wistfully at each other. Then* ARNOLD *drops to his stomach and kisses her*) I'm on my stomach now.

MISS SYMPATHY Yes.

ARNOLD I'm not even crawling any more. That's *real* regression.

MISS SYMPATHY Yes. (*He kisses her*) Before we do anything I want to tell you –

ARNOLD What?

MISS SYMPATHY Before – when I was feeling sorry for you – I felt you'd rejoin society if you were only made to feel like a man.

ARNOLD An expert analysis.

MISS SYMPATHY I was going to offer to go to bed with you to make you feel like a man. I couldn't offer myself in that spirit now.

ARNOLD I'm glad you told me. The social worker my folks had in last month went to bed with me because she wanted to make me feel like a man. I think she got more out of it than I did.

MISS SYMPATHY How many have there been?

ARNOLD One a month for four months. My parents keep bringing them around. They're very nervous about me.

MISS SYMPATHY (*Doubtfully*) You're not just using me, Arnold –

ARNOLD We're using each other, Miss Sympathy. That's what using's for.
      (*He begins to unbutton the back of her blouse*)

MISS SYMPATHY The all clear – What if the all clear should sound?

ARNOLD It won't. It's broken. That's what I did that was naughty today.
      (*They embrace as lights dim*)

BARRY (*Offstage*) Was that the all clear?

                              Curtain

Passionella

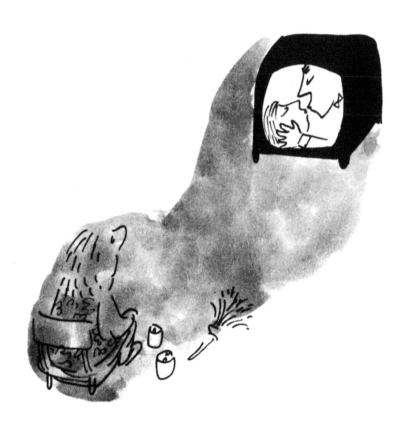

ELLA

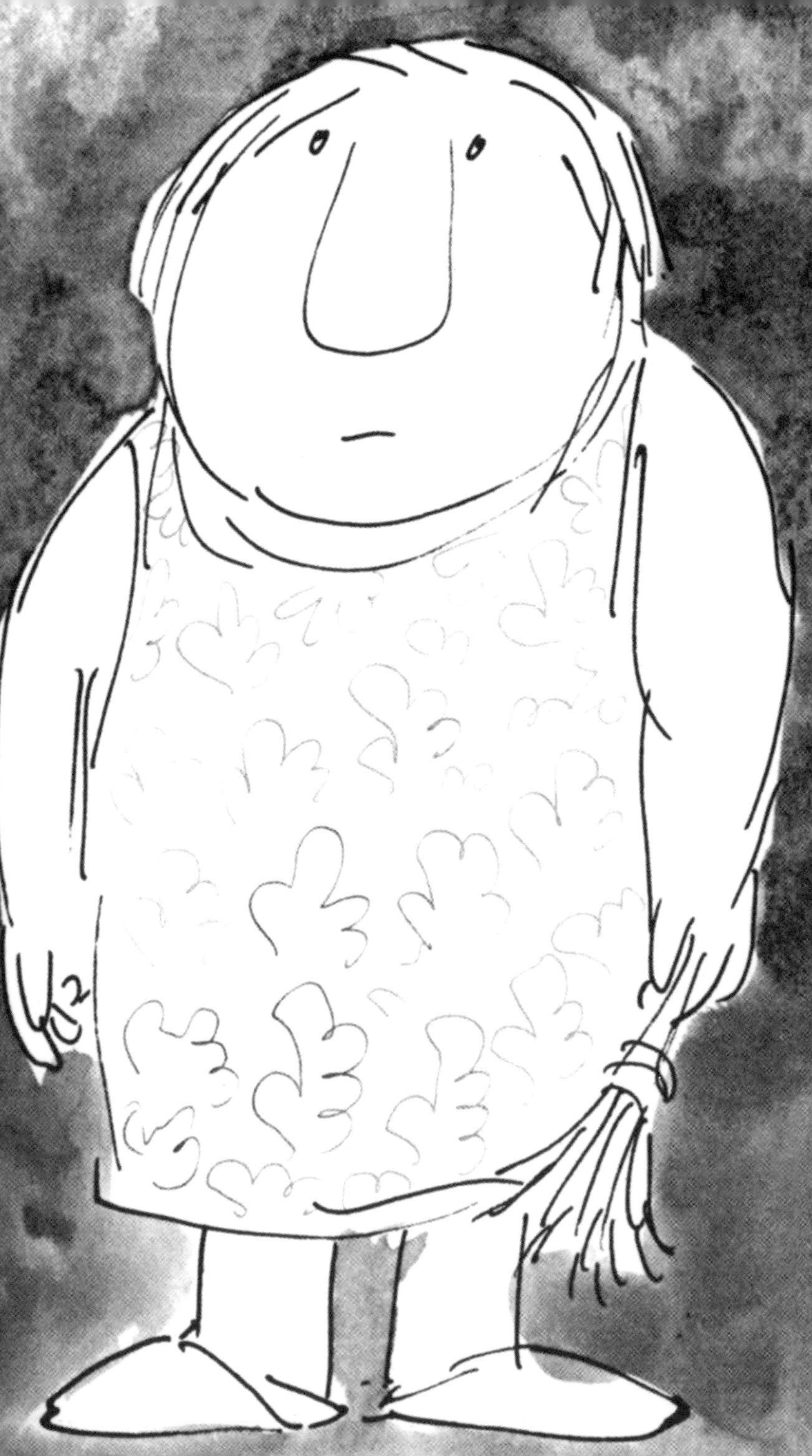

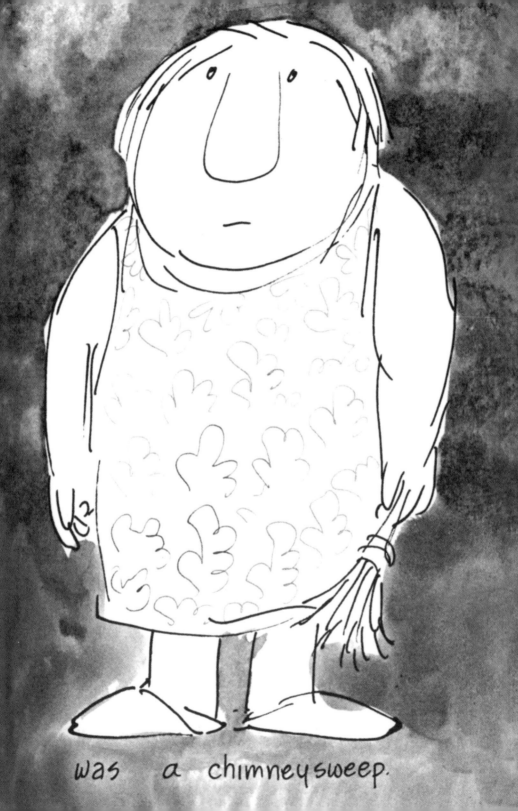

was a chimneysweep.

She worked in a big office building downtown.

But it wasn't what she really wanted to do.
As she often tried to tell people:

I'M ONLY DOING THIS TO MAKE A LIVING.

Every night after work Ella would go home to her lonely furnished room, and there she'd sit, all night, in front of the TV and think but one thought:

IF I
COULD
ONLY
BE A
BEAUTIFUL
GLAMOROUS
MOVIE
STAR.

And that was how she spent her days -

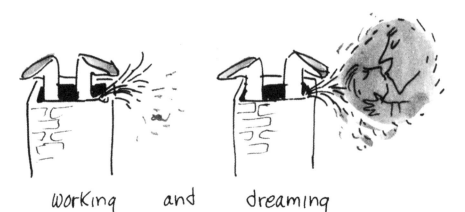

working   and   dreaming

Then one day Ella's employer came to her chimney and said: "ELLA WE WON'T NEED YOU AFTER NEXT WEEK AUTOMATION HAS COME TO CHIMNEY SWEEPING."

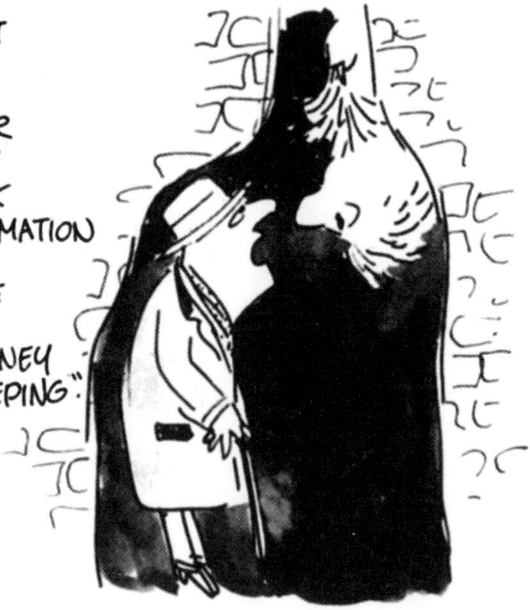

Ella was unemployed!

For weeks she wandered the streets looking for work. But nowhere was a good old-fashioned craftswoman needed.

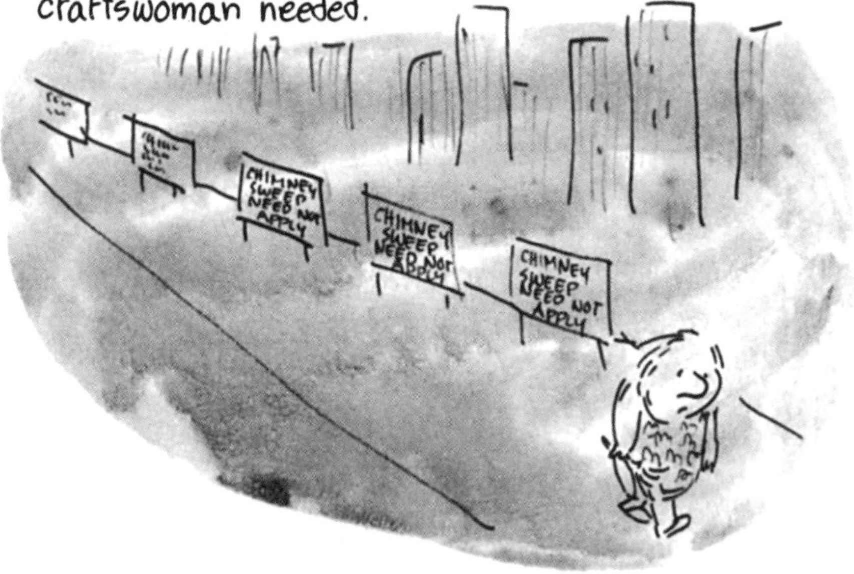
CHIMNEY SWEEP NEED NOT APPLY
CHIMNEY SWEEP NEED NOT APPLY
CHIMNEY SWEEP NEED NOT APPLY

She began to go hungry.

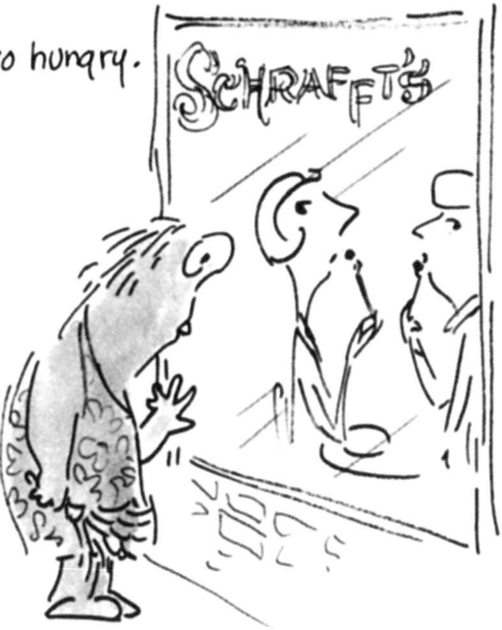
SCHRAFFT'S

Television was her only escape. From the time she arrived home till the time she fell asleep, her eyes never wandered from the screen.

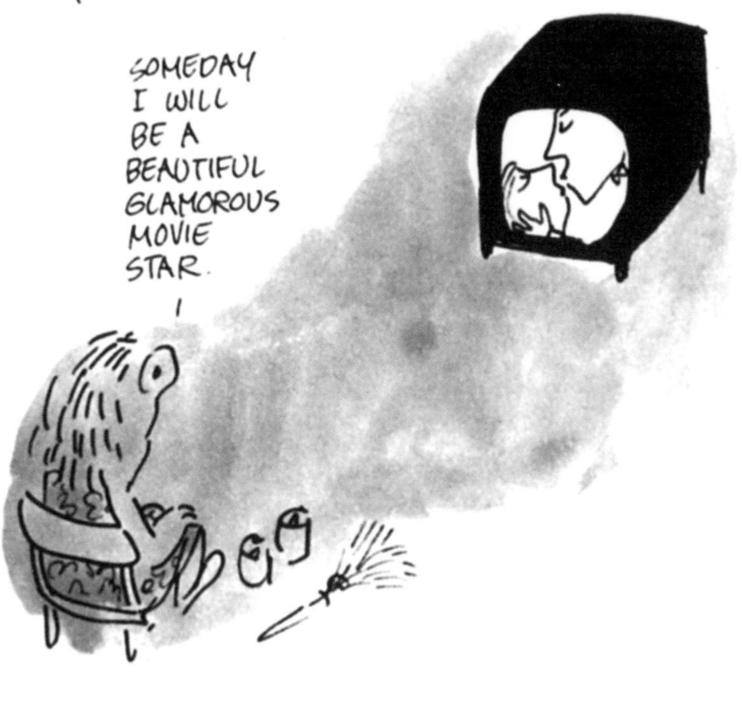
SOMEDAY I WILL BE A BEAUTIFUL GLAMOROUS MOVIE STAR.

Then one evening (it was the night of the full moon),
Ella returned from a thankless day of job hunting,
turned on the set and ... there was no picture!

She stood before the TV stunned, disbelieving, her
eyes searched the screen for the trace of an image.

NO PICTURE

NO PICTURE

NO PICTURE

Then Ella heard a voice:

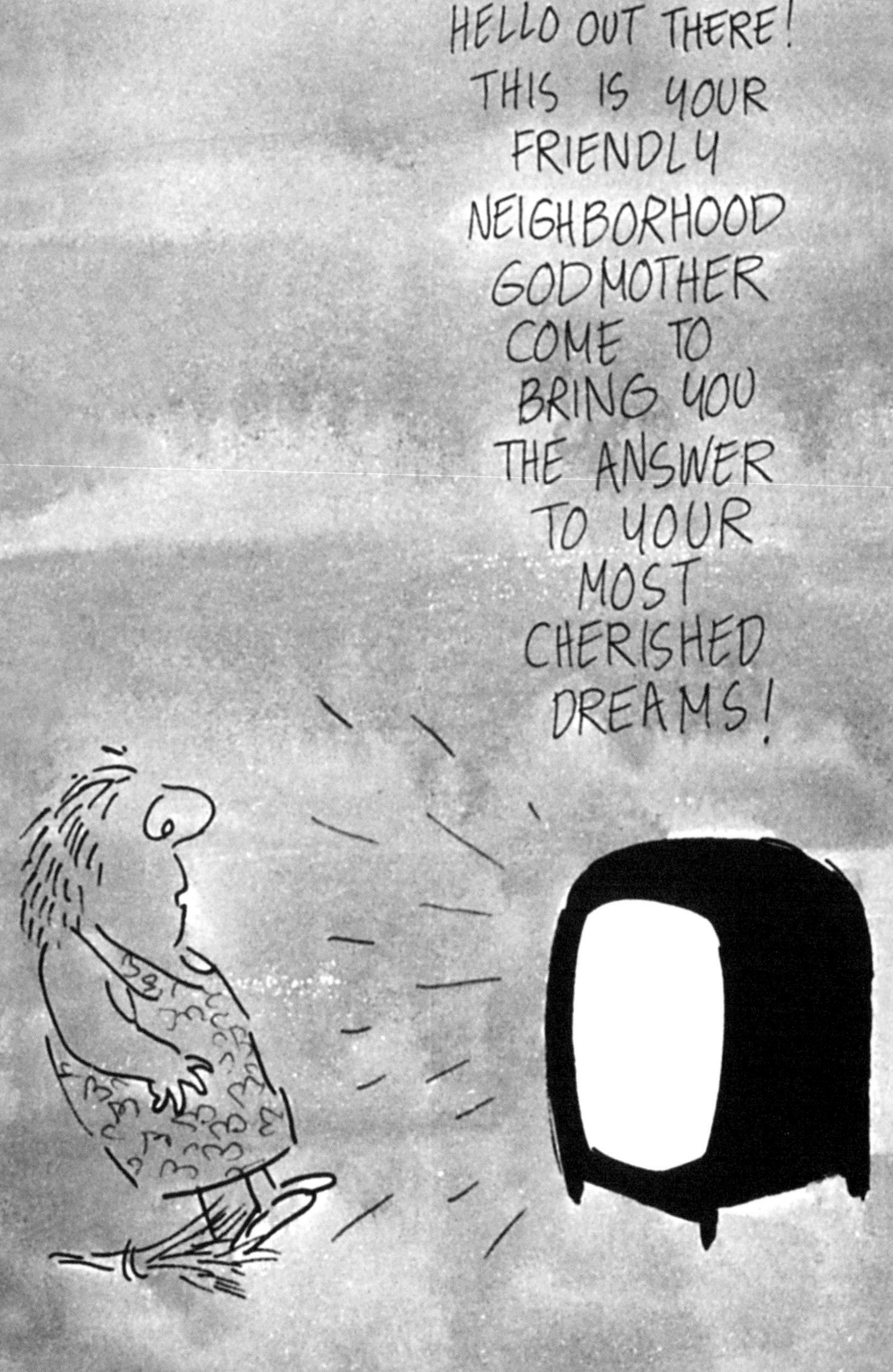
HELLO OUT THERE! THIS IS YOUR FRIENDLY NEIGHBORHOOD GODMOTHER COME TO BRING YOU THE ANSWER TO YOUR MOST CHERISHED DREAMS!

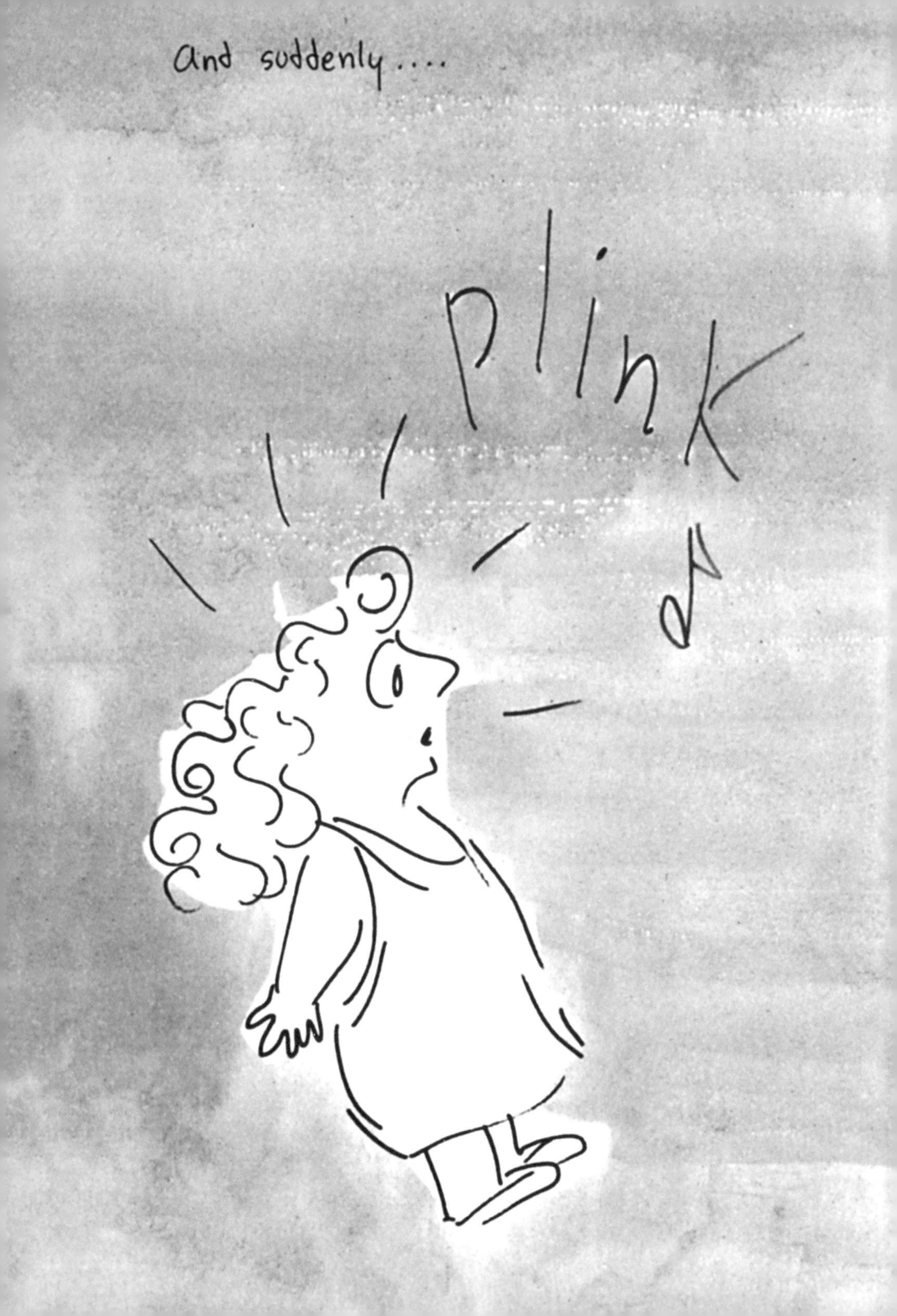
and suddenly....
plink

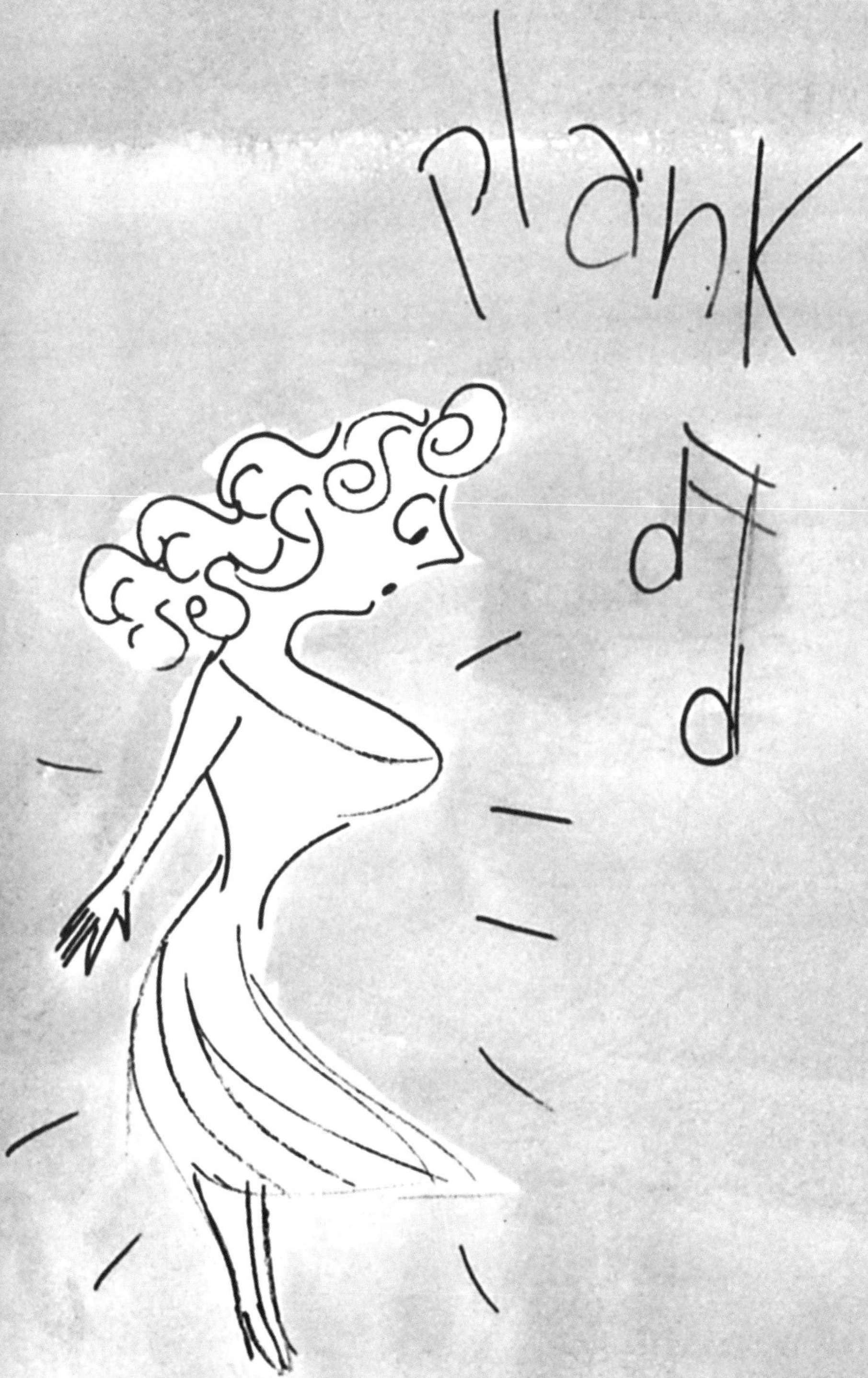
plank

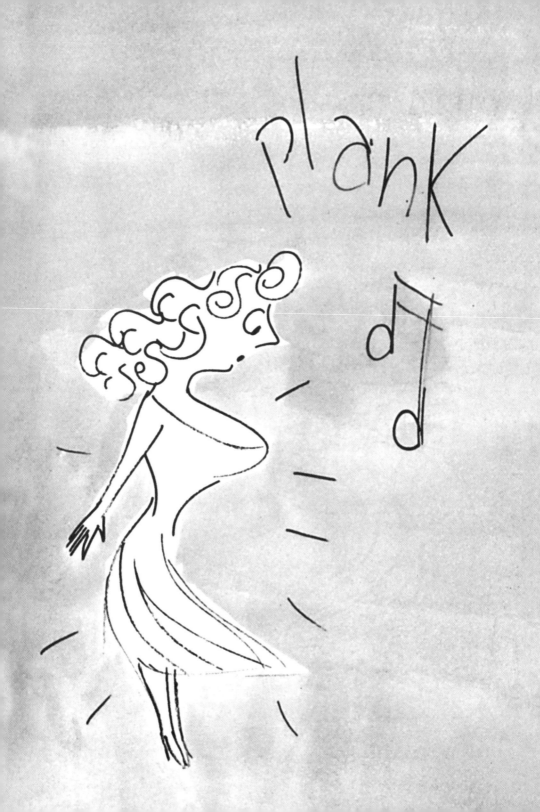

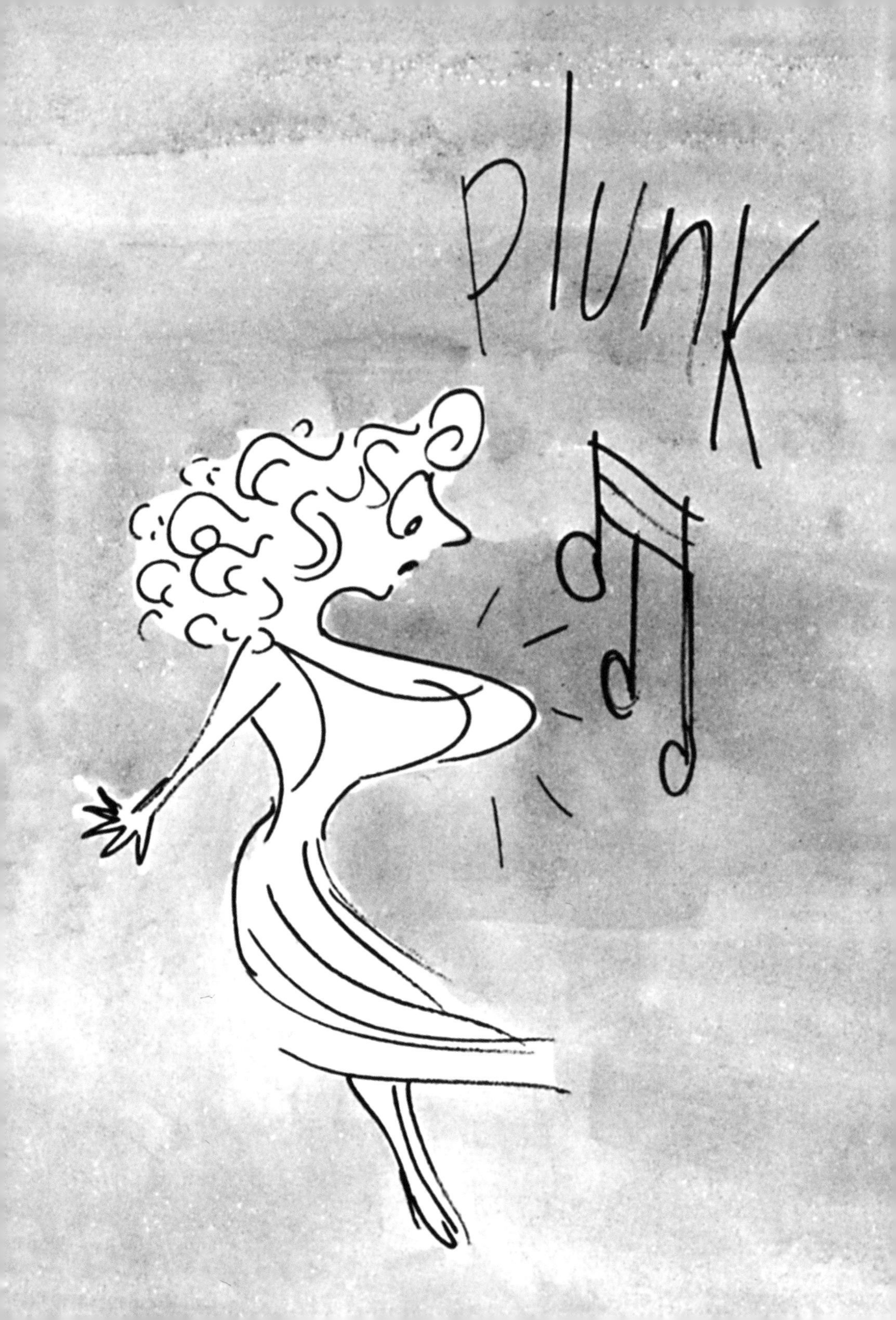
plunk

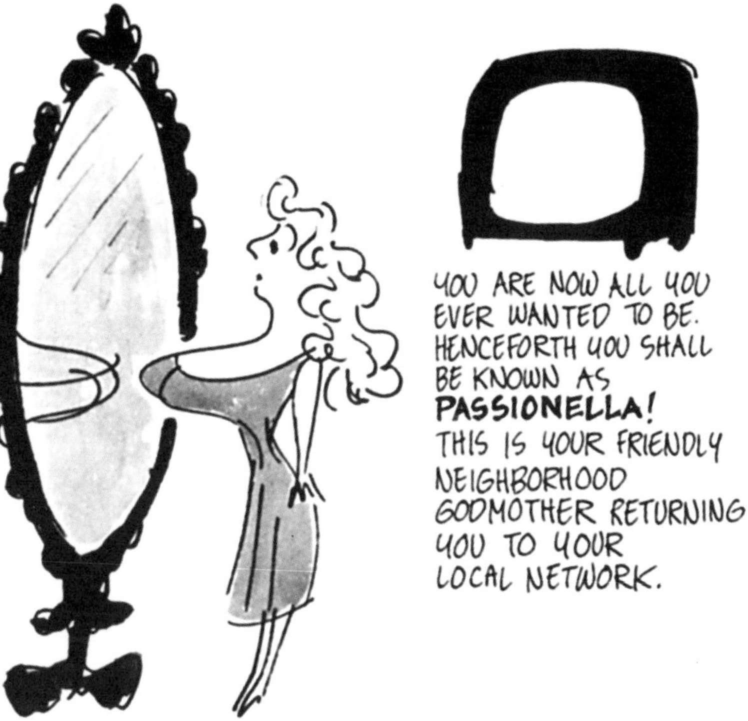
YOU ARE NOW ALL YOU EVER WANTED TO BE. HENCEFORTH YOU SHALL BE KNOWN AS **PASSIONELLA!** THIS IS YOUR FRIENDLY NEIGHBORHOOD GODMOTHER RETURNING YOU TO YOUR LOCAL NETWORK.

Ella could not believe her eyes. She was dazzling. "NOW I SHALL BECOME A BEAUTIFUL, GLAMOROUS MOVIE STAR!" she said and she ran off to El Morocco–

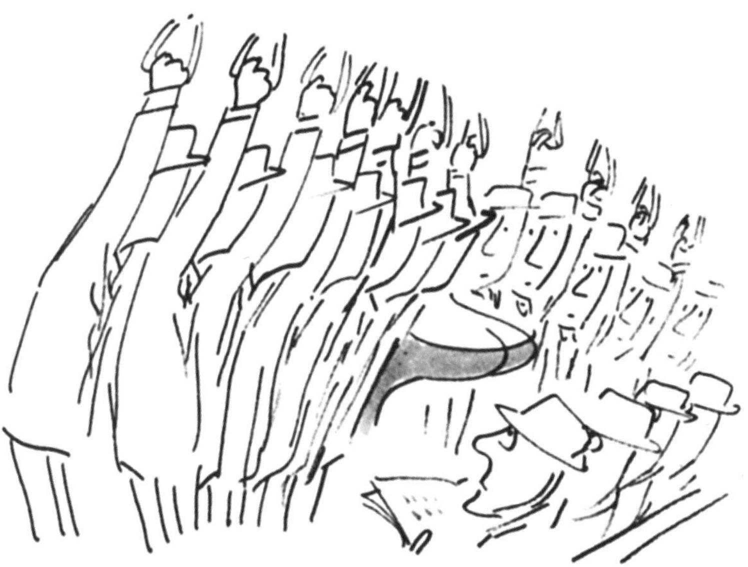

where she met Ed Sullivan, Walter Winchell, Earl Wilson and Cholly Knickerbocker - all of whom promised to do columns on her. And this also happened:

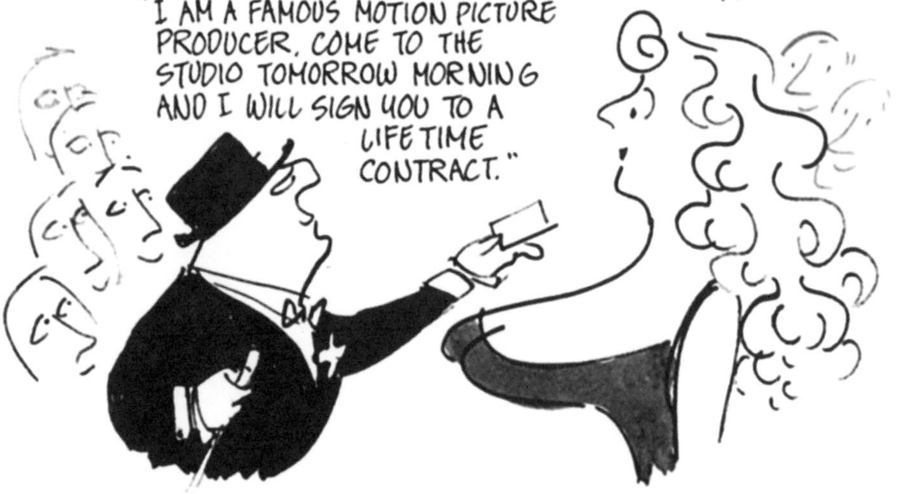
"I AM A FAMOUS MOTION PICTURE PRODUCER. COME TO THE STUDIO TOMORROW MORNING AND I WILL SIGN YOU TO A LIFETIME CONTRACT."

Passionella went home bursting with joy. The next morning, without bothering to look in the mirror, she rushed off to the movie studio.

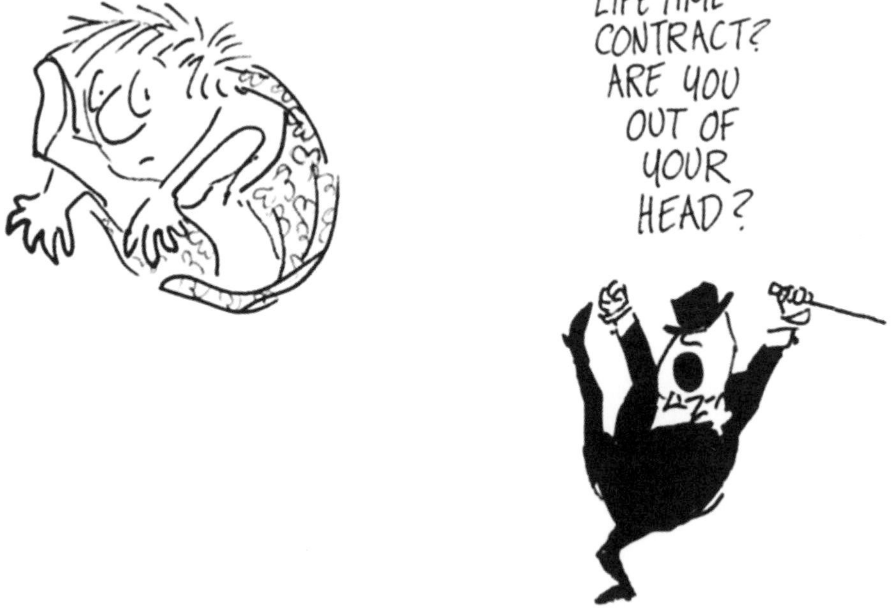
LIFETIME CONTRACT? ARE YOU OUT OF YOUR HEAD?

There she was —  her homely old self.

Then it was all just a dream!

Ella walked the streets
till the sun set.
'I'M NOT ASKING MUCH'
she brooded.
IT'S NOT AS IF I WANT
TO BE A **RICH** BEAUTIFUL
GLAMOROUS MOVIE STAR—
OR EVEN A **WELL LIKED**
BEAUTIFUL GLAMOROUS
MOVIE STAR. I
JUST WANT
TO BE A
BEAUTIFUL
GLAMOROUS
MOVIE STAR
FOR ITS
OWN
SAKE.

Then as the moon lit the sky she returned home.

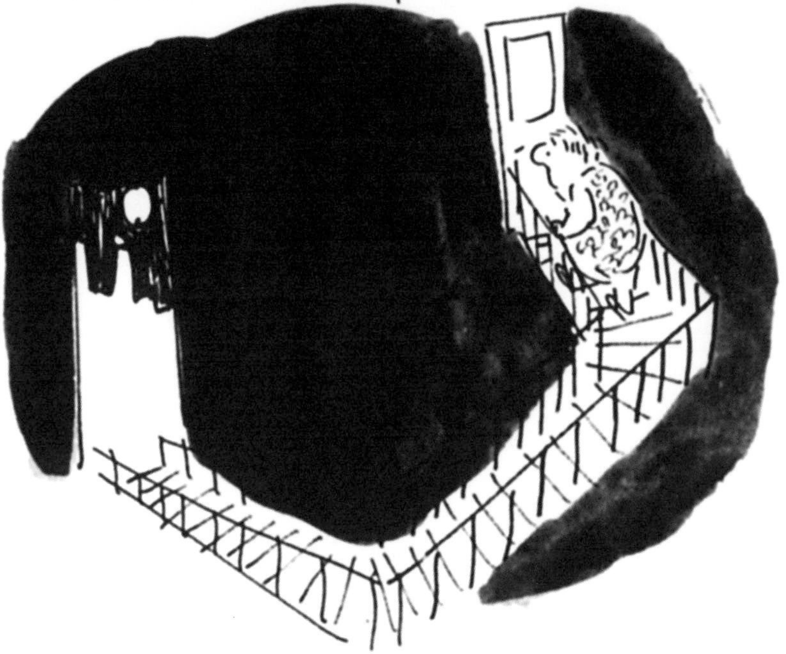

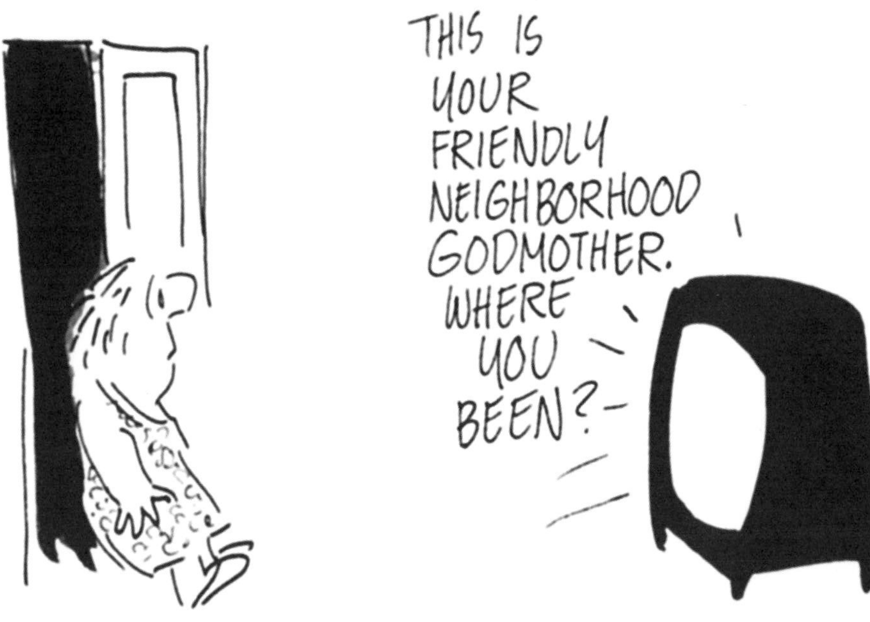
THIS IS YOUR FRIENDLY NEIGHBORHOOD GODMOTHER. WHERE YOU BEEN?

"LOOK AT ME!" cried Ella "I'M JUST THE WAY I'VE ALWAYS BEEN!"
"ARE YOU INDEED?" snickered the TV set and suddenly —

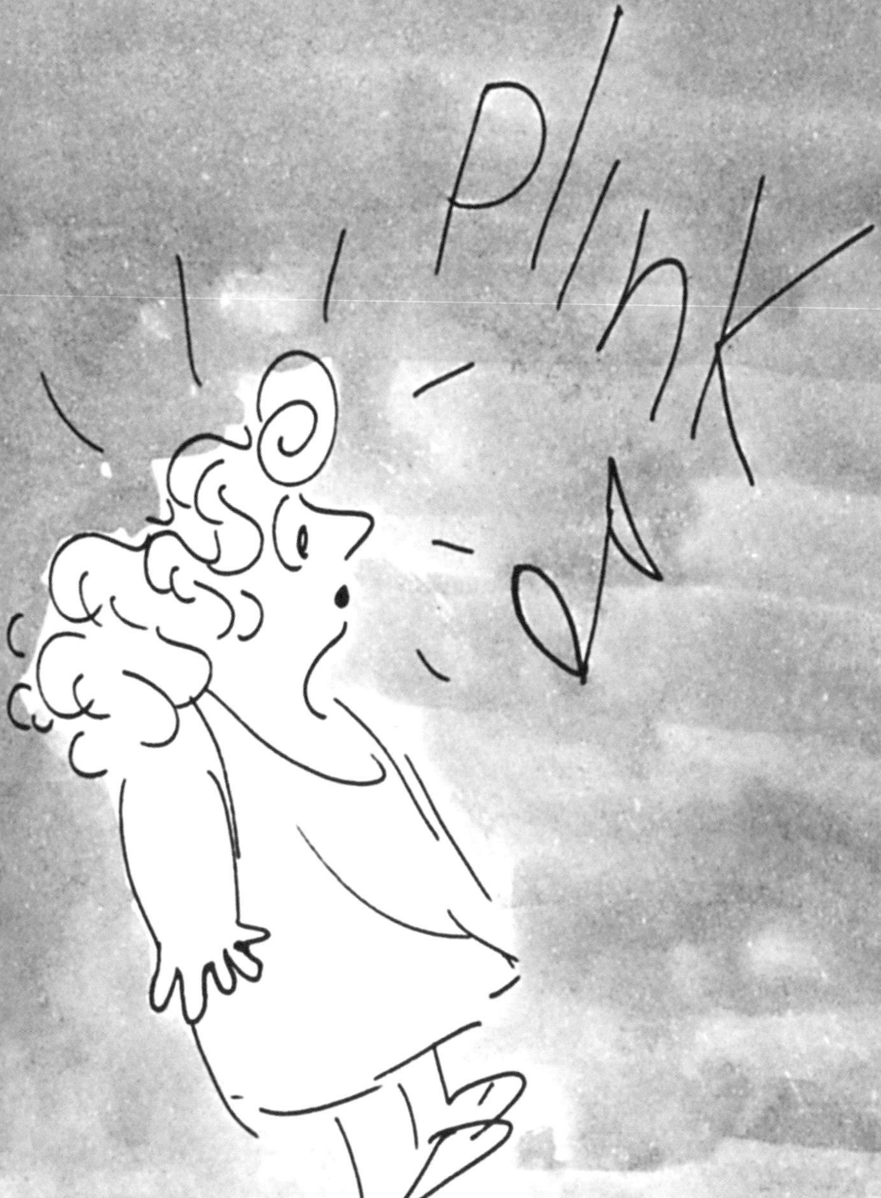
plink

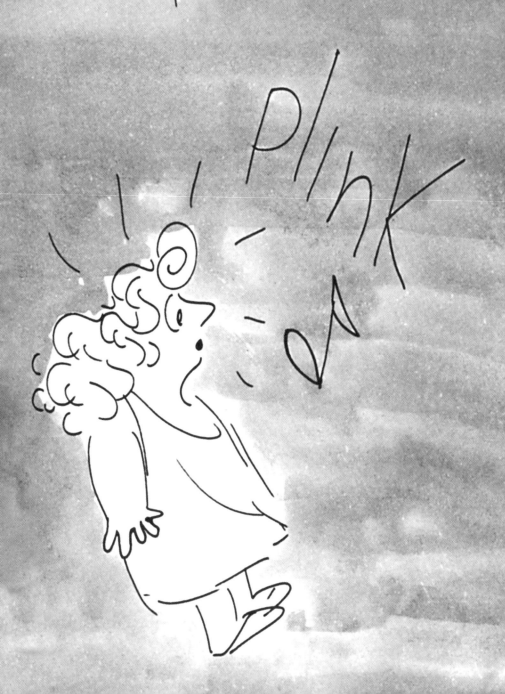

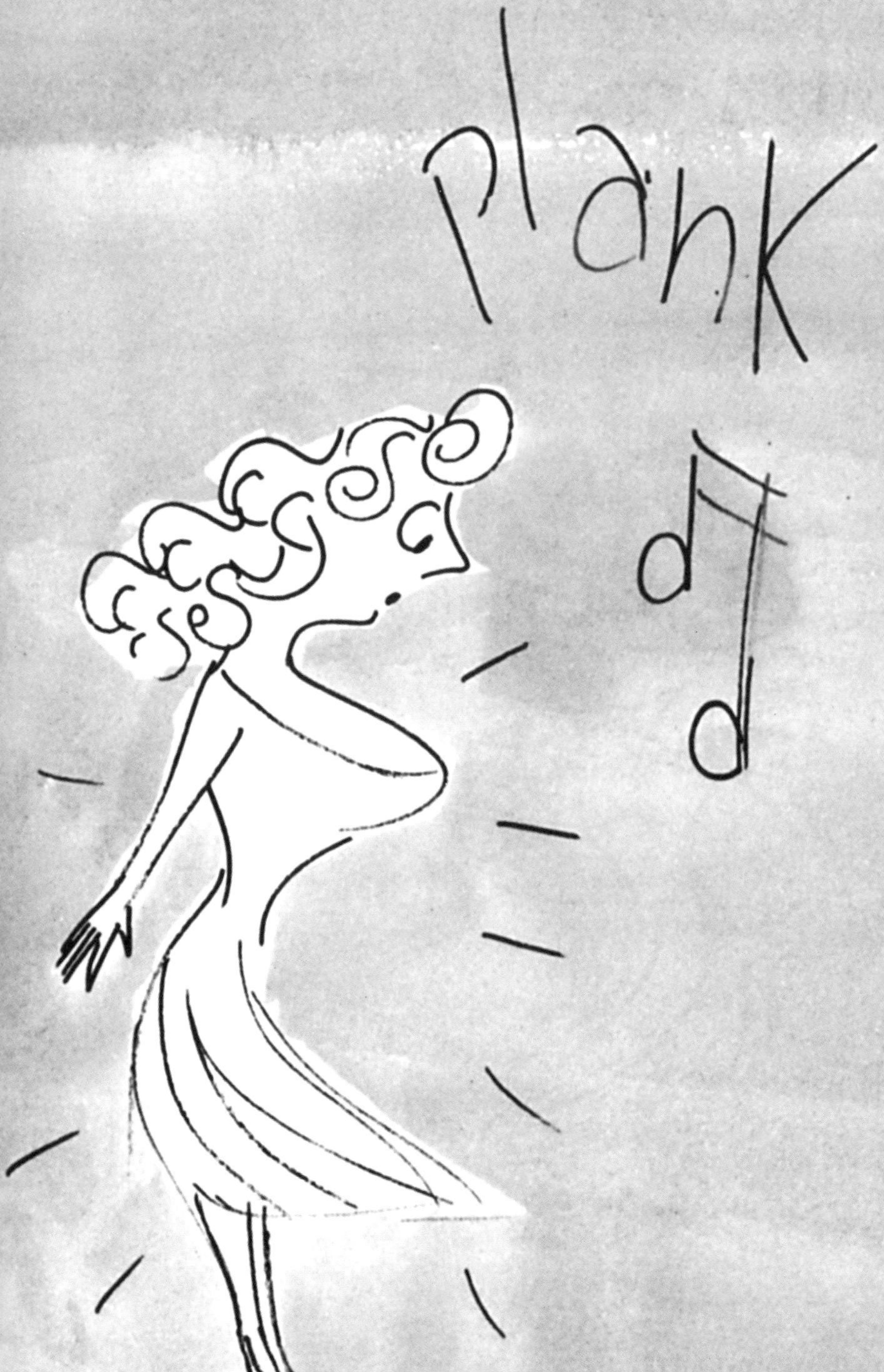
plank

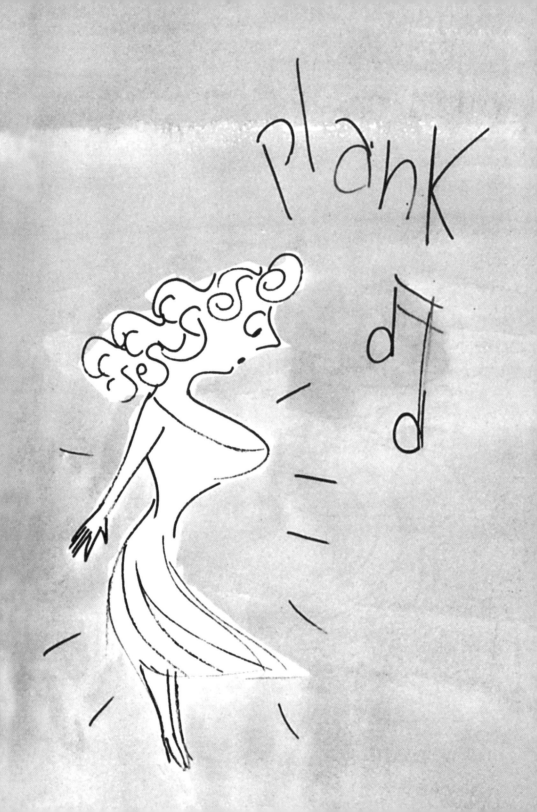

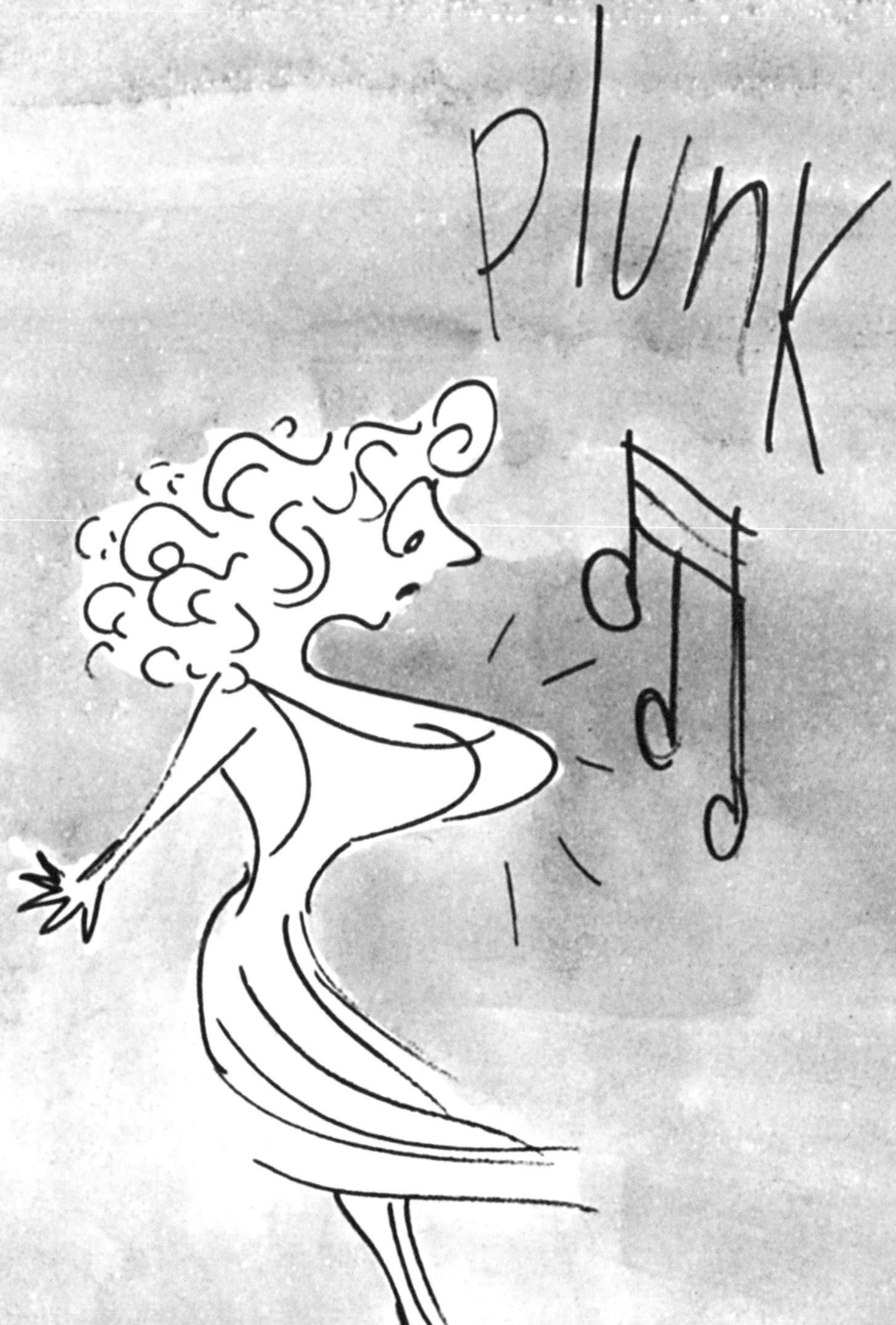
plunk

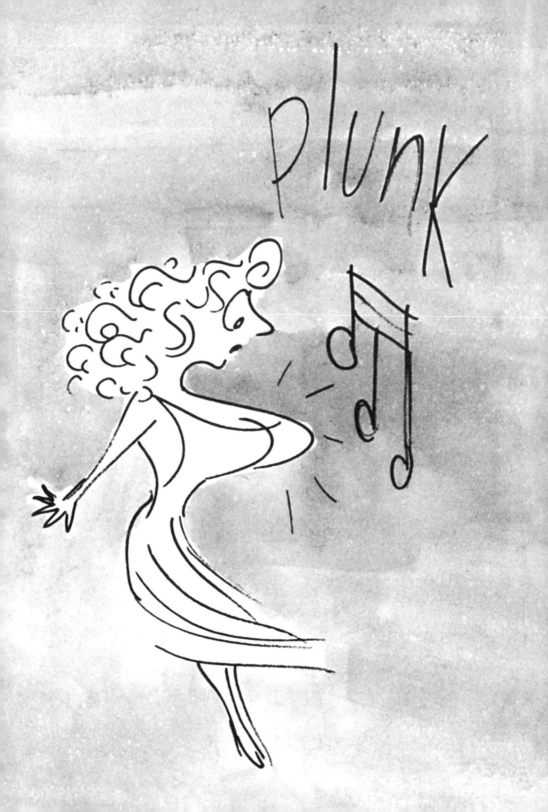

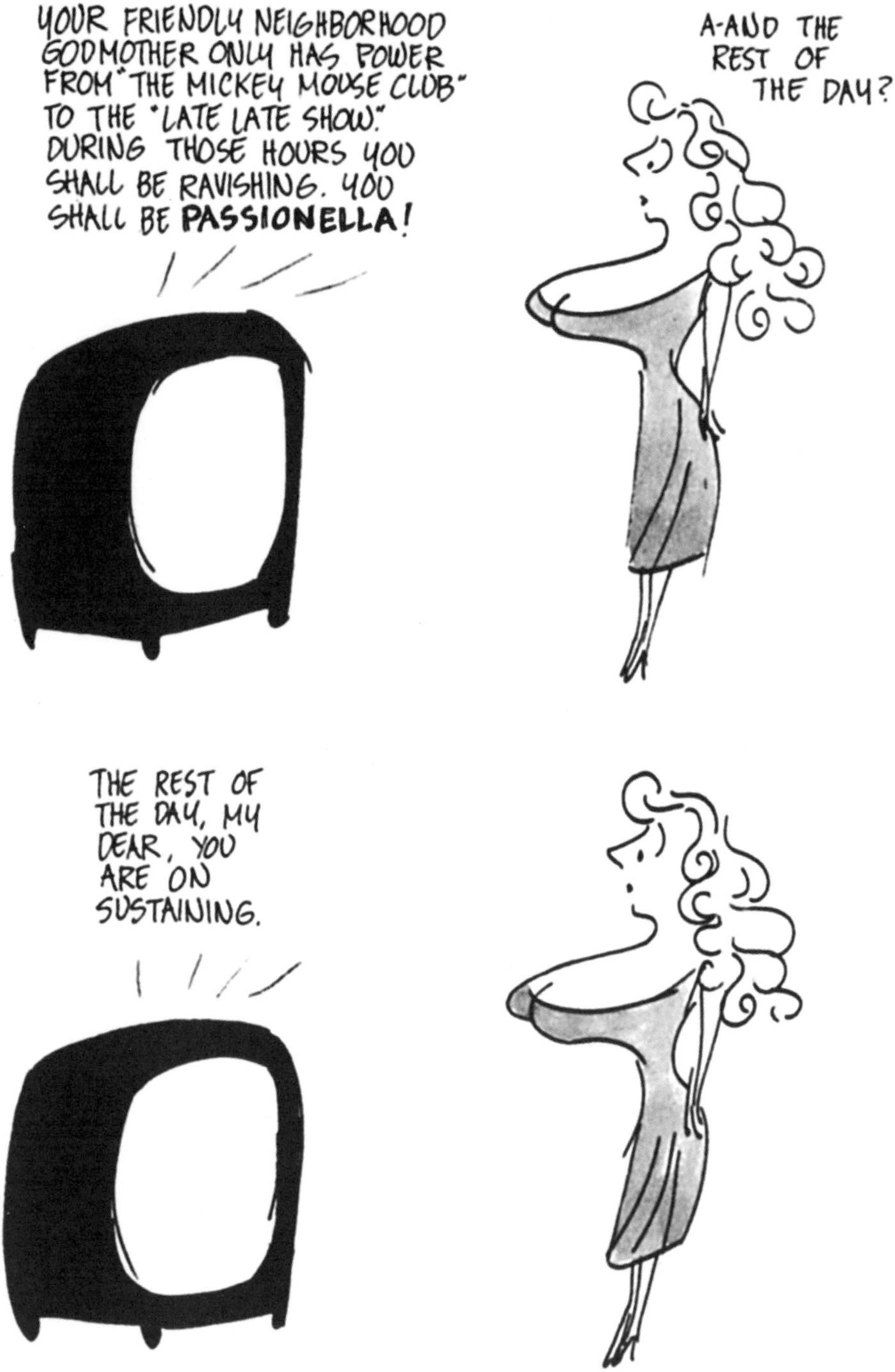
YOUR FRIENDLY NEIGHBORHOOD GODMOTHER ONLY HAS POWER FROM "THE MICKEY MOUSE CLUB" TO THE "LATE LATE SHOW." DURING THOSE HOURS YOU SHALL BE RAVISHING. YOU SHALL BE **PASSIONELLA**!
A-AND THE REST OF THE DAY?
THE REST OF THE DAY, MY DEAR, YOU ARE ON SUSTAINING.

And with that her friendly neighborhood godmother signed off.

in the months
that followed
a new star
was born :
the mysterious
exotic
bewitching
temptress...

Passionella

Prevue
PASSIONELLA
in
the SINNER

A legend grew around her. Strange stories circulated. Stories of how she would only allow her films to be shot between the hours of the 'Mickey Mouse Club' and the 'Late Late Show' and how at 3 a.m. she would hop into her sports car and vanish.

"WHO IS THIS MYSTERIOUS PASSIONELLA?" fans and columnists wondered. "WHAT IS HER SECRET?" asked show business.

And as her mystery grew, so did her popularity. Her pictures set new attendance records.

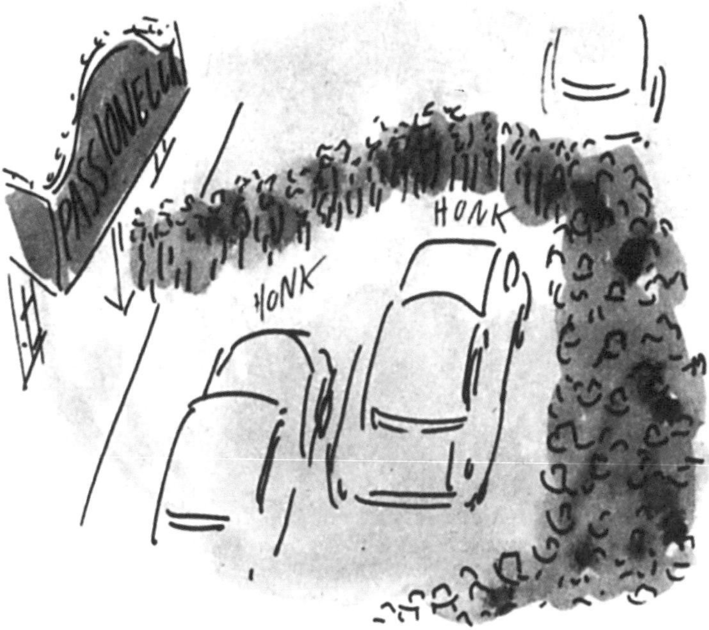
PASSIONELLA
HONK
HONK

Songs were written about her.

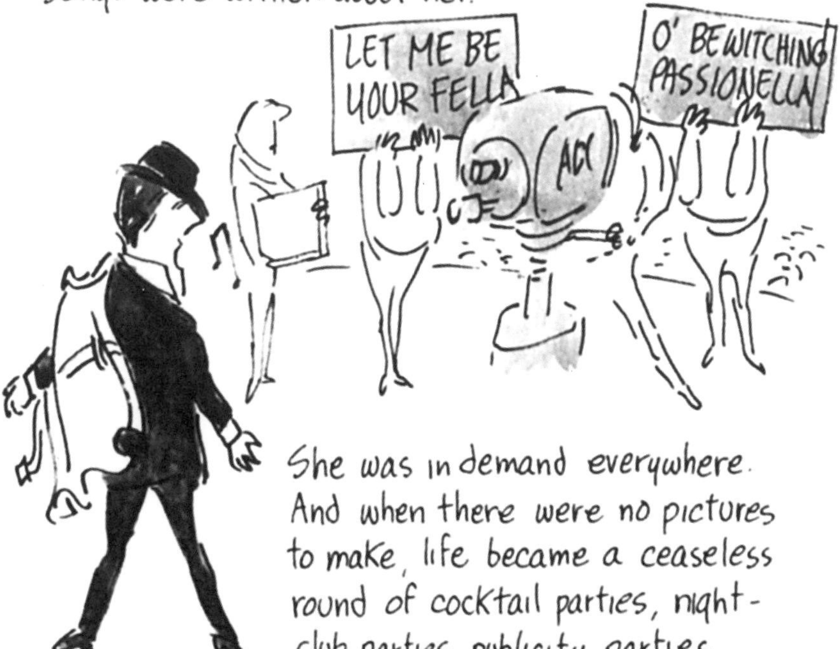
LET ME BE YOUR FELLA
O' BEWITCHING PASSIONELLA
ACY

She was in demand everywhere. And when there were no pictures to make, life became a ceaseless round of cocktail parties, night-club parties, publicity parties, beat parties.

But was Passionella happy? Now that she had money, fame, glamor, excitement - was she truly content?

Let us hear the answer in her own words.

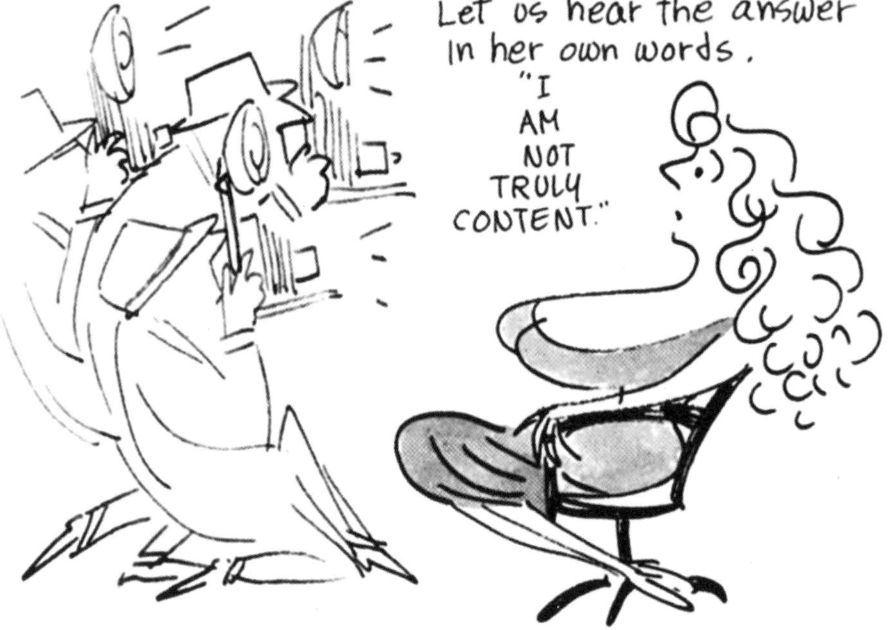
"I AM NOT TRULY CONTENT."

She began to feel a vague discomfort -

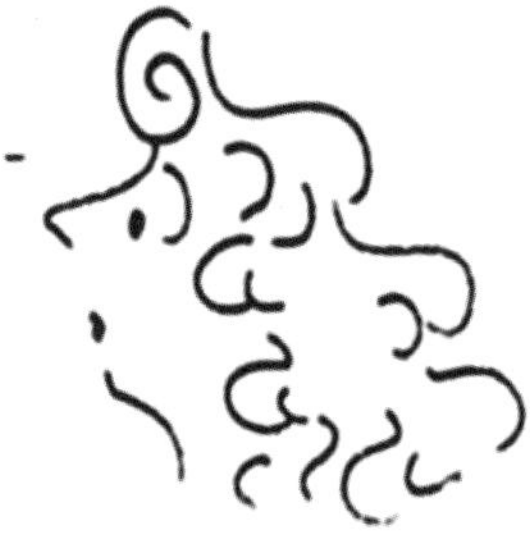

A certain indefinable unhappiness.

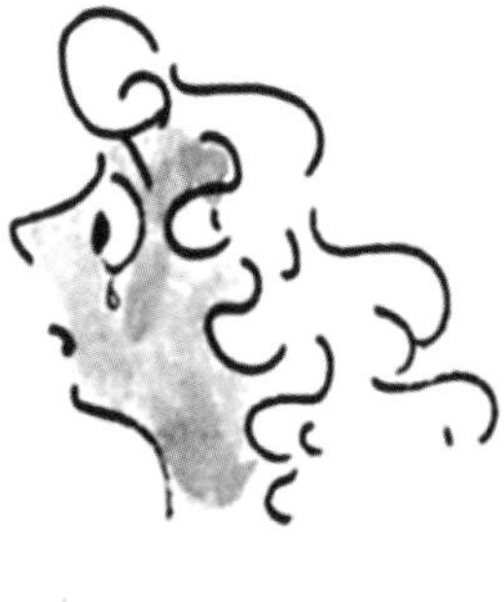

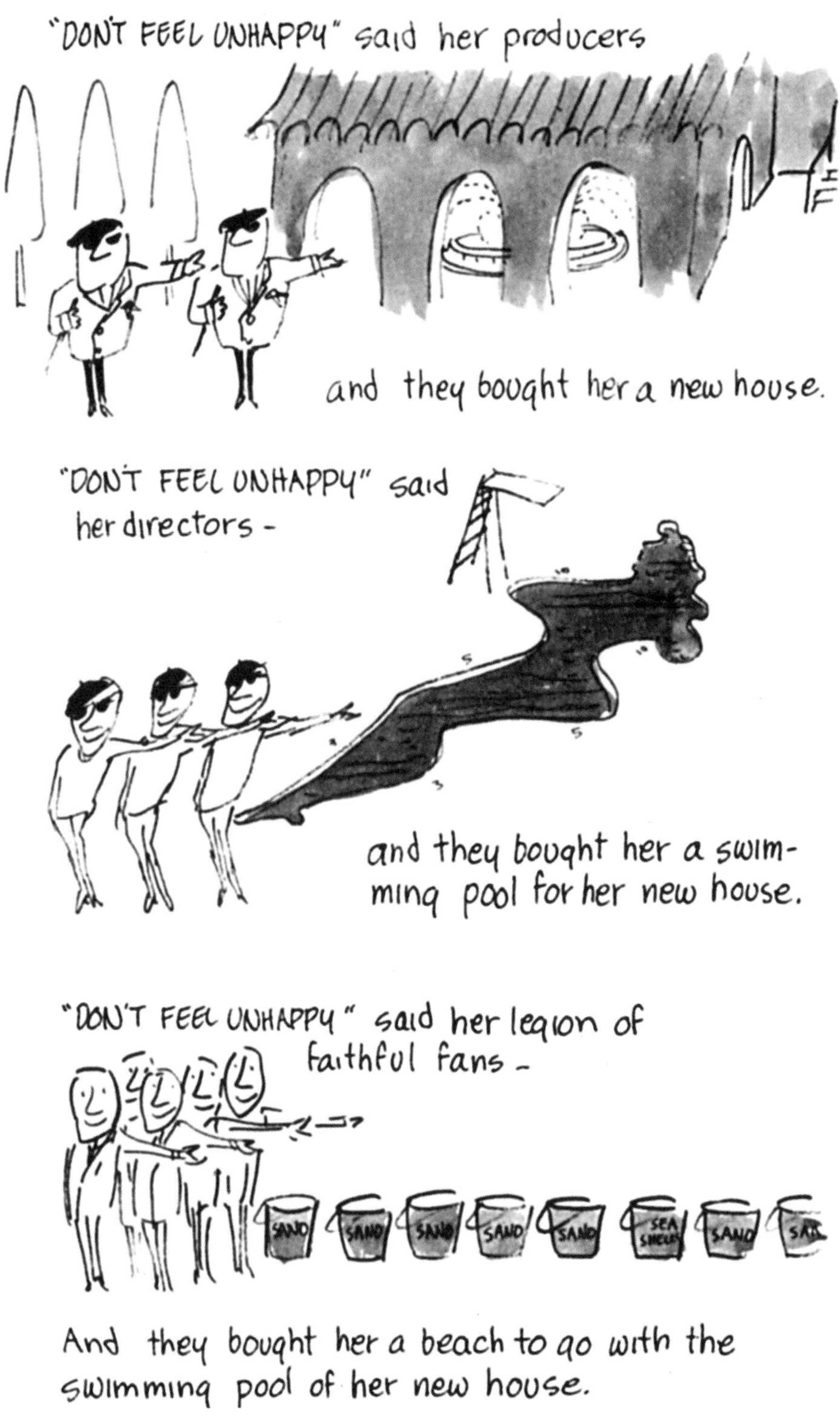
"DON'T FEEL UNHAPPY" said her producers
and they bought her a new house.
"DON'T FEEL UNHAPPY" said her directors -
and they bought her a swimming pool for her new house.
"DON'T FEEL UNHAPPY" said her legion of faithful fans -
SAND
SAND
SAND
SAND
SAND
SAND
And they bought her a beach to go with the swimming pool of her new house.

But Passionella was still not happy...

WHAT DOES
IT ALL MEAN
IF I CAN
NOT HAVE
LOVE?

She spent her nights acting and her days weeping.

OH HOW
HOLLOW
IS ALL THIS
BEAUTY
WITHOUT
THE RIGHT
MAN TO
SHARE
IT
WITH.

Finally she spoke to her friendly neighborhood godmother

MY FIELD IS STRICTLY PUBLIC RELATIONS. YOU'LL HAVE TO HANDLE YOUR OWN EMOTIONAL PROBLEMS.

And then one day Passionella met the right man...

CRAZY

her
new
co-star-
the
idol
of
a
million
teenagers..
FLIP
(THE PRINCE)
CHARMING!

snap
snap
snap

The Prince represented the youth
movement in Hollywood.

He hated cops.

He hated reporters.

He hated movies.

COPS STINK

REPORTERS STINK

MOVIES STINK

snap

snap

snap

Passionella had never met such a man.

YOU DIG - BECKETT, MAN?

WHO?

Glamor did not interest him.

YOU DIG BRECHT, MAN?

WHO? WHO?

Making love did not interest him.

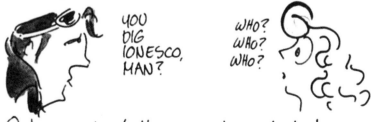

YOU DIG IONESCO, MAN?

WHO? WHO? WHO?

Only spiritual things interested him.

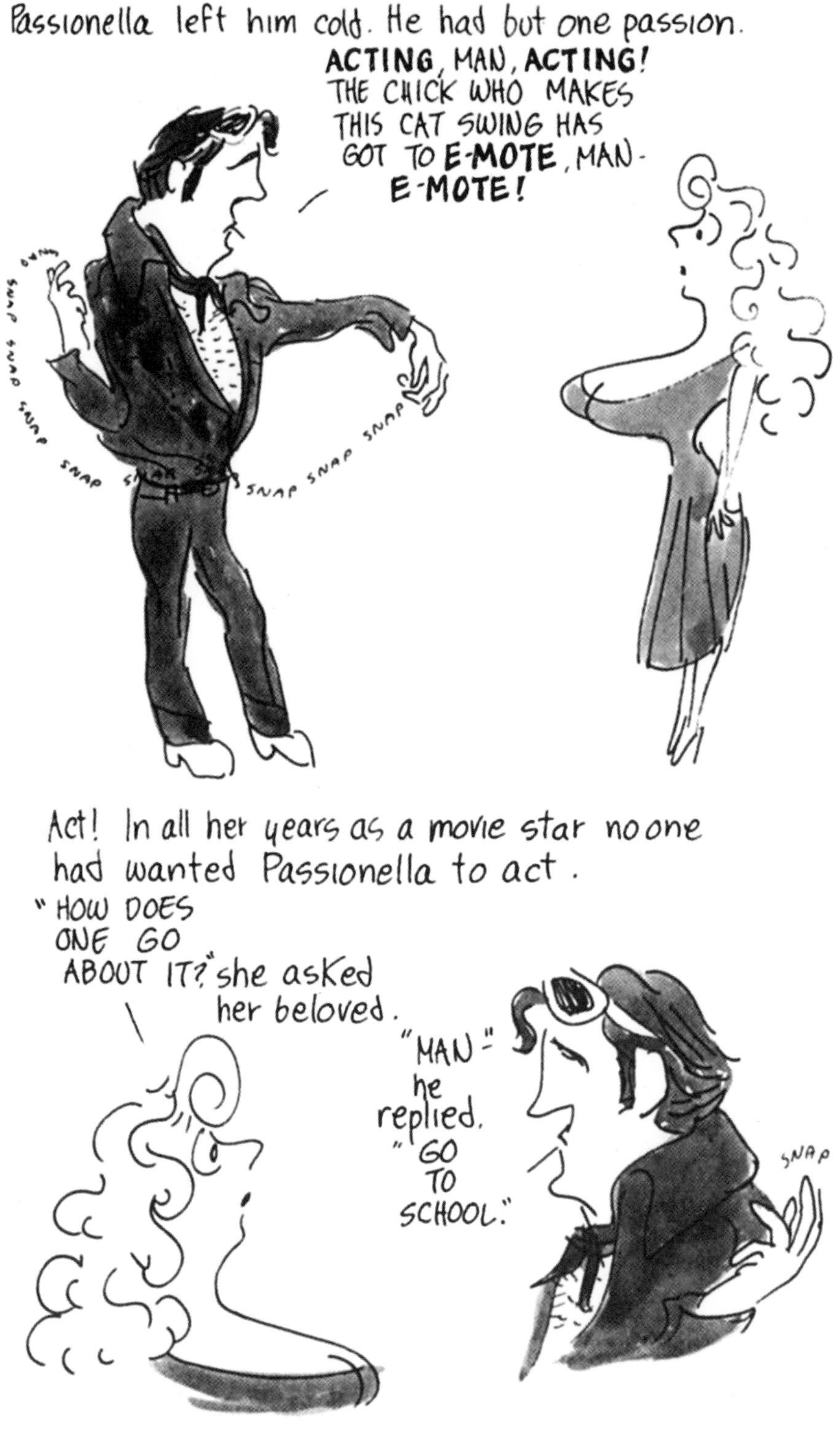
Passionella left him cold. He had but one passion.
ACTING, MAN, ACTING! THE CHICK WHO MAKES THIS CAT SWING HAS GOT TO E-MOTE, MAN- E-MOTE!
SNAP SNAP SNAP SNAP SNAP SNAP SNAP SNAP SNAP
Act! In all her years as a movie star no one had wanted Passionella to act.
"HOW DOES ONE GO ABOUT IT?" she asked her beloved.
"MAN-" he replied. "GO TO SCHOOL."
SNAP

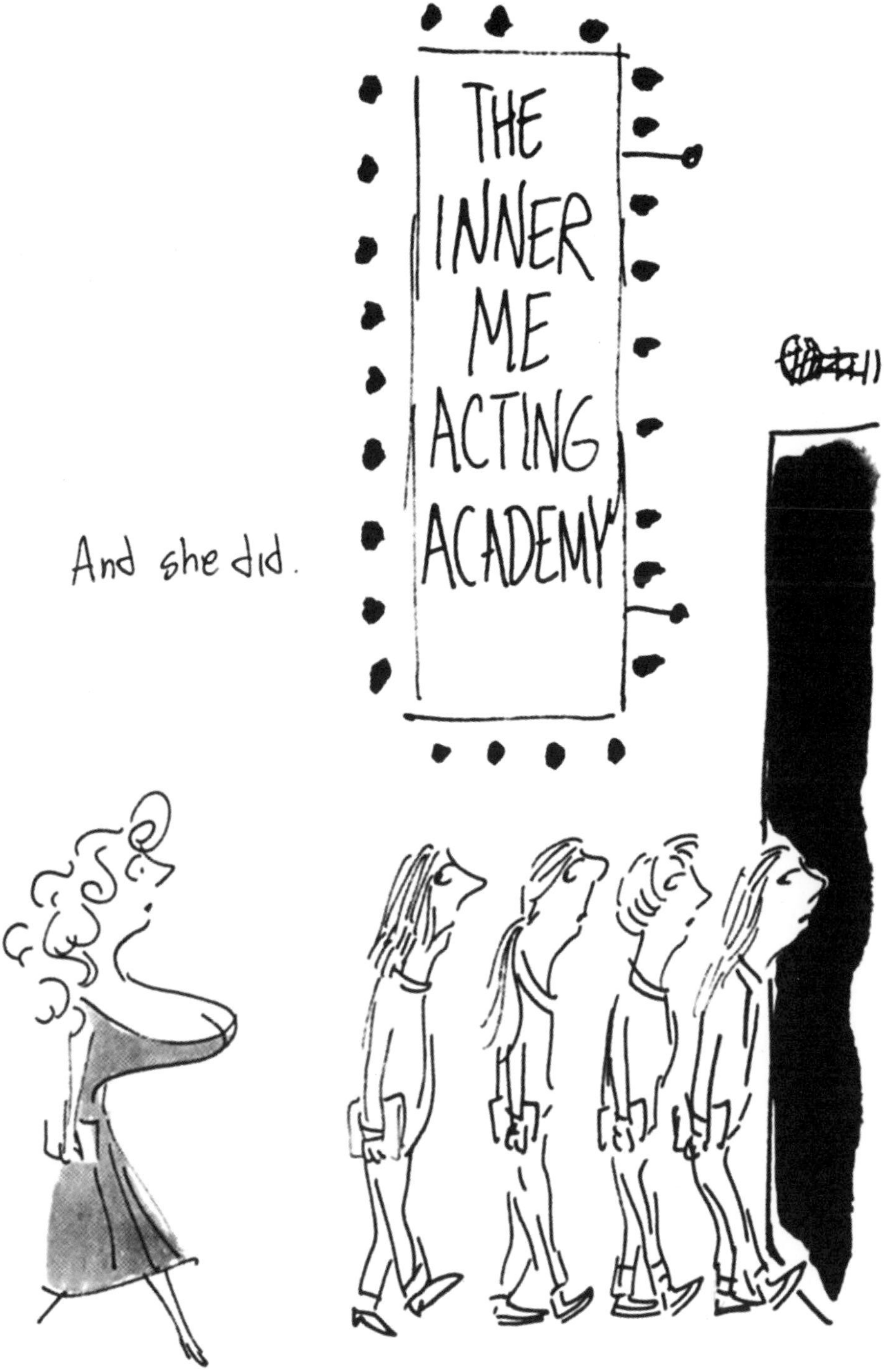
And she did.
THE INNER ME ACTING ACADEMY

Now, the 'Inner Me Acting Academy' was where all the movie stars went to learn how to act. It could take young, pretty, dimple cheeked starlets -

And after months of study teach them how to act like:

confused juvenile delinquents -   disillusioned drug addicts -   sensitive gun fighters -   misunderstood Nazis.

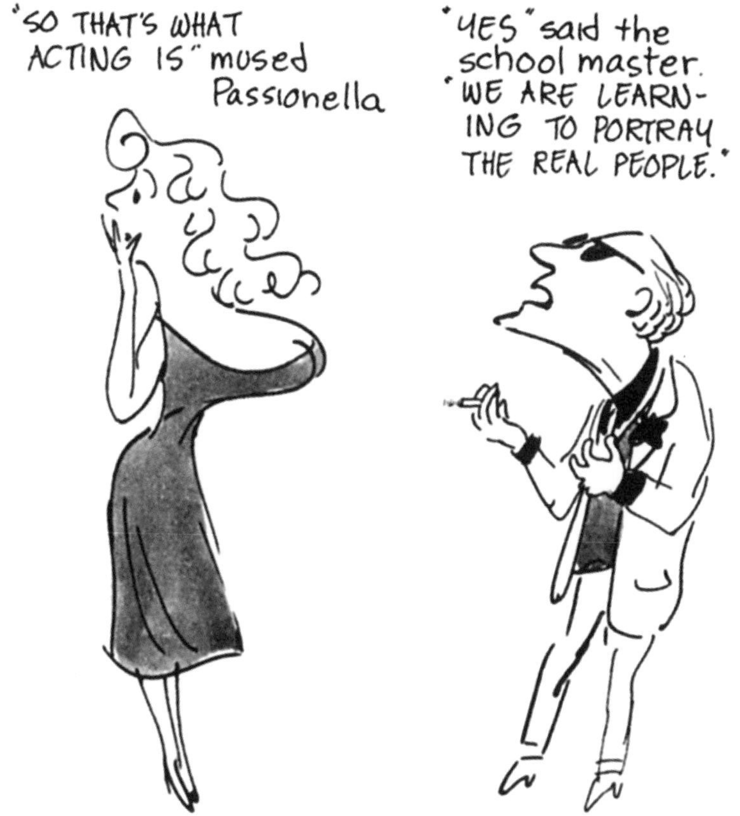
"SO THAT'S WHAT ACTING IS" mused Passionella
"YES" said the school master. "WE ARE LEARNING TO PORTRAY THE REAL PEOPLE."

The next day Passionella went to the head of her studio.

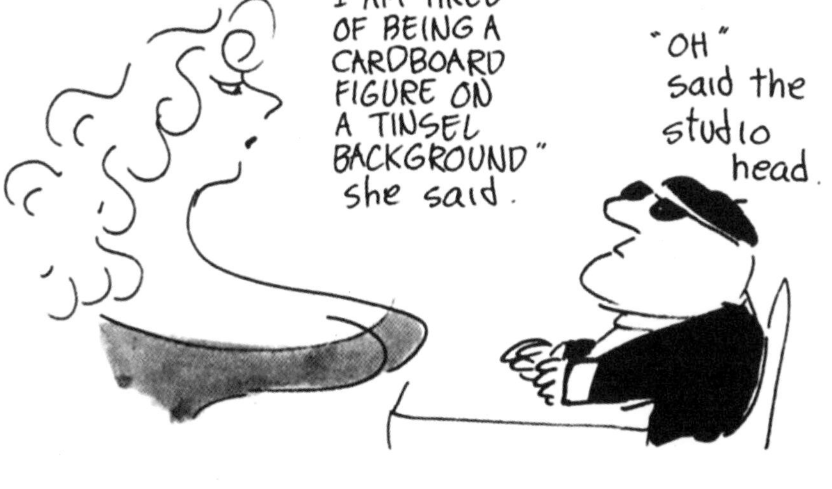
"I AM TIRED OF BEING A CARDBOARD FIGURE ON A TINSEL BACKGROUND" she said.
"OH" said the studio head.

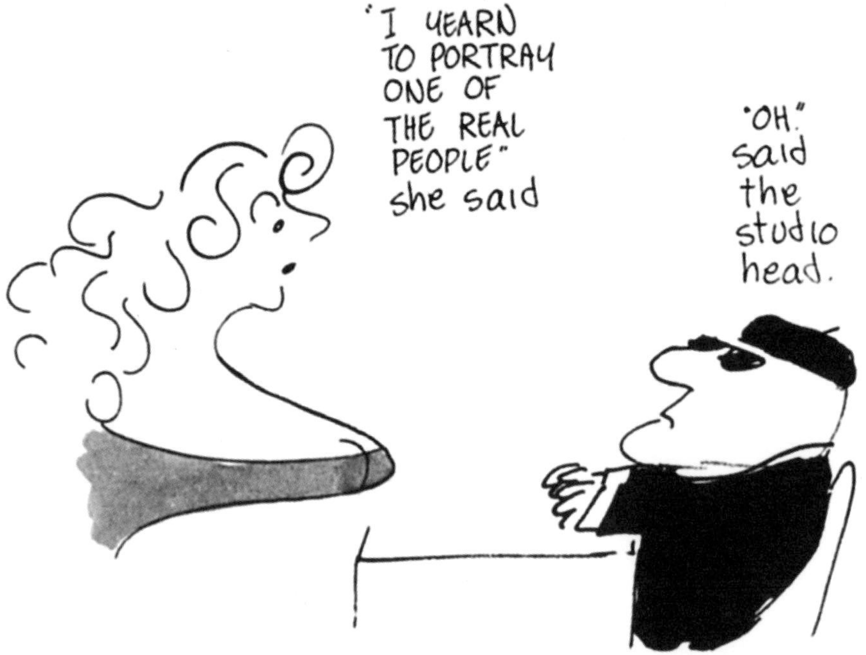
"I YEARN TO PORTRAY ONE OF THE REAL PEOPLE" she said
"OH." said the studio head.

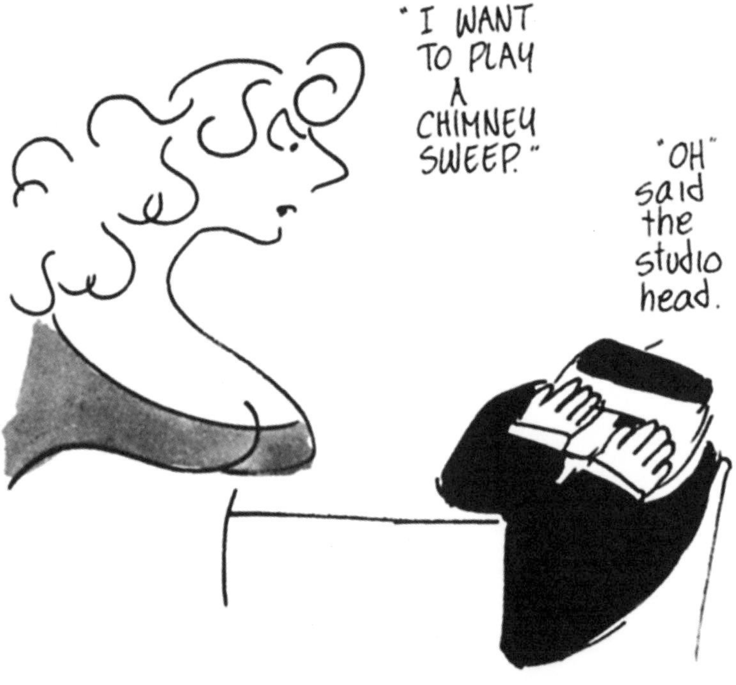
"I WANT TO PLAY A CHIMNEY SWEEP."
"OH" said the studio head.

So there it was. And there was nothing anybody could do about it. "IF I CAN NOT PLAY A CHIMNEY SWEEP I SHALL RETIRE FROM THE SCREEN."

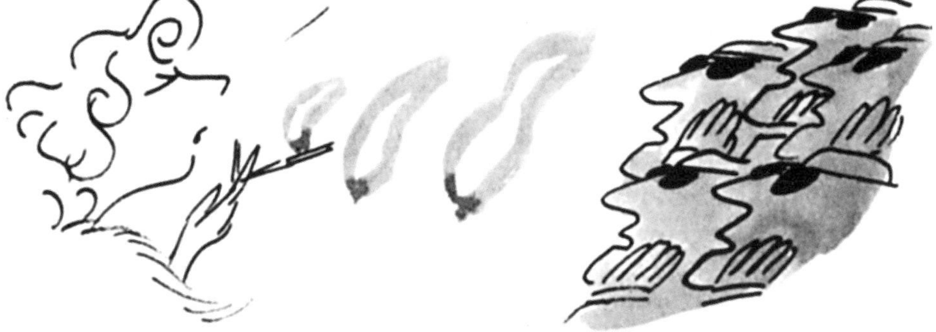

So the studio gave in.

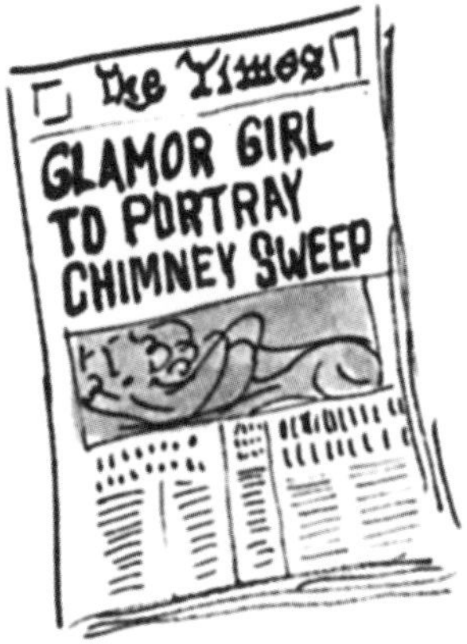
The Times
GLAMOR GIRL TO PORTRAY CHIMNEY SWEEP

cried the newspapers.

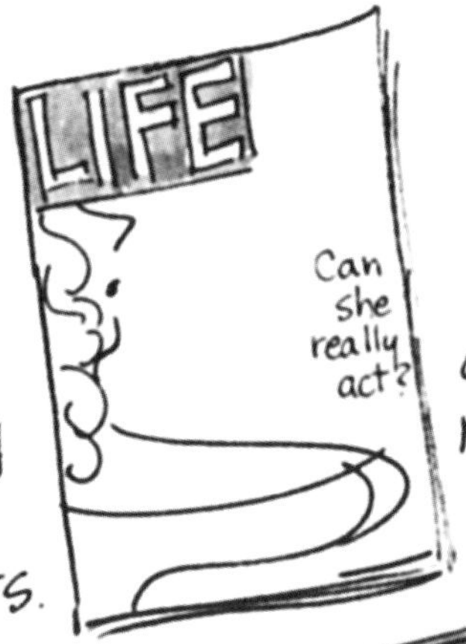
LIFE
Can she really act?

asked the magazines.

And the world waited to find out.

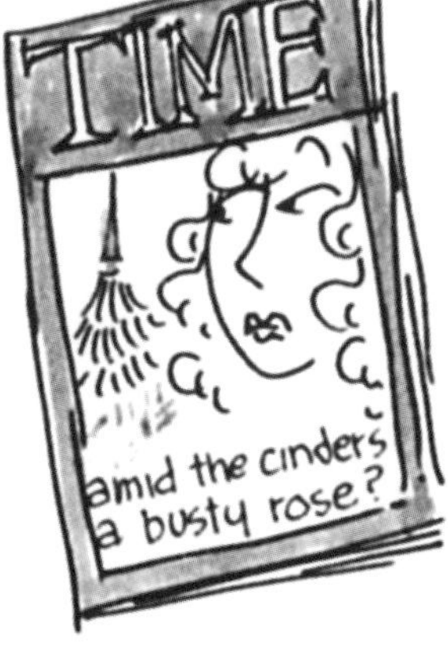
TIME
amid the cinders a busty rose?

"The Chimney Sweep" was budgeted as a twenty million dollar production.

NEVER BEFORE SUCH TURGID REALISM!

WE WILL EVEN SHOOT IT IN THE BRONX!

drummed the press agents

proclaimed the publicists.

No expense was spared. The very best blacklisted screen writers were flown in from England to do the scenario.

Then came word that Passionella had consented
to a **daytime** shooting schedule. A nation of
175 million reeled back, stunned. Passionella
went on "Youth Wants To Know."

"YES, IRWIN, FROM
NOW ON I WILL
PERFORM **ONLY**
DURING THE DAY."

In the weeks that followed the eyes of six
continents fastened on a secluded mansion
in Beverly Hills.

And then came the first day of shooting.
Half a state gathered to see the **new**
Passionella leave for the studio.

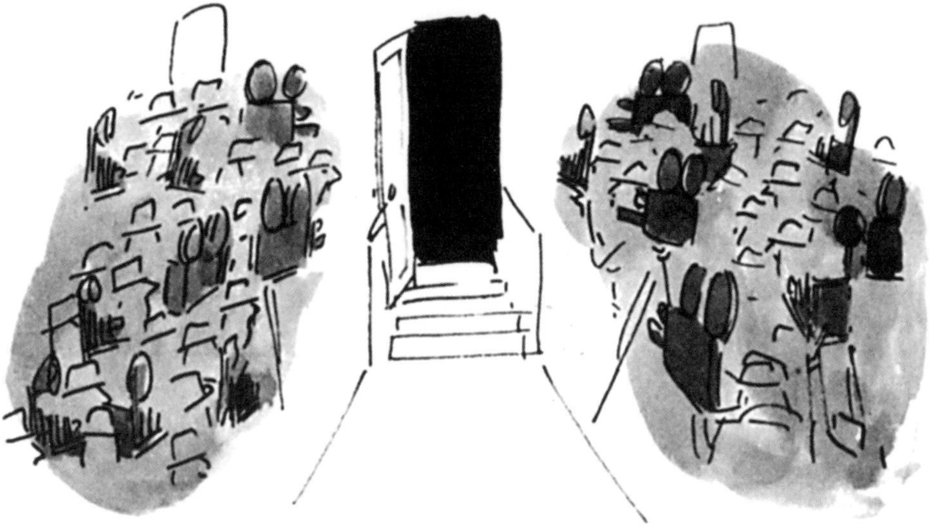

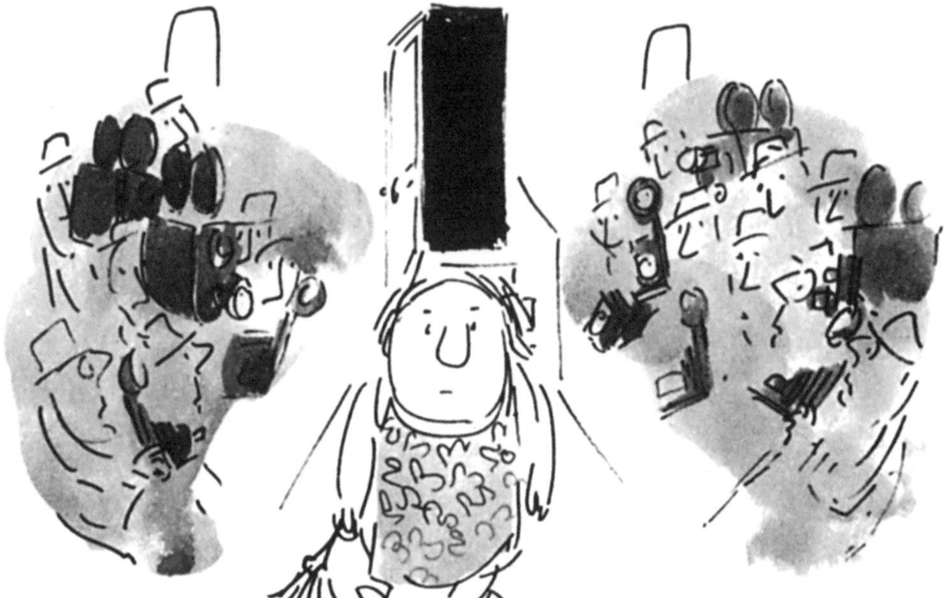

"MARVELOUS!" cried the
producer.
"UNBELIEVABLE!" cried the
director.
"I THINK SHE'S OVERACTING."
muttered a
jealous star
from a rival studio.

WE WILL USE
NO DOUBLES!
announced the studio.

PASSIONELLA WILL
SWEEP ALL HER
OWN CHIMNEYS!

No one could remember a screen personality ever fitting a role so perfectly.

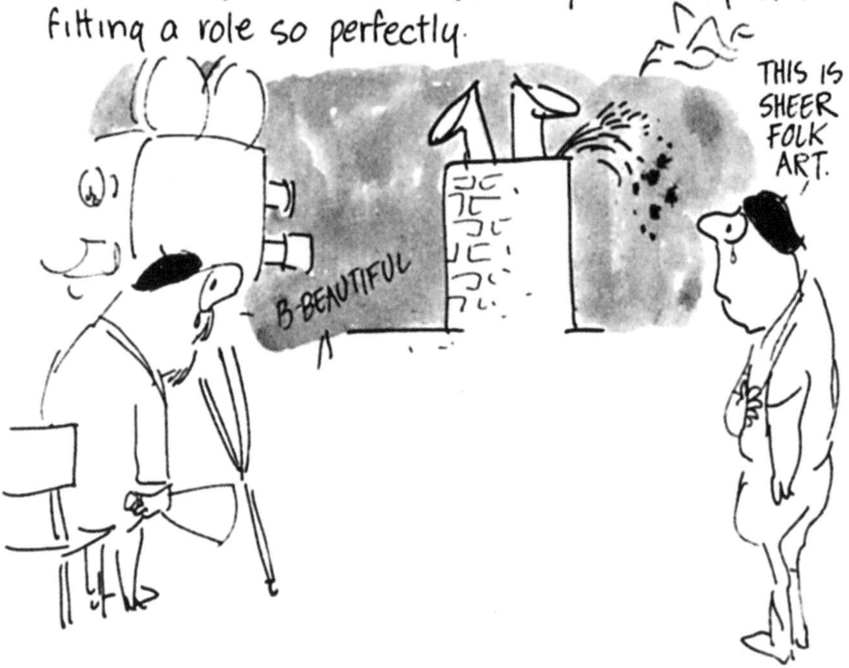
B-BEAUTIFUL
THIS IS SHEER FOLK ART.

But every day promptly at six, as the sun began to go down, Passionella would hop into her sports car and vanish.

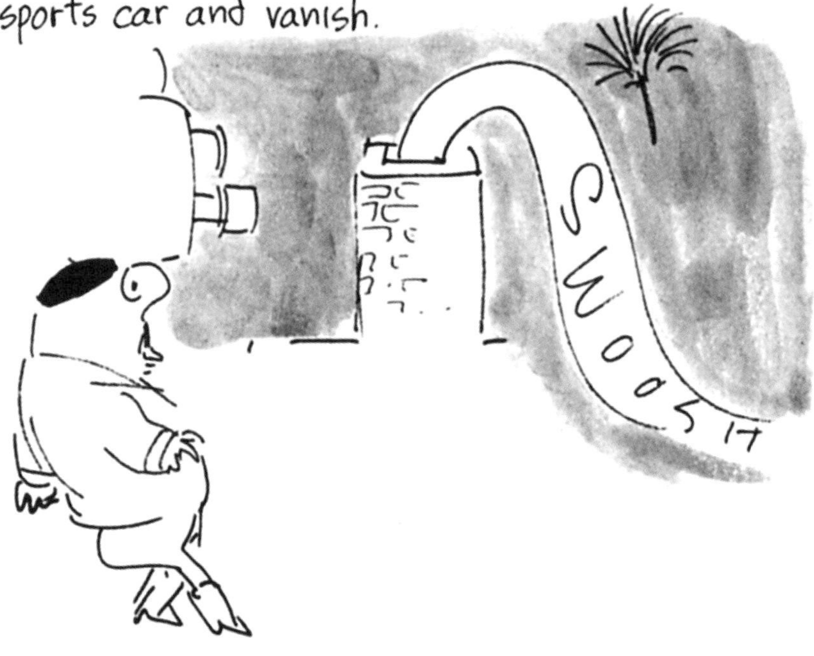
SWOOSH

Finally the picture was completed. 'The Chimney Sweep' was previewed at a special showing for landlords.

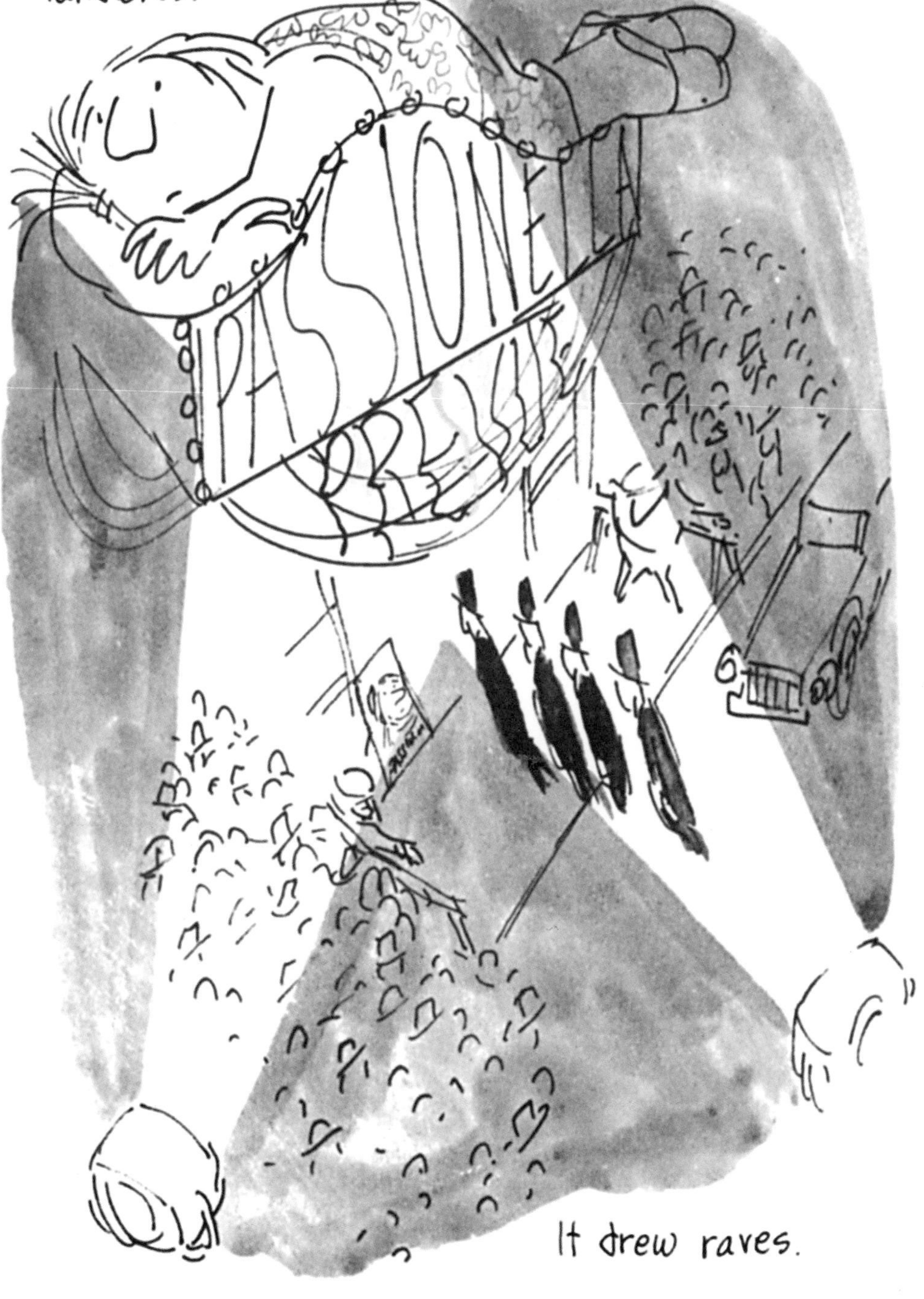
PASSIONELLA

It drew raves.

"AT LAST MOVIES HAVE COME OF AGE" said the Saturday Review.

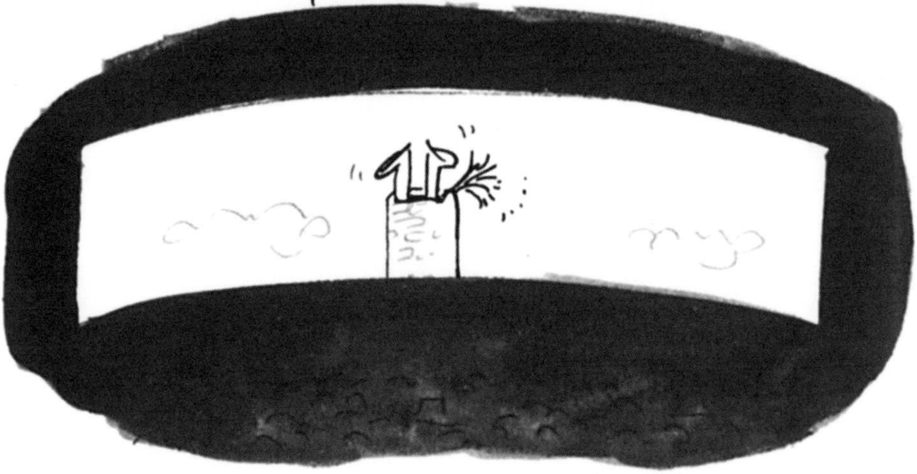

"PASSIONELLA IS A CINCH TO COP THE OSCAR" said Hedda, Louella, Sidney, Sheila, Hy and Cholly Knickerbocker.

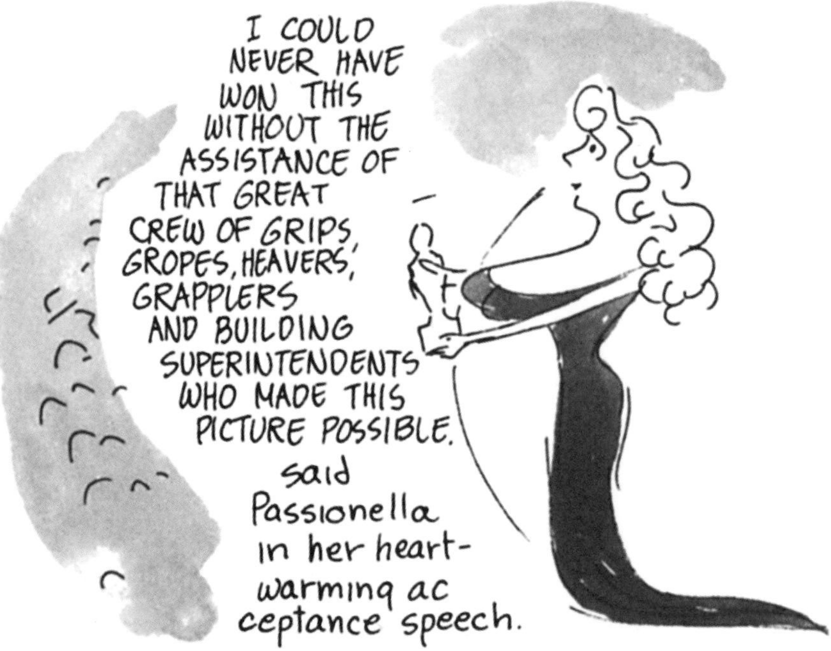
I COULD NEVER HAVE WON THIS WITHOUT THE ASSISTANCE OF THAT GREAT CREW OF GRIPS, GROPES, HEAVERS, GRAPPLERS AND BUILDING SUPERINTENDENTS WHO MADE THIS PICTURE POSSIBLE.
said Passionella in her heart-warming ac ceptance speech.

The award was presented by last years winner, FLIP (the Prince) CHARMING – who whispered:

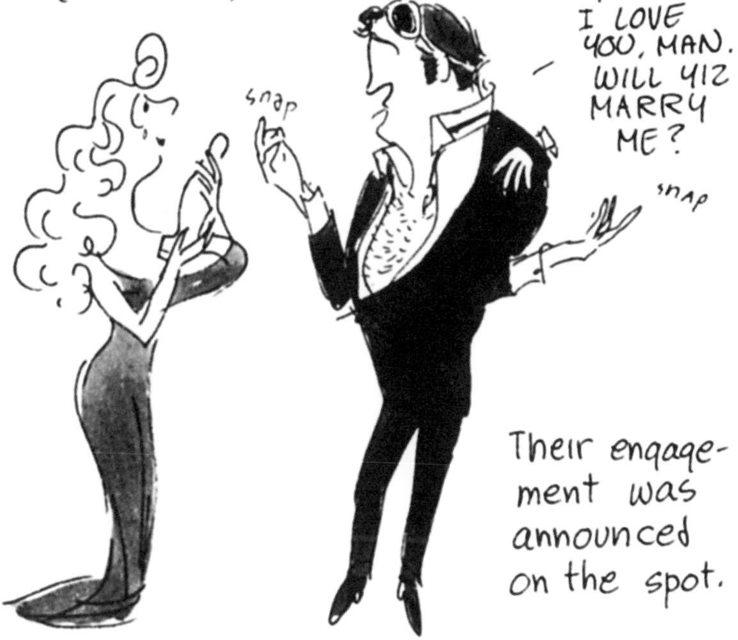
I LOVE YOU, MAN. WILL YIZ MARRY ME?
snap
snap

Their engagement was announced on the spot.

Dreamy eyed, the two lovers went home where they passed the night making tender love.

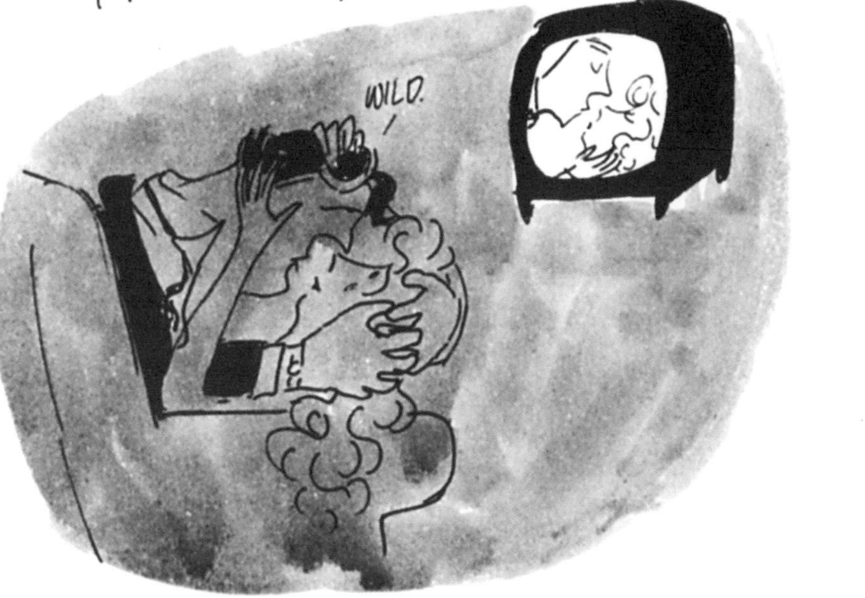
WILD.

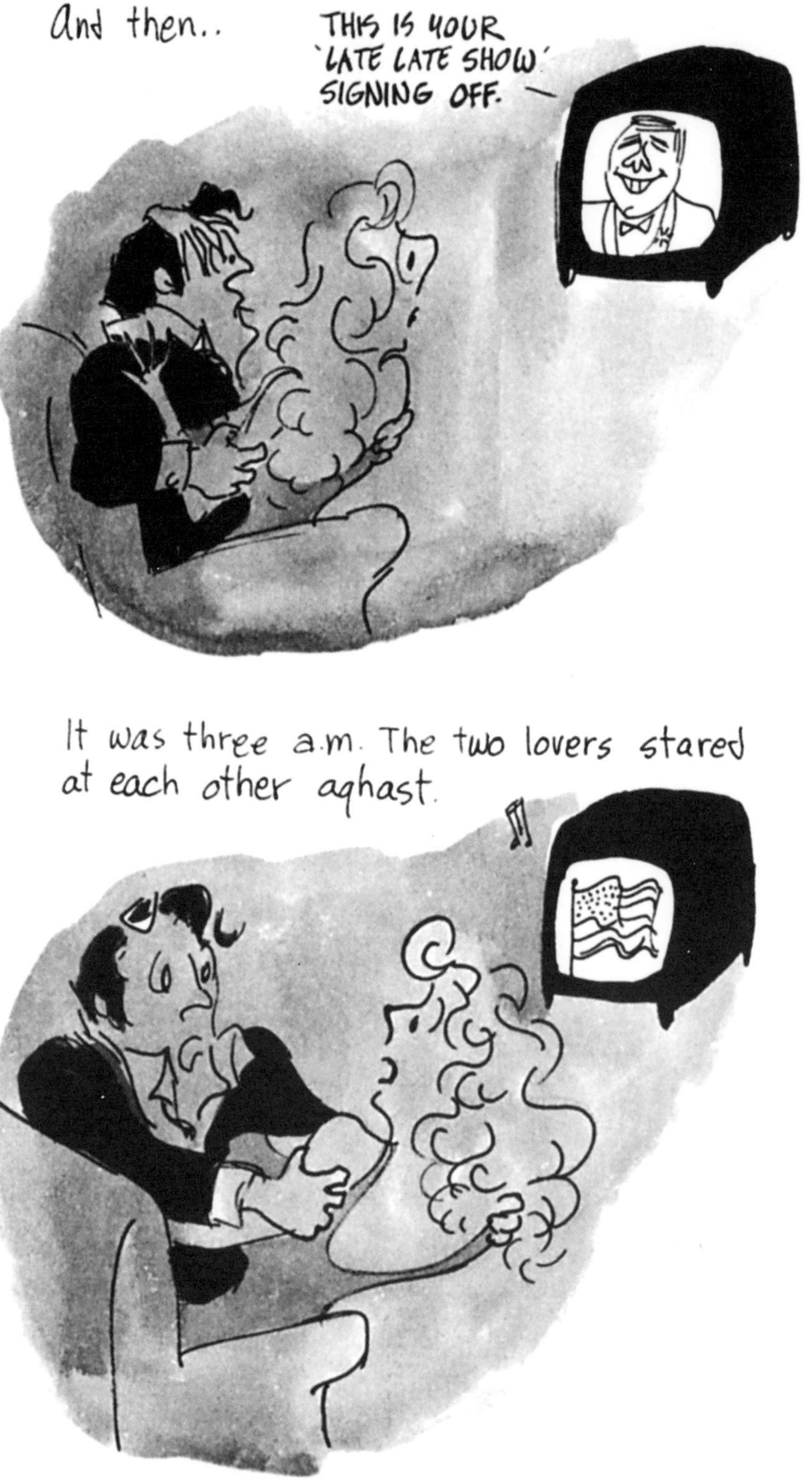
And then..
THIS IS YOUR 'LATE LATE SHOW' SIGNING OFF.
It was three a.m. The two lovers stared at each other aghast.

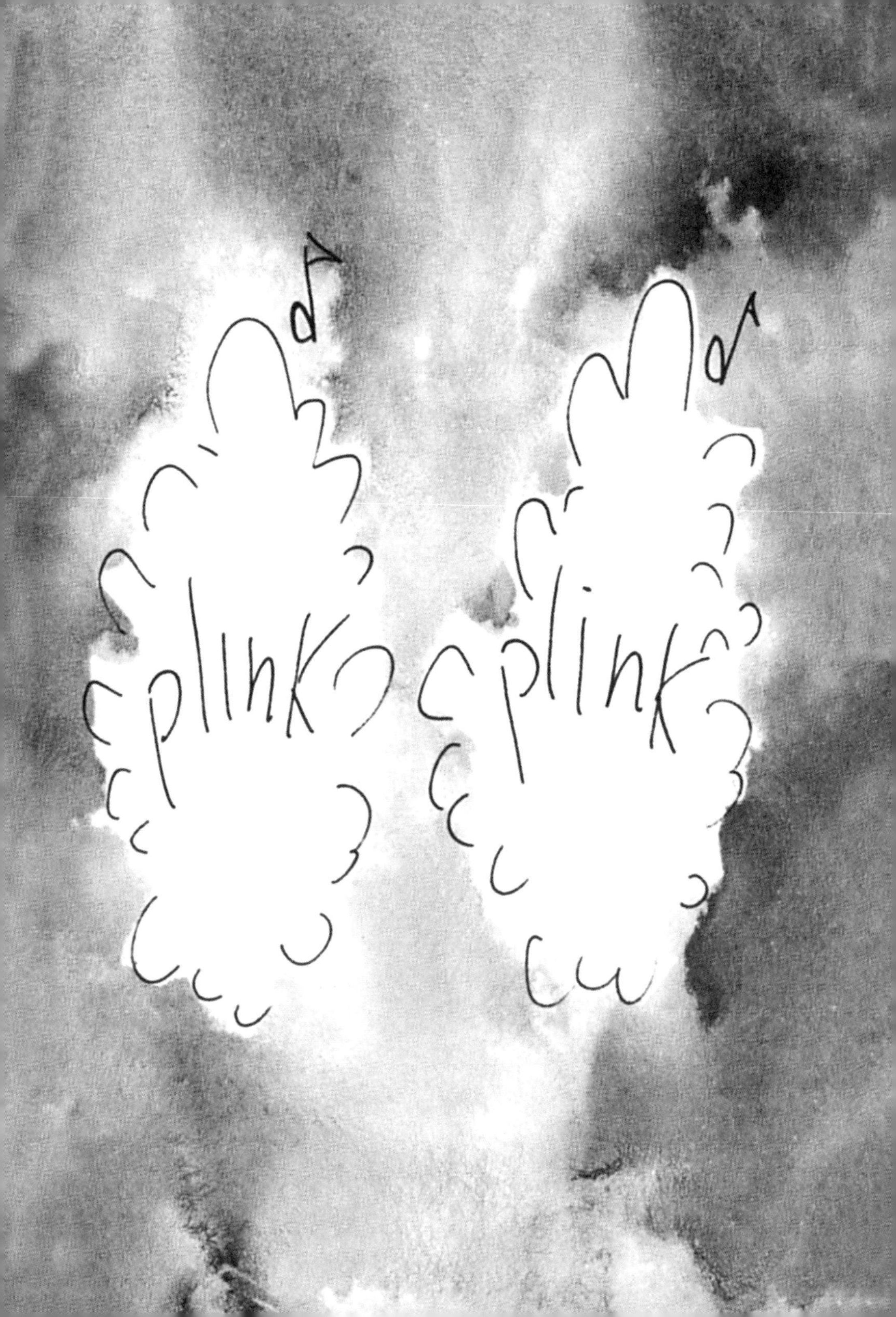
plink
plink

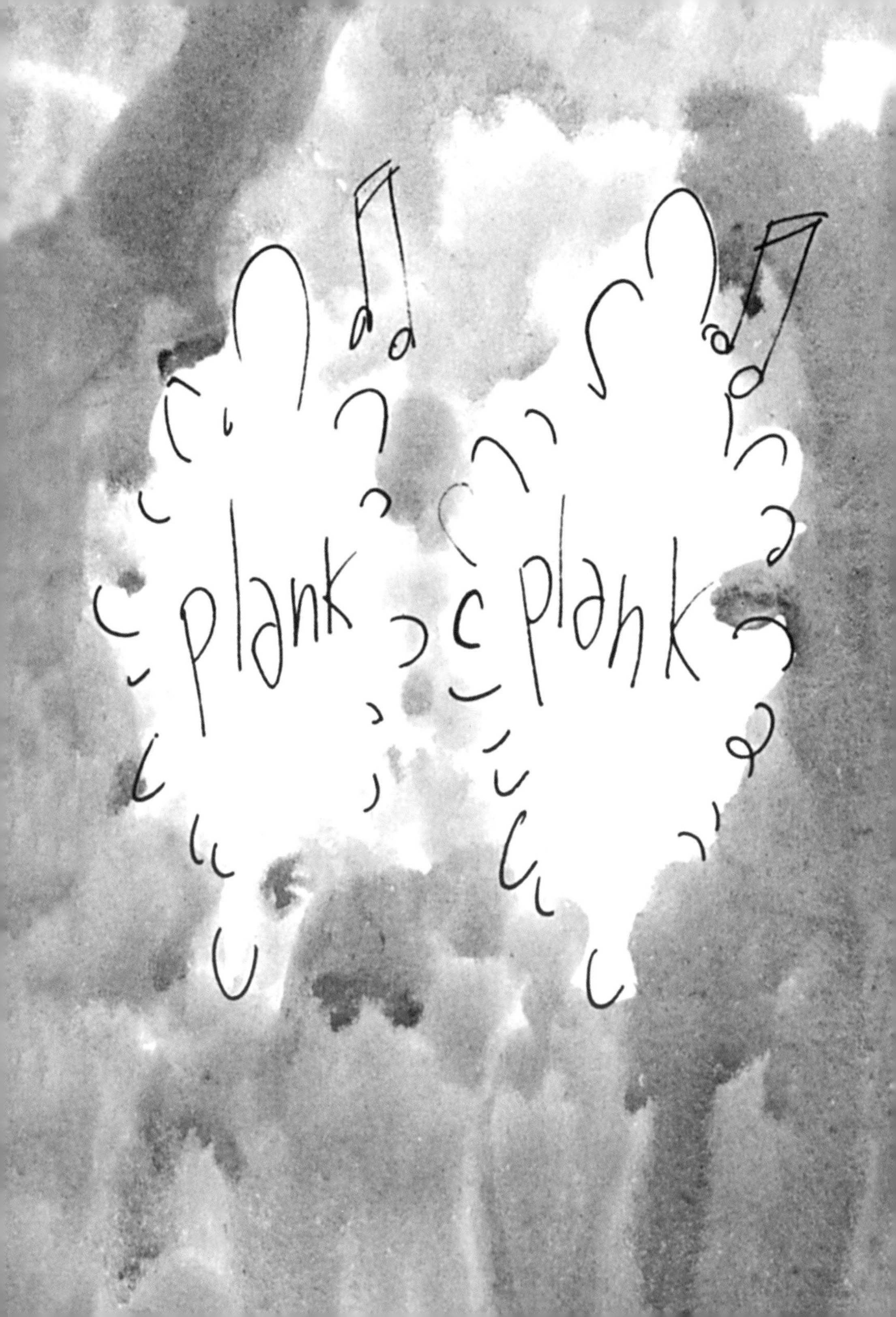
plank
plank

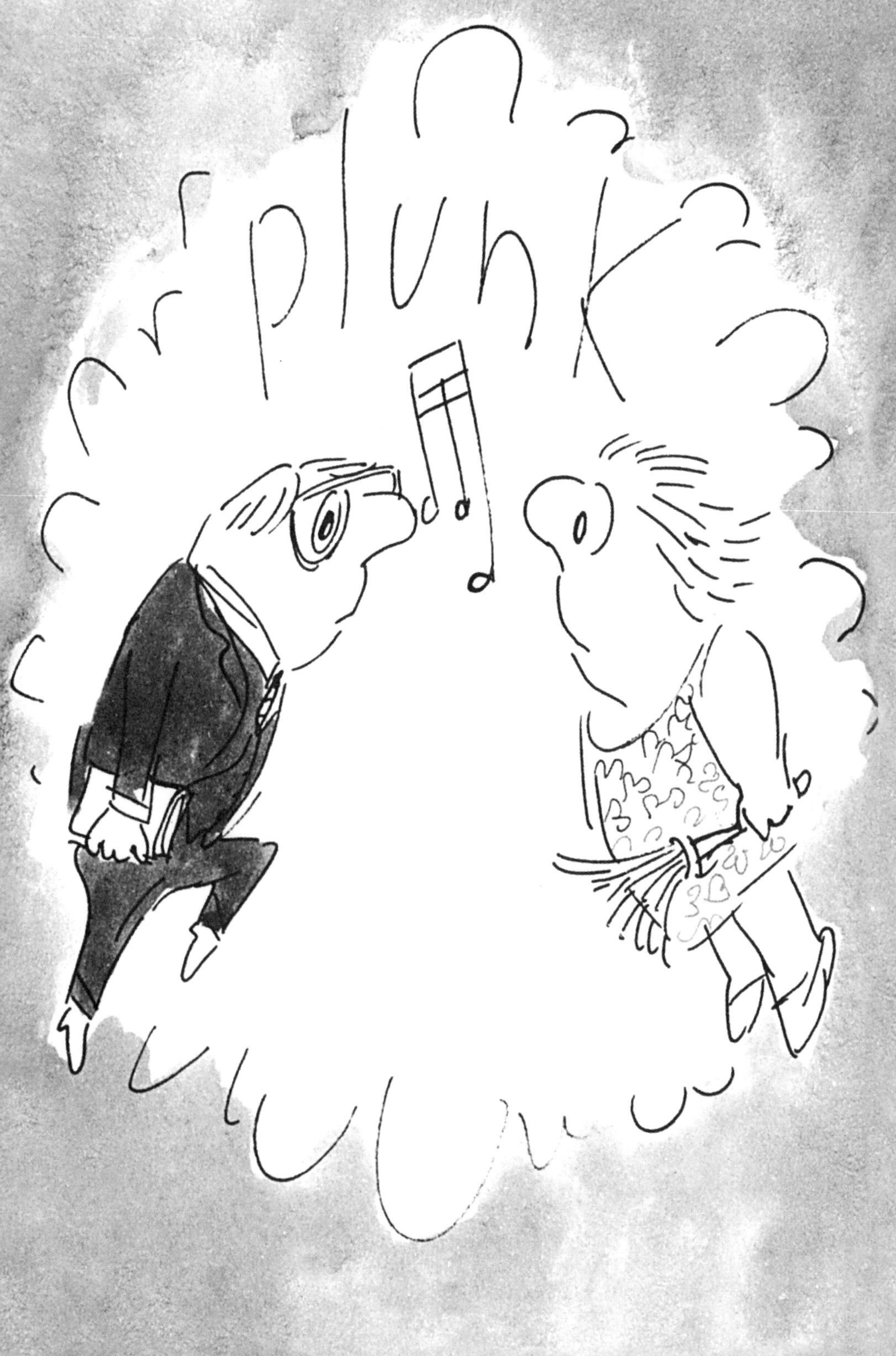
plunk

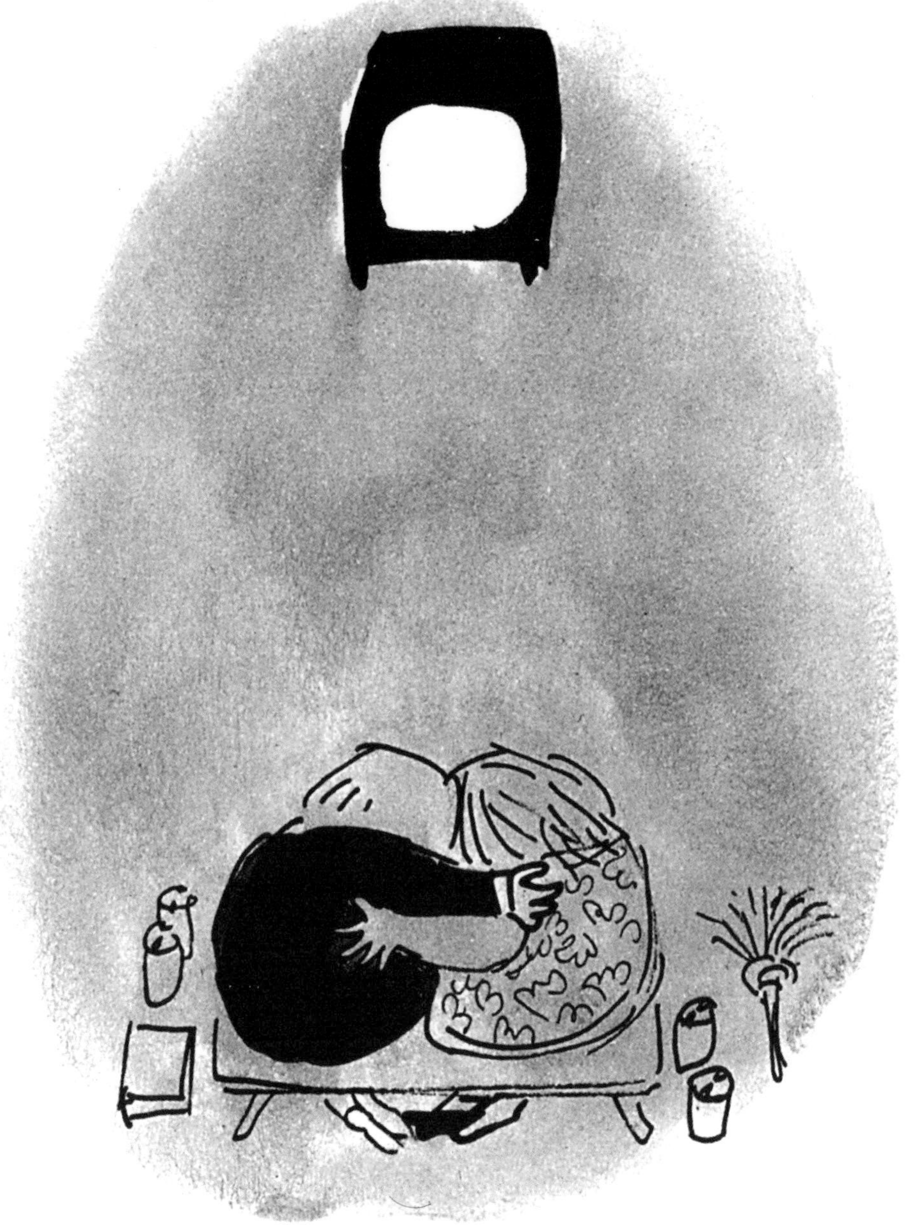

And they lived happily ever after.

The Relationship